PIVOT POINTS

POINTS

FIVE DECISIONS EVERY SUCCESSFUL LEADER MUST MAKE

Julia TANG PETERS

WILEY

For general information about our other products and services, please contact our Customer
Care Department within the United States at (800) 762-2974, outside the United States
at (317) 572-3993 or fax (317) 572-4002.

Wiley publishes in a variety of print and electronic formats and by print-on-demand. Some
material included with standard print versions of this book may not be included in e-books or in
print-on-demand. If this book refers to media such as a CD or DVD that is not included in the
version you purchased, you may download this material at http://booksupport.wiley.com. For more
information about Wiley products, visit www.wiley.com.

ISBN 978-1-118-89473-6 (cloth); ISBN 978-1-118-89395-1 (ebk); ISBN 978-1-118-89405-7 (ebk)

Printed in the United States of America
10 9 8 7 6 5 4 3 2 1

Contents

Preface

A Different Approach to Leadership and Careers

Leader. Not a leader. We judge who is and is not a leader quickly to summarize our overall impression of who should get our attention and support. In organizations large and small, a common complaint is that there are few leaders but many executives. Colleagues talk about strong leaders and weak leaders, but isn't *weak leader* an oxymoron?

Many surveys have shown that the primary consideration of career satisfaction and employee engagement has to do with how leadership at the place of employment treats people and how it runs the business. There are too few leaders—among bosses as well as all the people one must consider teammates. But the blame game compounds the problem, and everyone ends up stuck on a treadmill of unrewarding effort.

It's a quandary, even at companies making an admirable investment in leadership development programs—which are estimated to be a $50 billion industry when you include business schools. The trend of making leadership a performance measure for all levels of professional positions has only confused its meaning. Leadership has become the code word for judging the success potential of a 25-year-old, the promotion readiness of a 43-year-old, and the cost-value benefits of a 55-year-old. Why is the yardstick of success for individuals, teams, and companies so misunderstood?

We clearly need to approach leadership differently from the overdose of prescriptive advice that misses nuances of systemic problems, personalities, and cultures and that hinders authenticity. We need to think differently from the one-size-fits-all approach that can obscure real problems and become business-speak for people to hide behind. We need to look at leadership in its real context of specific dynamic forces and human relationships and eschew pedantic concepts that offer little practical value for the real life of organizations. Furthermore, we need to understand leadership from perspectives different from celebrity leaders whose goals and lives are in a different stratosphere from most people.

Also, we need to apply an insight about leaders who are by definition independent minded. Leaders play to win, not by following but by internalizing observations of other winners who captivate their imaginations. Real leaders know that 10-step recipes to fame, fortune, and success do not make leaders. *Pivot Points* is about leaders and experiences that will capture the imaginations of readers.

LEADER-MAKING DECISIONS

The best understanding of leadership would seem to come from leaders who are extraordinary in their achievements while being the kind of people we see as role models in our real communities of family, work, and friends. So I sought out industry-changing leaders, proven but without the swagger of self-importance, and had probing conversations about how they did what they did. I started out hoping simply to share the life journeys of very real people who became recognized leaders in their industries. I ended up getting that and much more.

What I learned from these leaders is that, first, leadership is about decisions—and not about dos and don'ts or leadership traits and habits; these authentic leaders cover the gamut. Second, the decisions that stood out in their stories were those made when they *held themselves accountable in a different way* and had to use more ingenuity than usual. Third, every one of them had exactly five decisions that turned their careers into leader-building journeys. Chapter 1 explores this framework of pivotal decisions.

Chapters 2 through 6 make this developmental perspective come alive with the stories of five leaders, based on the series of rarely granted intimate interviews I had with each of them. We look at their playbooks as well as their pivotal decisions. Each chapter focuses on one leader to show the impact of how each decision leads to the next and how the dots connect over a career. A different pivotal decision was the most important for the career achievements of each leader, giving us a deeper understanding of pivot points.

Chapter 7 looks at the overarching themes common to the very different leadership journeys. These themes dispel several myths about managing careers for success.

Chapter 8 explains the study that tested these observations by collecting and analyzing data from 500 professionals of all ages across America, representing nearly 40 million people. The study revealed that 80 percent of respondents have experienced pivot points and made pivotal decisions. Furthermore, analysis of the data on how people make pivotal decisions sheds new light on attitudes and performance along the career curve over time. Readers can immediately put to use findings about decision-making behaviors that separate leaders from managers, wanderers, and clock punchers.

The final chapter helps readers examine their own pivotal decisions and understand strategies for success. Chapter 9 poses questions for readers to assess where they are and where they want to go.

AUTHENTIC PEOPLE YOU WANT TO KNOW

With the array of leaders, personalities, industries, and pivot points presented, some parts of all their stories will resonate for every reader. They engage our curiosity because of their candor and authenticity as independent-minded and strong-willed individuals shaped by nature, nurture, and the school of hard knocks. They have insecurities about some things and confidence about others. They let us see both the long view of their career as well as the intimate moments at pivot points. Readers at any level on the career ladder can learn from their experiences. In fact, even the subjects themselves gained insights when they read their own stories.

By seeing great leaders in a realistic light, we can make sense of our own career highs and lows. With this understanding, we can reclaim dreams and take that next step—or leap—closer to fulfill them.

All the leaders in this book are entrepreneurs. This is neither deliberate nor coincidental. In my attempts to interview corporate leaders, they involved their corporate relations people and general counsels for terms and conditions and contracts. Entrepreneurs, however, supported what I am trying to do and just engaged in the interviews with openness and honesty, so I decided that corporate protocols placed too much constraint on corporate leaders and prevented them from freely sharing their experiences in the spirit of this book.

EVERYONE IS A DEVELOPING LEADER

It turns out that the experiences of entrepreneurs provide the perspective we most need today. According to the US Bureau of Labor Statistics (latest data are from 2012), a whopping 75 percent of private sector firms in the United States have fewer than 10 employees. Another 22 percent have 10 to 99 employees. Only 2.39 percent of companies that are owned and based in the United States have more than 100 employees, and just 0.2 percent has more than 1,000 employees. These numbers reflect, in part, the rise of the gig economy—an estimated 20 to 33 percent of the US workforce now works by freelancing instead of traditional employment; they are entrepreneurs. These trends point to the need for everyone to think like an entrepreneur and developing leader, whether he or she works in a Fortune 100 corporation or in a small business.

Here, I need to define how I use the word *leader*. My use of the term separates the person from the office. A person holding an official leadership title is not necessarily a leader. Conversely, a person without an official title can be a leader. Furthermore, a leader, I believe, embraces the Hippocratic Oath, "Do no harm." People who occupy leadership positions, who knowingly engage in destructive activities and do harm, should be referred to as what they are—unethical businesspeople, corrupt officials, or ruthless dictators—not leaders. Leaders have flaws and make mistakes like everyone else; a leader's intent, however, is always in the service of positive results benefiting more than self.

One further point: This book is about people who created a following, a culture, as they built real economic value and created jobs. The ideas, however, apply to making a positive impact on one person or many people—at work, at home, in schools, and in the community. Leading, according to this point of view, is an approach to living.

For everyone who believes that leadership and success are singular experiences of an individual journey, this book is for you. Understanding that leaders favor exceptions over rules and reach for exceptional goals, this book offers a framework and a road map—but no rules—for creating your own journey. My hope is to help achievers, whatever your age and accomplishments, answer this question: What pivotal decisions do you still need to make to realize your best self?

For all the bosses reading this, think how much easier your job would be if your people held themselves more accountable than you hold them and embraced ideas and solutions as their most valuable resource.

Acknowledgments

I have always had near reverence for the power of the published word. It can affect people a world away and generations to come. I dared to hope that one day I would have something to say worthy of a book that people would want to read. This has been a more difficult journey than I could have anticipated, but also more rewarding. It has been at times a very lonely journey, and getting to my destination was possible only because of all the love, support, and help many people gave me.

My deepest thanks go to the leaders who trusted me with their stories. I learned about the art of leadership from Dale Dawson, Bud Frankel, Al Golin, John Rogers, and Glen Tullman. In their extraordinarily busy lives, they were very generous with their time and spirit of sharing their stories. I am especially grateful to Bud Frankel, my mentor, my friend, and the first participant of this book, for giving me the most important opportunity—to just do it and start writing.

Leaders who inspired this book but are not in it gave me a vivid appreciation for what leaders do—and no book can fully do justice to what they give every day. My gratitude goes to friends, mentors, and clients for making the study of leadership such a gratifying endeavor. Special thanks to Robert Crutchfield, who helped me persevere through many conversations about leadership and by reading chapters as I finished them; and to Lucien LaGrange, whose understanding of my work encouraged me through the times I felt stuck.

What took this project to another level was the insightful research, designed and analyzed by two research experts whose fascination with the subject of the study made this book far richer. My thanks go to the dedication of Carol Foley and David Kuhn to finding the story in the data and empirically validating what was at first anecdotal research.

I got lucky in finding just the help I needed in the way I needed it from people in the publishing and bookselling industry, which was a whole new world to me. One of the most serendipitous meetings of my professional life was with Matthew Holt, publisher at John Wiley & Sons. Thank you, Matt, for immediately seeing the value of this book.

I got to the finish line with Charlotte Maiorana's enthusiasm and calm guidance as the editor for this project. Debra Englander gave me far more than her expert editing help; she was a guide, an encourager, a coach, and a friend.

My profound appreciation goes to my family. My daughter, Katherine Tang Newberger, has read every word of countless versions of manuscripts and given me astute editorial help and always gently. Feeling her walk alongside me from the starting line to the finish line has made all the difference in getting this book done. My son, Charlie Tang Newberger, gave me strength to persist by often reminding me that I should pursue my dream.

Without Michael, my husband, I could not have fulfilled my dream of being an author. He gave me loving support throughout a project that at times took over my life. And his always on-target feedback as a leader on leadership gave me confidence in the purpose and message of this book.

CHAPTER 1

From Ordinary Career to Leadership Journey

What Separates Leaders from Managers?

Whether a leader is made or born, whichever you believe, we see in the making of the five leaders featured in this book that they grew and *evolved*, one pivotal decision at a time. Their stories show how five pivotal decisions clearly stand out—from hundreds of other important work decisions they also made—as the ones that determined their journey to leadership. For these leaders, pivot points served as career builders, although they often presented at first as career stoppers. That is the dynamics of pivot points: They can show up as positive or negative events, and pivotal decisions can turn out for better or for worse. They can be catalysts of growth or leave careers to languish. The difference is what this book addresses: What turns a pivot point from being a potential career stopper or career trap into a career builder? How do certain decisions separate leaders from everyone else?

The industry-changing leaders in this book faced all their pivot points by consistently making decisions that unleashed a surprising reserve of leadership potential and produced outcomes exceeding their own dreams. Each decision triggered a quantum leap of learning and growth. By proactively making and executing these decisions, each leader avoided the career trap of daily operational and environmental issues becoming blinders to what truly mattered.

The framework of five pivotal decisions helps us understand the strategies leaders use to keep moving forward. Based on intimate, in-depth interviews and validated by research, this perspective examines more than decision-making skills, process, or style. It shows how certain decisions catapulted these individuals to extraordinary success because they *decided to change the story and hold themselves accountable* for changing the course of events. At other times, they created a pivot point to change the status quo. These were decisions to lead—although the decisions they made were not explicitly about being a leader or jockeying for position. Ultimately, leading is a purposeful decision for making oneself accountable for fulfilling a worthy idea that requires out-of-the-ordinary responsibility and effort.

DECISION-MAKING LEADERS, LEADER-MAKING DECISIONS

At the beginning of this book project, I interviewed a few handpicked leaders. I simply wanted to bring attention to great leaders who don't seek or need the spotlight. I ended up discovering that in all their journeys, a certain pattern existed in which a decision opened up possibilities that stirred their passion. They took on opportunities and challenges that involved skills to master, mistakes to make, and lessons to learn. Embracing this journey paved the way for the next career-defining decision, and that brought yet another new set of opportunities, challenges, and skills to master, mistakes to make, and lessons to learn. Each successive pivot point was not possible without the previous. Each pivotal decision built on the foundation the previous pivotal decisions laid and connected in a trajectory that turned these ordinary people into extraordinary leaders. Although each pivotal experience established leadership, it's the journey that made them great leaders.

All the featured individuals are ambitious, but none started out with the goal to transform industries. Their stories show that incredible achievements and personal growth come out of a decision to change the narrative from the expected course of events. Each success built confidence in exploring options as a better strategy than working within the confines of the status quo. Many decisions defied conventional wisdom; others put at risk the success they had already attained to achieve what really mattered to them, which perhaps is one of the most difficult pivot points to journey through. In all cases, midcareer turbulence instigated decisions that would propel them to great success they did not know was ahead.

This developmental perspective focuses on the decision to lead conscientiously as distinctly different from decisions motivated by personal gain only. Findings from our survey show that some people, when facing a decision that weighs heavily, focus on what's better for them, whereas others look at what's best for the business and team. Some people see only conventional or comfortable options, whereas others come up with unconventional ones, perhaps outside the comfort zone of an individual, team, or company. And so, some people keep making decisions that do not play a pivotal role but accrue personal benefits. Other people make one or two pivotal decisions and then lose their verve—usually without realizing it. The leaders in this book kept making pivotal decisions to build real economic and social value.

Leaders often cite luck for pivotal successes because they could not take credit for the exact time, place, and nature of those pivot points of opportunity. They know that their real opportunities to break out of the crowd arose from the complex interactions of people and organizations and of marketplaces and social change. In many cases, what catapulted them to success were adversities turned into opportunities. As heavyweight champion boxer Mike Tyson said when asked what he knew about his opponent's fight plan, "Everyone has a plan until they get punched in the mouth." Plans serve a purpose but in boxing or business, the champion is the one who instinctively connects with the spontaneous opportunity.

How these leaders handled pivotal decisions shows us what separates leaders from managers. Although managerial decisions are part of a leader's job, the pivotal decisions create and define the work of leading as distinctly different from the work of managing. By holding themselves accountable for a bold idea that changes the status quo, these leaders had to entrust others to manage all that is involved with business as usual. With each successive pivotal decision, they stood out from their cohort of high achievers; by the fourth or fifth pivotal decision, they were at the top of their game and their industry.

ARE FIVE PIVOTAL DECISIONS THE EXPERIENCE OF JUST LEADERS OR EVERYONE?

To answer the question of whether this framework of five pivotal decisions is a widely shared experience, I worked with a research expert to conduct a nationwide survey of 500 college-educated adults in professional careers, representative of 16 percent of US adults.

To study the relationship between pivotal decisions and leadership, we needed a new tool for measuring leadership decision making. Pulling from experience working with and learning about leaders, I peeled away all the values attached to leadership that are more descriptive than defining and zeroed in on its two most essential elements: accountability and ingenuity. Effective leaders hold themselves accountable to make something important happen; as part of taking full accountability, they also make others accountable for what was delegated to them. Ingenuity covers all the ideas, solutions, and vision that make up accountabilities.

When using these two variables in a matrix, four quadrants of behaviors emerge; I call these leader, manager, wanderer, and clock puncher. (See Figure 1.1.)

The study tested three hypotheses about leadership:

1. There are five pivotal opportunities to make decisions that determine the course of a career.
2. Both accountability and ingenuity drive leadership behavior.

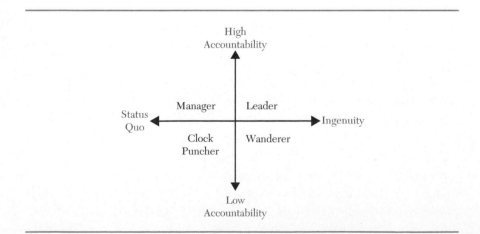

FIGURE 1.1   Four Types of Decision-Making Behaviors

3. When accountability and/or ingenuity fall short, other behavior sets produce outcomes less successful than leadership behaviors.

The study not only validates the pivotal-decisions framework but also shows how the five pivotal decisions can be career builders or career stoppers. In the self-reported perceptions, we see which behaviors produced successful and unsuccessful experiences. Collecting data for the same questions from the supervisors of the respondents would add another layer of analysis. However, this study's purpose is to understand the career experience of the decision maker as both story maker and storyteller.

Specifically, 78 percent (representing 29 million college-educated professionals) in the study have (1) experienced pivot points and (2) made pivotal decisions using the four behavior sets we postulated. Together, the findings, which I explain in detail in Chapter 8, identify the decision points where people need the most help.

As we can expect, men and women can experience pivotal decisions at different times; an obvious difference occurs when women make the decision to let go of, or postpone, the career they had at the time they opted to focus on parenting. Another important factor is that almost everyone in a professional career will encounter some of these pivot points, but not everyone will make an intentional pivotal decision. Some will not recognize the decision point, and others will simply not decide by waiting to see what happens. By the way, that is also a decision. People reporting they haven't had the occasion to make more pivotal decisions commensurate with their years of experience may, in fact, have faced pivot points with passivity—which was a decision but wasn't a pivotal decision.

The evidence strongly suggests that leaders walk the path to greatness by fully engaging with all five pivot points and that leaders make all five pivotal decisions with leadership accountability and vision. Between pivot points, they are human and can wade through times when they behave more like managers, wanderers, or clock punchers. At pivot points, however, they experience clarity and conviction about holding themselves accountable for fulfilling a worthy idea or vision.

The empirical study of the intersection of careers, pivot points, and leadership addresses the real needs people have for a new way to think about their careers in the changing world of work. Rare will be the career of our parents and grandparents with one or two employers over a lifetime, where tenure and long-term company relationships support career development. Instead, by defining leadership as holding ourselves accountable and tapping our ingenuity to fulfill our best ideas and our best selves, the individual is the self-aware decision maker who enrolls the support of supervisors, colleagues, and human resource executives in career development.

As technology, globalization, and social trends transform work, this worker-centric paradigm emphasizes personal responsibility for career development that counterbalances the traditional employer-centric paradigm. Shared responsibility benefits everyone.

PIVOTAL DECISIONS DETERMINE THE JOURNEY

In the journey of every profiled leader, pivot points do not mark events per se; they involve a chain of events building up to and immediately following a pivotal decision. At these decision points, these leaders responded with original critical thinking and were fertile with ideas. Some pivot points called for being a visionary leader, others called for being a crisis leader, and still other points arose from personal restlessness. Viewed as a whole process, the five pivotal decisions turned ordinary career paths into leader-making journeys.

"The measure of success," according to former US Secretary of State John Foster Dulles, "is not whether you have a tough problem to deal with but whether it is the same problem you had last year." Often, senior management stays stuck in the same problem, and their organization stays stuck for years, or even decades. Pivot points are really about preventing stuckness, so to speak, by taking on new challenges and moving forward.

What are these pivotal decisions that brought these gifted leaders to a series of new opportunities and challenges and stages of personal and business growth? (See Figure 1.2.)

1. The *launching* decision makes a commitment to gain mastery of specialized skills and do more than your job. (It's Malcolm Gladwell's thesis in *Outliers* that it takes 10,000 hours to achieve mastery.)
2. The *turning point* decision acts on an important opportunity or problem that usually creates a bold, new direction.

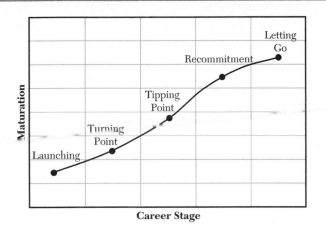

FIGURE 1.2   Five Pivotal Decisions Mark Stages of Career Development

3. The *tipping point* decision, involving significant risk, breaks through a fundamental barrier.
4. The *recommitment* decision focuses on purpose-driven leadership and sharpens the vision, moving the goalposts further out.
5. The *letting go* decision facilitates new sustainable leadership.

Let's take a closer look at each of these.

The *launching point* moved them out of their comfort zone. All these leaders started out in their careers to make a living. The launching point captured their imagination and work became more than about income. They had goals that riveted their attention, galvanizing them to turn dream into reality. It changed their work and their lives forever, although they didn't know to what extent at the time. The launching point established the platform on which the potential leader would become an actualized leader.

At a *turning point*, the confluence of a willful decision to do more and the pressing need—or opportunity—to take action unleashes an extraordinary verve to take the business to the next level. It's a decision to build a sustainable business that can flourish and not just survive. It tested their capabilities and capacity in various ways, stretching them far beyond their comfort zone and requiring their total commitment. The success curve at this stage strengthened their commitment to what would become their life work. The turning point laid the foundation for them to become leaders in their fields.

The *tipping point* catapulted them into the work of leading as distinctly different from the work of mastering their subject and running their business. Success already achieved allowed them to fully express their business vision, leadership values, and signature talents. They are honing the art of leading. At this point, they have built a team whom they trust with substantive responsibilities, freeing themselves to focus on the art of leading inside and outside their organizations. In this stage, they hit full stride and fully enjoyed wearing the mantle of power.

There comes a *recommitment point* when leaders look at where they are and where they want to go, knowing they need to renew their commitment or leave. In all the journeys examined, everyone experienced turbulence in his work or in his personal satisfaction after the tipping point, which for most occurred in their late 40s or early 50s. Quite simply, things happen—for many, disruptive change occurs because of being acquired or being the acquirer. For all, this stage is primarily a decision to recommit to self—to their North Star. For some, it was a decision to recommit to the same enterprise; for others, recommitment to self meant the decision to do something different. Whether the decision was to continue or change course, they moved on with new goals. At this point, they knew who they were as leaders and what they stood for, and they wielded their influential power with ease and confidence. They were as passionate about leading as about their vision. In their recommitment they intuitively attained and practiced the art of leading.

Everyone must face the *letting go point*. It can occur at any time when the leader decides another priority or opportunity beckons, when business conditions require a hold 'em or fold 'em decision, or when it's simply time to plan for succession. The ultimate test of leadership is letting go at a time of strength so that others can carry on the work. Letting go isn't just a decision; it is the practice and spirit of release so that others can establish their own paths and leadership. Because leaders by this time have developed such a symbiotic relationship with their work and people, this decision point is the most emotionally challenging. The letting go point is pivotal in defining the terms of the leader's legacy.

These five pivot points do not necessarily occur linearly; they can occur in a zigzag fashion. Over the long haul, however, one can pick out the most impactful decisions for a progressive march forward, despite setbacks, which result in career-defining achievements.

Two leaders profiled are now 84 years old. Their stories are particularly instrumental because the outcomes of their leadership are known. If we ended their stories when they were 50 or even 65, some decision points would be different from when we see the entirety of their careers. The other leaders profiled are in their mid 50s—old enough to have accumulated a record of sustained achievements, young enough to have more innings left in the game. The decision points having the greatest impact on their entire careers may look different later and are yet to come.

FIVE CHARACTERISTICS OF A PIVOTAL DECISION

The seminal moments of abundant energy and imaginative thinking came at different times and in different ways to the people you will get to know in this book. Also, the pivotal decisions having the greatest impact—without which their crowning achievements would not be possible—were different for different people. For Bud Frankel it was the launching decision; for Glen Tullman it was the turning point decision; for John Rogers, the tipping point decision; for Al Golin, the recommitment decision; for Dale Dawson, the letting go decision. But, in all their stories, we find five common characteristics of the pivotal decisions of leadership.

1. *They held themselves accountable.* They did not do it alone, but they took full accountability for making a decision and making that decision work. It was up to them. They did not point to people, issues, or circumstances. And in holding themselves accountable, they quickly learned they had to make the tough decisions because that's what leaders do. That included holding others accountable for their work and letting people go if they could not fulfill their role in, and responsibilities to, their work community. Personal accountability meant no excuses.

2. *There was a moment of truth when making a solitary decision.* Each confronted himself to answer the questions "Will I really? Can I? Should I?" They understood that the decision boiled down to its

essence was one of being true to self. The new path would bring more work, risk, and trade-offs. They explored and discussed their options with people whose opinions mattered. In their decisive moment, however, they knew they were making a solitary decision that would test their wings. No one could talk them into or out of it. It was their decision to make and theirs alone. It was their responsibility to enroll the support of family and secure resources.

3. *There was an impassioned inner voice.* The decisive moment transformed their way of thinking, from environmentally dependent to personally impassioned. They transcended logic and linear thinking, making a pivotal decision that, even with rigorous analysis, came down to a personal judgment call. Once that inner voice prevailed, often against the tide, their way of thinking became increasingly its own ecosystem. In that solitary decision, they had to trust and rely on their own acumen and judgment. It became a self-reinforcing feedback loop. The more progress they made, the more they trusted their own judgment. And the more they became leaders, the more other people turned to them for good judgment and leadership.

4. *They expanded their belief in the power of one person and increasingly believed in the magic that many people working together could create.* They knew they needed help. They had to make others believe in the direction they set. They used their vision as its own currency, something of real value that couldn't be fully monetized. They had to shape the workplace values and culture.

5. *Work became the source of renewable energy.* The decisive moment propelled them to make something out of the ordinary happen. The more they did, the more they wanted to do. Work became their passion. They entered a different zone of determination and energy beyond what they had known, which was considerable. Running through all their narratives is a genuine love for their work. Usually they speak of their passion for the field they are in, but it is also a passion for leading.

Real leaders don't have much use for job descriptions. The pivotal decisions they make shape their jobs and take them where one hasn't gone before and new lessons await. These decisions define what they want people to look to them for and not look to them for in their leadership. They choose the opportunities, threats, and headaches that they will take on as individuals and as leaders of people on a shared journey. Without making these clear decisions that set the leadership agenda, executives do the work of managing and not the work of leading.

When facing decision points, the choices are far from clear. Even with hindsight, the narratives in this book were not told to me as coherent stories of decision points that connect into a leadership journey. These stories, as they were recounted, cited opportunities, ideas, and luck. People usually see the proverbial door of opportunity as luck knocking on one person's door instead of another's. "Chance," according to the great scientist Louis Pasteur, "favors only the prepared mind." Through the lens of pivot points, we see in hindsight how chance favored these people who brought themselves to each threshold of change and door of opportunity. But the lens can also inspire *foresight*.

Chapter 9 offers ways to make pivot points in your career into defining successes. Readers can do an easy self-appraisal at www .juliatangpeters.com to see if your actual effectiveness is commensurate with your potential. Seeing where you can increase your leadership quotient helps you make the most of your pivot points.

THE ART OF LEADING AND THE SCIENCE
OF MANAGEMENT

Learning from leaders and learning about leadership are very different. It's the difference between art and science. The science of management can be taught, but the art of leading can only be cultivated. Research for this book has convinced me that effective leading is more art than science, and the science should be referred to, more accurately, as management.

My personal definition of leadership is belief in the power of one person and in the magic of many people. The art of leading creates this magic. By leading with mind and heart, leaders inspire others to join their mission and do more than they expected and achieve more than they thought possible. The work of managing, on the other hand, is about incentivizing and directing people to achieve short-term goals. Leading is more about navigating toward the uncertain future and anticipating possibilities that cannot yet be filled in with details. Managing works with the knowable today. Both are important, indeed, excellence is the foundation for leadership success.

Somewhere along the journey, these leaders crossed the threshold from the science of managing to the art of leading.

As with any scientist, they studied problems, came up with solutions, and validated methodologies. As with any artist, they brought together mind and heart on a very personal, sometimes lonely, individual journey that made a unique impact. Unlike artists, they know it takes a team to get the job done.

Each stage involves a new aspect to the art of leading arising from the paradoxes of leading. For example, how does a leader both trust one's gut *and* be genuinely open to different points of view? How does a leader both have control of the situation *and* not be controlling and micromanage? These dynamics not only can make or break a career, but they can also cause disasters. These questions loom large as heads of companies and governments explain major business failures in terms of being swept along by, or saying they didn't know about, mismanagement and misdeeds below them.

We demystify leadership when we understand it as a developmental journey marked by progressive stages of learning and mastery made possible through our own decisions. This perspective downplays the role of mystifying concepts that make leadership exclusive to those who have the X factor, secret sauce, success traits, DNA, and charisma. Focusing on decision points makes leadership inclusive; we can make the decisions that turn our untested abilities into proven accomplishments.

THE LEADERS WE SHOULD LEARN FROM

The leaders we are observing in this book have a profile that differs from those of the ones who have been getting all the attention. It's a good time to shine the spotlight on them when the Great Recession that began in 2008 has exposed stunning greed and failure of leadership.

The leaders profiled in this book accomplished much yet avoided self-promotion. They created real and sustainable value. Getting rich quickly was not their goal, although they did reap plenty of financial rewards. They significantly affected their industries. And, they could live next door: They are down-to-earth, hardworking people with simple values that keep them centered in their integrity. They come from businesses including investment and finance, marketing, public relations, health care, and not-for-profit.

We see in their stories that a leader is a way of being, not just a way of doing; it's from the inside out. As role models, they created and built cultures of excellence and achievement. As mentors, they created workplaces that developed people and their careers as well as social communities. As self-aware people, they made mistakes and got past them. They understood they were on journeys that keep going, recognizing there's always more to learn and more to do.

Despite their extraordinary accomplishments, these are real people who are leaders for the world in which most of us work. They don't pay much attention to cultivating their media image. They do what they do to improve something worth their commitment. They have insecurities. Their personal lives have issues. They are people with whom we can connect, and people we want to know better.

Decisions that were not leader-building decisions did not make it into this book. With that said, leading is also about all the decisions made moment to moment and day to day, one well-reasoned choice after another. For many people, poor judgments in these relatively small decisions can stall, distract, or derail careers. Real leaders make mistakes, but their overarching patterns of behaviors are rooted in values, principles, and vision. Also, a disdain for hypocrisy keeps them on track. Each of their chapters includes their playbook of leader-defining values and principles that sustained their drive and the trust other people placed in them.

They all invented themselves through the decisions they made. In the moment, it's a decision to try something. One thing leads to another, bringing them to new doors of opportunity as well as to unexpected problems. They became champions because they solved and resolved the challenges of leading. They turned risks into rewards.

They earned their place as leaders. This is why the debate about leaders being born or made is academic; in all cases, people evolve into leaders. Here are their stories.

CHAPTER 2

IDEA

Bud Frankel

Founder and Former Chairman of Frankel & Company

WHY YOU SHOULD KNOW HIM AND ABOUT HIS WORK

Bud Frankel, founder of Frankel & Company, built what he originally started as a sales promotion agency into a marketing powerhouse that spearheaded the creation of the $15 billion marketing services industry. During 40 years at the helm, he was an innovator of marketing ideas as well as how agencies worked. In 1979, Frankel introduced nationally the McDonald's Happy Meal, the most successful giveaway program in history. Frankel had also launched the first worthy cause promotion with Clark Gum Tree of Life program in 1969 and the first major promotion of the Olympic Games with McDonald's "When the US Wins, You Win" for the 1976 Montreal Games. Frankel was the industry pioneer of the commercial use of computer graphics in 1985 when a high-resolution system for print advertising was first available. *Advertising Age* named Frankel & Company agency of the year in 1989. That same year, Bud was the first inductee to the Council of Sales Promotion Agencies Hall of Fame. The company's success derived as much from the Frankel culture of work-hard-and-play-hard as from Bud's visionary leadership. Clients recognized Frankel for its combination of natural teamwork and effective sales-building marketing programs as what made the agency in a class by itself.

Frankel was the largest independently owned marketing services agency in the United States for nearly two decades. In 2000, Publicis Groupe SA, the third largest marketing communications company in the world, acquired Frankel. Bud stayed on as chairman emeritus until he retired in 2002 at the age of 72. He then created the Frankel Family Foundation to focus on philanthropic work.

Bud's transformational leadership began in 1961, when he decided to start a new kind of promotion agency at a time when vendors of printing and tchotchkes defined the industry. Bud's idea was for the agency to work, not as a vendor of things, but as the client's business partner in solving marketing problems. Instead of salespeople pushing the things they had to sell, client service managers would gain hands-on understanding of the *client's* products and services and go-to-market challenges. Instead of producing only collateral, the agency would produce big creative ideas and all that was needed to execute them by the people in the clients' distribution chain to the retail floor. As he looked for a business partner, Bud found that people thought his idea impractical and too ambitious.

The naysayers made Bud even more resolute to make it happen. He persisted and found a business partner. Bud and Marv Abelson opened Abelson-Frankel in 1962. They planted the seed that sprouted and grew, and the idea continued to inspire Bud right up to his retirement. This made the launching decision the most important in Bud's journey.

As Bud and Marv created this new kind of agency, the pair worked exceptionally well as a team. After 12 years of steady growth, however, the cofounders began to compete over staff and clients and clash over direction for growth. After seven years of escalating competition, the partners were moving in different directions. Bud decided he and Marv had to separate. His offer to Marv was to buy or sell. Marv sold. The decision to end the divisive partnership and move forward as Frankel & Company in 1981 became Bud's leadership tipping point. In reclaiming the clear sense of mission he had when first launching the business, he was making a decision to be true to his vision and values. In Bud's parlance, it was making a commitment to self, clients, and the company. Thereafter, he defined his job as maintaining the integrity of the idea and developing its full potential.

As Bud aligned people, capabilities, and operations behind one vision to meet the specific needs of a diversifying client roster, Frankel became a formidable competitor. Success with key clients, including McDonald's,

Citibank, Visa, Federal Express, and the United States Postal Service put Frankel on the map as an innovative marketing agency. By the end of the 1980s, major advertising agencies wanted to buy Frankel. Bud walked away from those overtures steadfast in his desire to remain independent.

Each of Bud's pivotal decisions built more momentum and took the company to the next level and continually established it as an industry leader. Believing that the idea had strength of its own, Bud underestimated the significance of his leadership and passion in bringing the idea to life. This made his succession plan and the letting go decision the toughest challenges of Bud's career. Approaching the millennium, a rapid flow of events in the marketplace and at Frankel intensified the letting go process. Frankel had prepared for an initial public offering (IPO), but then Bud decided selling to Publicis that already had an international network would be best for the company's future in the global economy. When Publicis retired the name Frankel & Company on April 2, 2007—seven years after buying Frankel and 45 years after the company's start—Frankel alumni posted messages paying tribute to Bud as the best boss who created the best company they had ever worked for. The outpour of sentiment inspired a few people to organize a reunion party that was attended by more than 500 former and current Frankel employees from across the country. The theme of the reunion was "Forever, Frankel"—the spirit of the company is more than a name.

Bud expressed his astonishment and gratitude. "Who'd have thought that people from all over the country would come to Chicago to say goodbye to a name? But I guess it's more than a name . . . it was a way of life; it had its own reason for being that goes well beyond a business." Bud's own words best express his enduring legacy of changing how marketing is practiced throughout the industry. And he showed that people and business flourish when ideas, not money, determine the journey and its purpose.

WHAT MATTERS TO BUD FRANKEL

Bud's Playbook

"The only reason the idea got off the ground and we survived those early years was that I never doubted the idea was worth all of my energy and total commitment."

Bud's path to success started when his boss rejected his idea. As the top salesperson at a small promotion agency, Bud was assigned to help the other salespeople increase their sales. Instead of coming up with the expected solution—how he could help them give better sales pitches— Bud proposed that the company change the way it operated from a sales culture to a client-service culture. This was classic Bud Frankel: thinking in terms of the big idea instead of incremental improvements.

For Bud, big ideas are those that call for a commitment to see them through. Bud was committed to making commitments. With an unwavering sense of responsibility, determined belief, and persistent hard work, he turned ideas into crusades. It was his competitive strength. Even when someone disagreed with him, or simply did not get his idea or vision, he or she had to defer to Bud's certitude. He saw it as commitment— the measure of the strength of an idea and of a person's character and leadership. He says:

> It's great to have an idea of where you want to go, a vision of what you're trying to achieve, but most important, you have to have the willingness to make a commitment to it.
>
> Idea and commitment are a very strong part of the Frankel story. The other part of it is we weren't focused on the money; we were focused on our clients and our work. The courage part was really a belief in what we were doing. It may have been ignorance—but there was a real confidence in the idea and what we were doing.

Bud's founding idea—marketing from firsthand understanding of the client's business and operations—was his constant source of inspiration for innovations in Frankel's operations, capabilities, and creativity. The idea was his North Star for leading day to day and for planning the future. Fundamentally skeptical of institutionalized processes, he thought they squandered creativity, common sense, and acumen. Instead of judging a proposal from an exhaustive report, he preferred a rigorous discussion stimulated by his stream of penetrating questions about the idea and how it would be executed. Instead of relying on forecasts for financial planning, Bud acted on ideas and his instinctive timing. His measure of success was being consistent with the power of the idea, including having the discipline to say no to walk his talk.

Although not focused on the money, Bud appreciated Frankel's financial success because it was proof that his ideas worked and made his clients' businesses more successful. He supported his family with a very comfortable, but not lavish, lifestyle while he continually reinvested in the business.

With so much emphasis today on pursuing one's passion when making career decisions, Bud's story highlights the true meaning of passion: energy that nurtures (1) commitment to turn an idea into reality, (2) persistence to find solutions and to make continuous improvements, and (3) discipline to not compromise the long-term vision for expedience or short-term gain. Without that commitment, to say one is passionate about something is self delusion.

At the core of Bud's commitment to his idea was making the human investment that went far beyond training, which he called indoctrination. Indoctrination—which included Bud's personal drop ins, storytelling, case studies, role modeling, company outings and events, as well as training workshops and learning lunches—turned employees into believers.

Bud's Playbook

"I'd rather have people who are happy to work with each other than 'performers.'"

Bud hired people, not résumés. He valued the person over credentials. He saw employees as individuals, not as a rank or function. He genuinely relished knowing everyone by his or her name and the names of employees' spouses, partners, children, and even their parents. He looked for people motivated to make money but driven by more than money. He wanted to know what made the person tick. He looked for people with varied interests and hobbies because a person of many talents brings fresh dimensions to the work and culture. Until the head count grew to more than 400 people, Bud personally interviewed for key hires, and he worked at indoctrinating new hires to become believers in the Frankel way.

I used to spend a lot of time talking with the staff. I called it MBWA, Management by Wandering Around. I dropped in asking, "What's going on? What are you working on? How's the family?" When I saw the work, I was always asking people, "How is that going to work? Does the client have the manpower to execute it? How would they advertise it, communicate it? What kind of support are you going to get from management? Can we make the idea bigger?"

The people who were happy working with each other in that environment were able to come up with some really phenomenal stuff. I could always get more and better work out of the happy group than the others.

Bud was more like a mayor than a chief executive officer (CEO), creating and building a community that would attract and retain the kind of people who would make good citizens and neighbors. He didn't warm to people overly occupied with self-importance to truly join with the community. Company parties were not for networking; quite the opposite— they were for having fun because all employees, regardless of position, should have fun together.

Chuck in the mailroom was highly regarded for both prompt delivery of the mail and enriching the company culture. He wasn't much of a conversationalist—which made the mail rounds timely and efficient— but he was the definitive expert on the Chicago Cubs and arranged company outings to Wrigley Field. Bud loved people like Chuck, who considered no job too trivial and who had hidden talents and passionate hobbies. In valuing his employees as human beings, Bud was more likely to ask people in the hallway or elevator about their hobbies and families than about their work.

Making employees feel they belonged to this community was the secret to having people who were happy while getting them to work hard. Bud pushed relentlessly for more and better work but always with genuine caring for his people and the work culture. MBWA was what he enjoyed most, and people knew Bud really *was* interested in how they were doing. Even though several of the top executives thought Bud meddled to the point of disrupting decision making, most people enjoyed knowing the chairman of the company was always accessible and thought each person's work was equally important.

Bud's Playbook

"Creative tension is great; political tension is a waste."

Bud disdained political manipulation and pinning blame as a waste of energy and shut it down with a steely glare, making clear that he saw through self-serving politics. The work was what mattered. By focusing everyone's attention on the work, and squashing time-wasting politicking, Bud set the example for fostering trust. Even when people disagreed with him, they trusted that his heart was in the right place, from making strategic decisions to arbitrating conflicts.

We used to have creative arguments all the time. They were terrific because they provoked creative energy. If the argument is political, it's a waste of time. We had a guy who was a great creative director because you could argue with him about his ideas and that challenged him. He would walk away grumbling and swearing, and he'd walk back with a great new solution. And he was happy with the new solution. There were people you could never argue with.

Every now and again I had to settle a creative argument. I used to get so excited about that. I loved that because you have two people who were so committed to their ideas that they'd fight for them.

On the other hand, when we had someone start a dispute over who was to blame for a mistake, the blamer was fired. When it was explained to him that he had abdicated responsibility that was his, he understood why we had to let him go.

These experiences shaped the culture to value creative tension and shut down political tension. Bud took every opportunity to set this tone. Everyone knew that Bud got information firsthand and looked on politicking with disdain. Bud knew to push harder here and to encourage more there. Although staff and clients knew they could count on him to declare what was wrong with what they were doing, they implicitly trusted Bud had their backs covered.

During the 1990s when Frankel's head count quadrupled—in 1998 reaching the peak of 980 employees—the growth pains were very personal for Bud. Once the company topped 500 employees, Bud could no longer be everywhere. He not only did not like feeling less connected with employees, but he increasingly realized that he relied too much on the executive committee for information and situation assessments. He could no longer have his finger on the pulse of the company through his personal queries while making his MBWA rounds. "I had a clue there was trouble when there were no more creative arguments. We were spending a lot of time compromising. That was followed by the loss of an important account." Taking responsibility, Bud thinks he didn't spend enough time mentoring his successors on the value, to the leader and the led, of MBWA for information flow, trust, and commitment to the idea. Nonetheless, the core of the agency that had direct client responsibilities carried on with the values and principles that had built strong client relationships.

With 20/20 hindsight, Bud saw the importance, especially when becoming a much bigger company very quickly, for the leader to take a fresh look at leadership needs and continue being personally involved in hiring, development, and succession planning in all parts of the organization.

I'd really dig down and understand what the person's ambition was about. I look at people I've known who I consider to be strong and effective leaders: Fred Turner, Ray Kroc's successor at McDonald's; Steve Reinemund, chairman of Pepsico; Maurice Levy, CEO of Publicis; Martin Sorrell, CEO of WPP; Sally Rynne; Mary T., former chairman of the board of the American Refugee Committee; Joe Sullivan, co-founder and former chairman of Vigoro Corporation, who was the best leader I ever knew.

What they all were are what I'd look for: very smart, high energy and hard working, all had the ability to communicate, all had vision, all are straight talkers without any b-s, none are braggarts, they were all interested in making money, and they had an ambition that was more than about making money. They all had a pretty good idea of what the future is about. I don't think you can train people to think strategically about the future. There are people who always think about the future. And there are people who never think about tomorrow.

Bud's Playbook

"We preached commitment to self, commitment to clients and commitment to the agency—in that order."

Bud's 40-year journey of starting and building Frankel & Company is about the humanness of leadership. Whoever coined the phrase "It's not personal; it's business" never met Bud. He believed business is, and *should* be, personal in several ways. First, he saw his leadership as a personal responsibility to all the employees, clients, and suppliers who depended on his effectiveness to do their jobs well. Second, he walked away from business if having the business meant compromising Frankel's values. And most importantly, commitment to self meant defining your own personal values and meaning of success, and doing things to fulfill your own expectations.

The toughest decisions for Bud were at the intersection of people and business. Does he make the decision that's good for the human side of business or for the financial side of business? Bud usually found ways to do both. He succeeded in not having a layoff for 35 years. When he had to fire someone, he treated the person with dignity.

I felt a tremendous responsibility that so many families were making a living from Frankel. That was a heavy responsibility, particularly when business was slow. The popular thing to do would be to let people go. I would get charged up and energized to get business and not have to let people go. I used to say to myself, "Do you know how many people are depending on you?"

Commitment to values came to life in a culture-shaping event that became company legend. Having a large tobacco client, Bud found himself in a dilemma when he discovered that his 13-year-old son was smoking cigarettes. After a conversation with his son, he knew the company's tobacco account now posed a conflict of interest: What was good for his business would make the father a hypocrite for his son.

One night I got home and my wife said she found out that our son was smoking. I lost it. He and I had a big to-do. While driving to work the next morning I said, "What kind of jerk am I, where are my values if I do work for a tobacco client—which we did—and I'm beating up my son for smoking?"

I got down to the office and spoke with Marv. I went to New York and told the client what had happened, that I felt hypocritical and could no longer work for the cigarette brands. I expected him to explode. He said, "I understand what you're going through, absolutely no hard feelings. You can continue to work with the safety razor division and the gum division, and we'll continue to be good friends."

That experience really impacted our culture about doing the right thing as a commitment to oneself. We preached commitment to self, commitment to clients, and commitment to the agency—in that order.

This became one of those culture-building experiences of a company that has far more impact than a corporate values statement—it gave Frankel a soul. When an employee would consult with Bud about a personal decision, Bud would invariably advise him or her to make the decision that made a commitment to him- or herself. He rarely if ever brought up the company in that advice. Commitment to self meant living up to your own expectations.

Success is fulfilling what you set out to do. I don't think it has numerical values, nothing to do with money. It's something you feel personally and you don't need someone outside of you to tell you that you're successful. You know you are. Nobody else can make you feel successful.

That's why I used to tell people when they made a great presentation and the client didn't get it, "It's not your fault. You did a great job. What's sad is the client doesn't see it. So you have every right to feel successful about what you did."

Despite his achievements, Bud never looked at the entirety of his career as successful—there were successes but there was always more to do. "Frankel and Company was always a work in progress. It was never done. I never felt successful. I felt proud of many things we achieved, but I never felt successful."

Bud's Playbook

"I committed to working harder than anybody else."

Bud always saw himself as just one of the guys, and working hard was the only way to earn a living. He says, "I never thought of myself as the underdog or the 'overdog.' I thought of myself more as Joe six-pack than anything else." Working hard was also a way for him to compensate for having left college because of a football injury. By working harder than others, he figured he could do at least as well as all his friends with college degrees.

This admission would surprise most people who know Bud; he has such certitude and confidence. He projects natural leadership. He looks like a CEO with his 6-foot-tall trim and broad stature and has the comportment of self-assuredness and executive presence. It was his socially relaxed attitude and love of a good poker game with beer and buddies that revealed his Joe six-pack side.

> I was never afraid of work; it never bothered me. When I was a kid, I always had a job or two or three. When I was a teenager working on a pop truck, they gave me a bad route. But I had the best book every week because I'd go out at 7 at night while other people would finish by 4 in the afternoon. Every job I had, I would be number one because I worked harder. That was simple.
>
> I was injured playing college football and never finished college. Everyone else I knew had a college degree or more. I thought they were smarter than I was. I felt I had to work for what I got and everyone else was already there. So I had to outwork them just to stay even. I committed to working harder. In the process of working hard, I saw things and opportunities and capitalized on them.

Believing in the value of work and of all workers, whatever the task and position in the business, was the cornerstone of Bud's idea and leadership style. He saw that great marketing programs depend on understanding not just customers and client executives but also the work of people in the warehouse, in the kitchen, and at the sales counter. Mistrusting academic approaches that lack conviction and common sense, Bud had little patience for people who had all the answers without getting out in the field and understanding the day-to-day experience of the stock boy, the store clerk, and the cashier. Being an uncommon blend of Joe six-pack and chairman, Bud was as comfortable working alongside hourly workers as boardroom executives.

One story showing how Bud defined working hard became company folklore. In the early years, Bud, Marv, and a team of freelancers worked for 72 hours straight, catching naps in the office, fulfilling a last-minute assignment that the client knew had an impossible deadline. Bud finally went home late Sunday night before the work was completed. When he returned to the office early Monday morning, he found a stack of finished art boards of advertisements with a note: "Go get them, Tiger. We'll see you when we see you." This story helped foster a culture that took pride in working hard, in taking on challenges competitors would not, and in a team where members had each other's back.

Working hard for the client didn't mean always saying yes to them. Bud fiercely believed in the agency's role to lead the client and not just be an order taker. Never able to be passive about client direction that he disagreed with, Bud preached to his team to stand for what they believed and pushed them relentlessly for big ideas, even if the client gave directions that generated small ideas. Bud was not popular with all the clients, but they knew there was a Bud Frankel behind his people and the work.

Although some people considered Bud's MBWA and queries micromanaging, he was the ultimate role model in encouraging employees not to settle for the commonplace, even if it meant working round the clock. Although the staff grumbled about the long hours over work that was not a matter of life and death, they always took pride in their work. This was the art of Bud's leadership: getting more out of people and garnering results that made them proud.

BUD'S PIVOTAL DECISIONS

Pivot Point: Launching Decision

"Think about how you can, not about how you cannot. There are a lot of people who operate that way: 'We can't do that.' There's always a way, particularly if it's the right thing to do."

A single statement instantly made Bud decide to start his own business: His boss said, "I don't want to work that hard." The response to the idea Bud proposed on that seminal day in 1961 sparked his entrepreneurial instincts to prove his idea could work. Perhaps, more accurately, the idea of a boss not wanting to work hard provoked Bud to prove the merits of his idea. "At that second, I was intellectually out the door. I immediately began looking for ways to go into business working off this concept," Having joined the small promotion agency for a chance to become partner, he failed in that plan. But he ended up more successful than in his wildest dreams.

Since the birth of his first child, Bud had gone "from being an employee to thinking ahead in a big way." On that day of rejection—one year into the job, at age 32, with a wife and two babies—he found his boss too complacent. Five sales jobs and five bosses taught Bud more about what not to do when he became a boss than what he aspired to do. He was ready to start his own company and make a commitment.

> I always had in the back of my head that I'd have my own business. I came by that naturally; my father was a business owner. The real energy in the business was my mother. She was a grand dame and a tough old broad. She lived to be 103. She learned to swim at 77. She used to bang into my head, "You can be whatever you want to be. You're in America."
>
> They were both born in Poland. My mother emigrated from Poland; my father, from Germany. When he was 13, he apprenticed with a master watchmaker in Germany and became a master watchmaker himself. My mother talked my father into starting his own business. She was the hard worker. He was more concerned about having a cigarette and coffee with the guys down the street. At his funeral, there wasn't an empty seat. He was a good guy.

From his mother, Bud got the "tough" gene and from his father, the "good guy" gene, an effective blend. Most people respected his persistence but his intractable stubbornness was not as easily accepted. They were two sides of the same coin that helped Bud be an entrepreneur with a singular focus. Naysayers only strengthened his commitment to prove the merits of his idea. That launching decision catapulted him from being a super salesperson to becoming an industry-changing leader.

When I made the decision to start my own marketing agency, I never doubted we'd get business; I just never dreamed it would get as big as it got.

When I would tell people in the industry what we were going to do, they all said it wouldn't work. Clients won't pay for marketing ideas and thinking. They pay for *things*, the ads, the brochures, the promotion giveaways. The more I talked about the power of ideas, and the less enthusiastic my audience, the more convinced I became that this was a viable idea.

For the next 45 years, Bud worked with single-minded obsession to prove how big the idea could be. His first test of commitment was finding a business partner. He approached six owners of art production studios and got six rejections. Without a financial and operating partner, he would be another freelancer in an industry filled with freelancers. This was not what he envisioned for his future. Beginning to lose hope that he could pull this off, one day he walked in on a client talking on the phone with Marv Abelson, a production manager Bud had worked with at Kling Studio. "I literally grabbed the phone out of my client's hand and said, 'Marv, this is the most expensive phone call you ever made in your life.'"

Bud and Marv opened Abelson-Frankel on April 1, 1962, on the second floor of a brownstone in downtown Chicago. Bud was the copywriter, client service representative, and business developer. Marv took care of operations. Freelancers did all the labor-intensive work of hand-rendered illustrations and production-ready materials. The company started with two of Bud's former clients from his previous job.

Bud and Marv established the company DNA for never settling for good-enough work. They gave everything they had to coming up with ideas with staying power and making them even bigger and better. "I remember times when we were working on projects until 11 at night, then look at it and say, 'Not right. Yeah, we know it.' And we'd start all over again."

Bud and Marv quickly got their next test: Unable to secure a bank line of credit because they were unproven entrepreneurs, they had business but negative cash flow. Bud's mantra, "Think about how you can, not about how you cannot," carried them through the first year of survival and a second year of reinvesting in the business. In 1965, they hired a new creative director, John Forbes, who became a financial partner. By the end of the third year, they had proven they had a sustainable business model.

Marv and I didn't take any pay for the first year. We took nothing. In the beginning of the second year, Marv and I took salaries of $600 per month. At the end of that year, we had nine employees and everybody got a bonus. As we were able to grow and hire staff, we got people who were better than we were at functions that we were doing but not well.

There was never a doubt in my mind we wouldn't succeed. Of course, my picture of success in the beginning was not grand. Success was really proving the viability of the idea because so many people said it wouldn't work. But the naysayers were not part of the proof. I was in a place where I had to prove to myself that my idea worked. That became my screen. If all my competitors said you couldn't do it, I'd do it. I honestly believed clients wanted to have partners, not vendors.

With growth, we took additional real estate and worried whether we could fill it up or not. Those numbers were terrifying. When we took 2,500 square feet at 740 North Rush, it was so much space. In about a year, it was all filled. Then we moved to 360 North Michigan Avenue into 8,000 square feet. We thought, "Oh my God, what have we done. We have all these empty offices." We had to take a second floor. In 1979, we moved into 111 East Wacker and all that space was unbelievable. What were we going to do with all of that? We ended up with four floors and over 120,000 square feet.

Bud's prodding and expansion risks paid off. His timing was perfect as marketing was increasingly recognized as the key driver of business growth. Companies became marketing driven.

On that day in 1961, Bud didn't know the phenomenal trajectory marketing would enjoy. He only knew that he believed in his idea but his boss had rejected it. He could have sulked and complained about his boss's aversion to change and risk and begrudgingly decided to develop a better sales presentation for the sales team. He could have decided to start interviewing with another company. He could have made these decisions and even advanced his pay and title, but these decisions would not have ushered in all the opportunities of his leadership decision. The natural leader in Bud had turned a rejection into his opportunity. His launching decision was a decision to challenge the status quo and pursue what he ardently believed was a better way for business and for achieving his goals.

Was Bud inspired by his idea, or was he challenged to prove himself right? Both. Because Bud was inspired, he inspired others. Because he was determined to prove he was right, he had the sustained intensity of drive to build a game-changing company.

Pivot Point: Turning Point Decision

"You reach a point when you have to clearly define what you are."

Ten years of steady growth proved the validity of the idea, giving Bud the confidence to take the next bold step. He decided the time had come to bill clients for labor and talent as professional fees in the same way as law and accounting firms. He had delayed the inevitable decision to break away from the industry's conventional billing practice that marked up production and media to cover labor as a hidden cost. This practice conflicted with his founding idea that the human investment in partnerships and creative ideas is the real value proposition. The change was a big and risky move that was about more than billing practices. It made marketing an expertise and professional service that required talent and training, which should carry its own value.

> Every business starts out having trouble defining who they are. It's really tough because the name of the game when you're starting out is survival, and so you're compromising as you go. But then you reach a certain point when you have to clearly define who and what you are. And at that point the business is going to either fall off or it's going to take off. That point occurred for us when we had been in business for 10 years. We had to put our money where our mouth was—and that was the human investment we made in our clients' business.
>
> We got our clients believing in us because of the visible commitment we made to understand their business. If it meant riding the bread truck, we did it. We went to the bakery at 4 in the morning, met the drivers, and rode the route with them. Doing

this kind of thing really paid off in how we helped our clients. That's what clients were really paying us for, so we decided we had to work on a fee basis. It was a scary move at the time as we struggled to gain credibility as a national agency.

Bud's timing was again impeccable, or he was lucky; it was probably a bit of both. In 1973, McDonald's was looking for a new promotion agency and was interested in a fee-based relationship.

Luck came our way. McDonald's decided that they would work with an agency on a fee basis. That was manna from heaven. They put together a list of over 60 promotion agencies. Six Chicago agencies made final presentations.

In the finals, we were selected to work on the children's business and another agency got the adult business. At the end of six months, it became clear we were head and shoulders above the other agency in our commitment, our service, and our understanding of their needs. By the end of the year, McDonald's also gave us the adult business.

Everything we did for McDonald's was highly visible. It gave us confidence to be selective and work only with clients wanting long-term relationships. When we got calls from potentially large clients inviting us to discuss projects and they said they wouldn't pay for our pitch ideas, we declined those meetings. It was very difficult to turn down work, but we had to do it to maintain the integrity of the idea.

Other agencies followed us. Today fees are the standard. This was a defining move for the industry and for our company culture. Our success was the power of the idea. The idea had strength of its own. All we had to do was be consistent with it. And that really became my job.

By aligning the revenue model and financial management with the partnership idea, Bud clearly defined Frankel and its marketing expertise as a professional service. Frankel delivered on its value proposition to McDonald's, and that marked the turning point for the regional agency. Not only did Frankel establish a national reputation as McDonald's marketing agency of record, but it also did some of its best work ever for the fast-growing company that believed in marketing and new ideas. Three years after winning McDonald's business, Frankel created McDonald's When the US Wins You Win promotion for the 1976 Montreal Olympic Games. It was a huge success for McDonald's and for Frankel—a tour de force that was a turning point and established Frankel's reputation for powerful marketing. The agency grew to 100 people servicing a growing client roster.

Pivot Point: Tipping Point Decision

"Real growth kicked in about a year after Marv and I separated. Everybody was focused on growing the business; there were no compromises from trying to serve two masters."

Prosperity brought competition between the founding partners. During the early years, Bud and Marv had worked well together, complementing each other's strengths with a clear division of labor. Marv had been the inside man, running operations, while Bud ran client services and creative development. Competition started after Marv called on clients, at first because the agency didn't have enough account people, and continued to do so because he was having success. Competition turned into division.

Marv and I were a very good team when we started out. That lasted about 12 years, although we were business partners for close to 20 years. We were an "us" team when we started out. Then competition between us brought out insidious kind of stuff—that's my designer, that's my copywriter, why isn't your guy billing as many hours as my guy, all that kind of stuff. And we couldn't agree on how to grow the agency. Marv was having successes with medical products accounts and wanted to turn us into a medical advertising agency. We were Abelson-Frankel yet operated as two separate agencies. People chose sides. There were Marv's people, and there were Bud's people.

In order to get rid of the problem, I put this plan together to buy or sell. I could have gone either way, buy or sell. It didn't make any difference to me. But we had to stop what we were doing. He chose to sell. So we separated in 1981. At that point, we had about 100 people. It was a fairly smooth split. Marv got a lot of money plus the right to hire any of the people he wanted and to take his clients with him. The only thing we could have done was to separate. That's clear. That was the right decision.

The punch line for all of this is it worked for both of us. He created Abelson-Taylor, and I created Frankel & Company. And we were both successful.

If Bud had not approached Marv with the decision to end the divisive partnership, the company would have struggled or perhaps been destroyed. Instead of trying to win the competitive disagreements, Bud took the high road. The leadership decision was to separate as equals—no winner or loser.

After being in business for 20 years, the disruptive partnership gave Bud clarity about what he had to do to provide fresh leadership. It was a decision to lead a team united behind one vision and one growth strategy, ushering in the tipping point of his leadership journey. The company embarked on a winning streak that lasted almost 20 years. In the process, Bud grew from being a very good entrepreneur to being a great leader.

Moving forward as the new Frankel & Company mobilized all of Bud's energy, taking his leadership to the next level. He applied an important lesson from the dissolution of the partnership: For teamwork, there must be clear division of responsibilities. He turned an informal operation into an organization with more functional structure and more cross-functional teamwork. He hired an accountant. He built a production and purchasing department. He expanded the project management department. He hired more senior client service people.

With functional experts to manage day-to-day operations, Bud worked on establishing one team, with one vision and one leader. The coming apart of a great team left a deep imprint, and Bud set out to create a workplace without competitive rivalries that ensnare people in destructive politics. He led the way by focusing everyone's attention on the work. He stepped up his involvement with all the account and creative teams. He devoted much of his time to MBWA, dropping into meetings and people's offices and cubicles. He hired team players. The culture of teamwork and camaraderie was able to develop an immune system that rejected grandstanding and backstabbing. Bud used MBWA with all clients, paying regular visits to have his finger on the pulse of the clients' businesses and their relationship with Frankel.

Known primarily as McDonalds' agency, Frankel won recognition in 1985 for the successful launch of a major new product for Citibank's New York Banking Division. Not only did Citicorp quickly become the agency's second largest account, it established Frankel as marketing experts for any industry.

> The banking industry in the early 1980s was not yet market-ing oriented. Citibank called us because they wanted our retail expertise working for McDonald's. They hired us to work on the introduction of the first electronically linked banking account. It had the highest visibility, because John Reed, CEO of Citicorp at that time, wanted to make technology Citibank's competitive advantage.
>
> We worked with their marketing department, their branch managers, and their operations people. All the thinking we did, all the training, all the retail merchandising, and all the internal communications got total organizational support and everyone on the same page—it got everyone's attention. The introduc-tion was a huge success with consumers but also with Citibank employees and management. After that success, we didn't need to pitch Citbank for more business; they gave it to us. We worked with almost every part of the bank.

The work that Frankel did for clients just didn't fit the traditional work of advertising agencies or promotion agencies. The Frankel way defied conventional capabilities defined by what was produced—print advertising, television advertising, radio commercials, press releases, marketing events, direct mail, merchandising, giveaways, and bro-chures. Instead, Frankel was working on marketing campaigns and cli-ents' annual marketing plans and executing them. The value of a client grew exponentially from hundreds of thousands of dollars for a project to millions for year-round marketing.

In 1993, Bud hired Dick Thomas for new business development; "he turned out to be a *very important* hire." From 1994 to 1997, revenues grew 30 to 40 percent annually, and the number of employees more than doubled to 650.

By 1994, we had more business than we could absorb even as we were hiring people by the boatloads. We got the new business rhythm down pretty good. We were hotter than a $2 pistol. We had to literally put a halt to all new business activity. Our confidence was off the charts.

Frankel's capabilities had expanded to include strategic planning, promotion, database marketing, direct mail, digital marketing, public relations, event marketing, research, merchandising and retail design, sampling, and on-site training. Along the way, Frankel had taken the lead in creating the marketing services industry.

We had client successes. We were getting all kinds of new business. The key was we were keeping clients. We weren't turning them over as we were getting new clients. We had very good staying power with our clients. We worked very hard to keep it.

We got the new business rhythm down pretty good. Our presentations talked more about our potential clients than talking about ourselves. Once we figured that out we were on a roll. Once you got the client talking about their needs, you could pretty much tell you were on the right track. We were batting 600—we'd win two out of three pitches.

We encouraged the potential client to talk about their issues and their problems and their desires. We then responded with similar experiences with other clients. That made those presentations really good. You didn't have to spend a lot of time talking about what you've done. And that was relatively easy and straightforward, and very brief.

Frankel's success brought growth pains; no one felt them more than Bud. Once the company topped 500 employees, the executive committee pushed for more process and more power to make decisions independent of Bud.

The company was getting very big and very fast. I used to do all the interviewing. I used to think I could get through to people and figure out if they were going to be any good for us. Then it became very difficult to do, and we had a human resource department that took it over. They were hiring résumés; they weren't hiring people.

Then you get so big, everything gets departmentalized. You get leaders for the departments. You start talking with the leaders and hope they'd pass it on to others. And I wasn't where I wanted to be. I wanted to be with the client. I wanted to be working on projects. I wanted to get my hands dirty. Instead, my time was spent on financial issues, healthcare and employee benefits, negotiating office space leases. It was for me the drudgery of management.

Recognizing in 1994 that the much larger and still growing business called for more leadership, Bud handpicked an external advisory board of "three of the brightest people" he knew: Joe Sullivan, chairman of the Executive Committee of International Mineral & Chemical Corporation; Larry Erhlich, a labor lawyer; and Wayne Fickinger, the retired chairman of advertising agency J. Walter Thompson. From them Bud got expert counsel, a peer group of trusted advisors, and objective guidance.

Also, in 1994, Bud's son, Peter, joined the company. Bud sharpened his focus on the company's next level in the changing business landscape of consolidation and globalization.

Then in 1995, Bud's daughter was killed in an automobile accident. "That blew me apart. That was the toughest thing I've ever gone through. I lost an awful lot of energy after that. I was less involved for a period." The company and clients rallied around Bud and his family. The company had momentum and continued its spectacular growth.

Pivot Point: Recommitment Decision

"You start, move along, define the business, go up drastically, level off again, and define again where you are; and hopefully you take off again."

After several months, Bud dealt with his grief by throwing himself back into work. He focused on the company's future. In 1996, Frankel's sales were surging 40 percent per year. The marketing communications industry was consolidating into four major global networks: WPP Group, Interpublic Group, Omnicom Group, and Publicis Groupe.

Bud thought about their acquisition strategy to get a bigger share of clients' marketing dollars. He saw the opportunity to create synergies. He believed no one was working on the whole marketing picture for the client and Frankel could play that role. With the client at the center of a network of communications capabilities and media, Frankel could orchestrate the work of various agencies to deliver a coherent brand message and experience that would stand out in the noisy marketplace.

He thought about ways to expand internationally along with Frankel's global clients, including McDonald's, Nestle, and Microsoft. That required capital for acquisitions, changing Bud's long-held conviction to stay independent and "have control of our own destiny." Bud explored various options to go global and to create synergies.

> I thought I could pull this off—build a global organization that serviced the client at the center—if I got the right partner and the money to do it. This was a different mode in a different time than when I set out with my original dream. When I started the business, rejections only strengthened my verve to do it. This time I couldn't do it because I didn't have the money. I knew it was going to be expensive.
>
> Our first thought was to acquire agencies in key global markets. We looked at a lot of agencies and a lot of people. It became clear there wasn't anyone out there doing business the way we were. Our next thought was to join forces with someone who already has an international organization. We started talking with the global communications networks to create an alliance. Almost everyone wanted to make a deal for stock, not for cash.
>
> We then thought we could have an IPO to get the money to do it ourselves.

In 1997, Bud started working with investment banking firm William Blair on an IPO. He also hired Paul Gipson, who had IPO experience with Goldman Sachs, to be his independent advisor. Acting on William Blair's advice, Bud set aggressive financial targets to make Frankel & Company attractive to investors. The company invested heavily in developing a new digital platform. It hired a senior executive to spearhead electronic marketing initiatives. In 1998, Frankel put together a preliminary offering memorandum. It formed two business units, Frankel &

Company with Jim Mack as CEO and New Ventures with Dave Tridle as CEO, both reporting to Bud as chairman. Since 1991, Jim and Dave had been copresidents, Jim as chief client officer and Dave as chief operations officer. Also in 1998, Bud paved the way for his 34-year-old son, Peter, to become vice chairman. In January 1999, Frankel announced this appointment, signaling that Peter would succeed Bud as chairman at some future date.

> We had some work cut out for us in order to have an IPO. We figured we'd get this done in early 2000. We put a lot of work in developing technology-based marketing tools under the New Ventures unit. It was slow going and had a high cash burn rate.

Preparations for an IPO triggered clashes between the executive committee and Bud, most intensely in 1998 over corporate strategy and the shareholder agreement. To Bud, the other shareholders were losing the spirit that got Frankel to where it was. To the shareholders on the executive committee, Bud was disrupting their management decisions. The committee handled Bud by deciding what he needed to know, when he should be told, who would tell him, and how. Bud ended up with an information bias that was his blind spot.

> Don't accept everything that you're told. People who were bucking for sergeant were out to create a good face for themselves. There was such bad information coming back to me about client relations and internal matters. You have to dig for what's really going on.
>
> I don't know the answer but I do know you cannot police people. You can't spend your time worrying who's going to tell you and who won't. The only thing you can do is work on the culture and hope that the culture stops that kind of thing.

As the undisputed visionary, Bud focused on the future rather than on the conflicts. It was a time of "irrational exuberance," borrowing from then–Federal Reserve Chairman Alan Greenspan. Frankel had unstoppable momentum. In 1998, revenue rose to $100 million, headcount had quadrupled since 1992, and Frankel had four offices in the United States. Bud focused all his energy on going where he knew the market needed to go—global and digital. And, Bud wanted to hand over to Peter what he knew would be the driver of Frankel's future growth and success. He invested heavily in building value for a successful IPO.

Although this was a controversial time within Frankel, Bud demonstrated that Frankel still had entrepreneurial energy and the courage to transform during an inflection point of technological change that was transforming marketing communications.

Pivot Point: Letting Go Decision

"The emotional letting go took a long time."

On a paper napkin at Manny's Deli on the south side of Chicago, Paul Gipson jotted down two numbers. Bud looked at the numbers with intensity detectable only by those who knew him well. For this pivotal meeting in 1999, Paul had picked Bud's favorite lunch place, where the Formica tables, linoleum floors, and cafeteria trays are as unpretentious as the corned beef is famous. Bud likes unpretentiousness.

"The bid is going to be between here and here," Paul explained. "This is the high end." Paul paused and then asked cautiously, "Bud, will you be satisfied with that?"

With characteristic candor that is part regular-guy humility and part boardroom confidence, Bud responded, "Yeah, I'd be satisfied with the low end." Relieved, Paul outlined preparations for the change of course from going public with an IPO to selling Frankel & Company.

This would become both one of the best financial decisions and one of the most bittersweet decisions of his career.

> When Paul proposed that we put the company up for sale, I had come to the conclusion that the only option was to join an organization that already had an international presence and could get the idea done. It was clear we didn't have enough money to buy a big enough organization. It was clear we couldn't get enough money through an IPO. And, it was clear that Peter wanted to leave. Peter said, "I don't feel comfortable here. I don't like doing this." So, it was time to sell.

In part, letting go was an emotional decision Bud made when it became clear that no one in the family would be part of the company's future. In part, it was a pragmatic business decision. At the time of the lunch at Manny's, the IPO market was slowing and Frankel was having some setbacks in its New Ventures initiatives. In part, it was a visionary decision with Bud still in the recommitment mode to steer the company to a new global model.

The all-cash deal closed in January 2000 for $5 million more than the high number on that napkin at Manny's and $50 million more than the low end. The undisclosed selling price delivered a very high valuation and to Bud, who owned two-thirds of the company, significant wealth. The winning offer in the bidding war came from Paris-based Publicis Groupe, a global organization of 42,000 employees in 104 countries. Maurice Levy, its CEO, voiced support for Bud's goals throughout negotiations.

Being bought by Publicis was our opportunity to create the kind of global partnership that we had envisioned. The conversations with Maurice were always positive. It was always, "We'll do that. We'll get someone to help you. Let's put together a team to do that." He was very smart that way—Maurice could tell where people's hearts were.

Immediately after the sale, Bud traveled the world to find companies he could buy. He found that *"No one in the free world was doing business the way we were."* The economy was also working against him. Two months following the closing of the sale in January 2000, the dot-com crash began to take down the equity markets and dry up the IPO market. NASDAQ peaked on March 10, 2000, and quickly nosedived; a year later, NASDAQ had lost 60 percent of its value. Furthermore, on September 17, 2001, when the stock markets reopened after the 9/11 terrorist attacks, the Dow Jones Industrial Average lost 684 points; by that Friday, US stocks lost $1.2 trillion in value for the week.

On one hand, Bud's timing to sell was almost prescient. On the other hand, he did not have the time, nor were conditions right to start a new global Frankel. In the economic downturn of 2001, Frankel lost business and the parent company put a halt to expansion plans. In 2002, Bud retired at 72 years old.

THE LEADER'S LEGACY

In the process of working as the clients' indispensable partner, Frankel changed an industry. Even Bud's detractors agree that his vision, perfect timing, and leadership advanced marketing and the whole industry. Bud's fans believe he built the best company to work with and for; it not only changed an industry but also changed lives. It was a success driven by the founder's commitment to do the right thing for the integrity of self, the company, and its clients, which filtered down to thousands of people who regarded Frankel as giving them their best opportunities to learn and do their best work.

Frankel grew and succeeded because Bud had the vision, verve, and nerve to tell clients they could get better marketing if they changed how they worked with their agencies. His launching decision, to create a different kind of agency-client relationship, turned sales promotion into a full-fledged marketing discipline. His turning point decision, to charge professional fees, elevated the role of marketing services in clients' brand building and sales growth. His tipping point decision, to be a unifying leader, propelled Frankel on a trajectory of innovations and growth that changed the industry. His recommitment decision, to build a new global organization, paved the way to service multinational clients. His letting go decision, to sell to the organization that could best get the job done, secured help to build a new model for the global economy. Selling Frankel also provided significant financial remuneration that enabled Bud to create the Frankel Family Foundation for advancing justice in the world.

Bud received the 1999 Silver Medal Award from the Chicago Advertising Federation for his contributions to the advancement of advertising as well as to the community for the betterment of human welfare.

> The model we created was right; it's still right. The power of the idea and my total commitment to it propelled us forward to a certain level of success. I wanted to keep pushing the idea to new levels.
>
> It was a great ride for a long time. I loved all of the work. I loved the idea of having a problem to solve and getting everyone around it. We all got our hands dirty. We worked our tails off and had a lot of fun. Those victories were so sweet.

I achieved more wealth than I ever dreamt possible, by a long shot. But the important thing to me is not the wealth. I really think I created an industry where there wasn't one. I believe I helped a lot of people in my lifetime. And I'm still doing that through the Frankel Family Foundation.

Bud's leadership journey started with an idea for a new company. He ended up redefining marketing services in ways that extend far beyond a single company. He also ended up being a role model of leadership principles before they became part of the business lexicon, such as client partnerships and alignment and the importance of the emotional quotient (EQ) in leadership. Yet, Bud feels that Frankel was still a work in progress. There was more to do to achieve his vision where "one happy marketing family" addressed the clients' total marketing to connect better with customers and deliver a consistent brand experience. In retirement, Bud couldn't stop thinking about how it could be done.

I want my legacy to be about persistence. Think about how you can, not about how you cannot. There are many people, even in high places, who operate that way—"We can't do that because." There's always a way to get something done, particularly if it's the right thing to do.

Bud's journey is about the equal importance of a great idea, an unwavering commitment, and the courage of conviction to defy naysayers. Bud's story reminds us that loving the journey is as important as the destination reached, because on a great journey, there is always more to see and do than there is time. Bud's legacy is best expressed in his own words: Frankel became "a way of life; it had its own reason for being that goes well beyond a business." When asked what title he would give to his story, he replied, "Keep Dreaming and Keep Working." Bud loved the journey and had the courage and tenacity to walk on unknown paths, the mark of a true visionary. And he is still loved by the Frankelites who still speak of Frankel & Company as the best place they had ever worked.

CHAPTER **3**

CHANGE

Glen Tullman

Managing Partner of 7wire Ventures; Former CEO of Allscripts Healthcare Solutions

WHY YOU SHOULD KNOW HIM AND ABOUT HIS WORK

Glen Tullman, chief executive officer (CEO) of Allscripts Healthcare Solutions from 1997 to 2012, transformed a failing drug repackaging company into a $1.4 billion leader in electronic health records (EHR), laying the foundation for a fundamental change in the cost and quality of our health and health care system. By building the industry's most widely used system, including more than 180,000 physicians, 1,500 hospitals, and 10,000 post-acute-care centers using Allscripts software, the company established the infrastructure for patient-centered care. Allscripts software allows patients to walk into any doctor's office, hospital, or nursing home in the network and have their medical records, with permission, instantly available for medical staff to coordinate diagnostics, treatment, and therapeutics. Putting the patient at the center of information technology took tenacious visionaries, such as Glen, first to create and then to advance the fledgling EHR industry as a tool for improving medical care. Among his awards was recognition with President Obama as one of the two most important figures in health care in 2009, selection as an EHR Game Changer by Health Data Management in 2010, CEO of the year from Illinois Information

Technology Association, and the Lifetime Achievement Award from the Chicago Area Entrepreneurship Hall of Fame for his work driving innovation and change across a number of businesses.

Glen also focuses in a big way on giving back to the community. Although he supports many charities, he is most committed to the Juvenile Diabetes Research Foundation (JDRF), in part because of his youngest son being diagnosed at age eight. He has held a number of leadership roles, including his efforts leading a $100 million campaign for the newly conceived artificial pancreas, which, six years later, is now in clinical trials, for which he received the JDRF Best of Illinois honor in 2009. He has also led by example, with his family foundation contributing millions to causes. He currently serves as a chancellor for the JDRF International Board and most recently chaired the most successful gala in JDRF history in Chicago.

Glen's career has been a series of successes and challenges, some self-imposed and others foisted on him by external forces. He likes to say, "The world often turns upside down on people who thought they were standing on top of it." His experiences and the decisions he made have shaped his always-ready and always-alert approach. It's no surprise that on his booklist is *Only the Paranoid Survive* by Andy Grove. Glen's trial by fire came early at Allscripts, when he braved the conflicts between managing to meet short-term goals and leading to make sustainable long-term improvements—both important but involving different perspectives, decisions, and accountabilities. Shortly after he completed Allscripts' initial public offering (IPO) in 1999, the burst of the dot-com bubble sent the stock in a freefall from $89 in 2000 to $1.60 in 2002 in a market further devastated by 9/11 terrorism. Glen was standing on the proverbial burning platform with employees fearful of losing their jobs, physicians unimpressed with Allscripts' software, and analysts and investors bailing out.

He saved the company from ending up on the pile of dot-com rubble by listening to doctors explain what they wanted his software to do. To build the product line his clients really wanted while needing to move into a more lucrative market segment, Glen leveraged what he had: Allscripts stock. This was a bet-the-company move, his first among several. Sealing a strategic partnership in a stock deal with IDX Systems Corporation, the leader in physician practice management for large practices, Allscripts ultimately signed up 50 percent of large physician practices—the strategy worked. The stock clawed its way above $10 in early 2005 and to $30 in 2007, while revenues grew to $280 million with more than

$20 million in earnings. The decision, initially scorned by the market, was the right bet and helped Glen crystallize a vision of how information technology can improve health care outcomes. It also emboldened Glen, turning a passionate entrepreneur into a determined visionary. This makes the turning point decision the most important on Glen's leadership journey, galvanizing him to build a better and stronger platform.

Each bold decision enabled the next bolder decision for growth and more connectivity in the health care continuum. Those decisions usually left financial analysts perplexed at the time they were announced. Frustrated with their line of sight and fixation just on quarterly results, Glen moved forward, knowing that managing only for short-term goals would only delay the company's demise. His initial success paired with his survival instinct freed him from the doubts of critics and second-guessing of investors. "At a certain point you get brave and say, I'm not going to be afraid anymore. That's freedom!" Over time, results validated his strategic acumen, and Glen ultimately won the growing confidence of stakeholders.

Stable growth soon aroused Glen's entrepreneurial instincts to make a game-changing move. The merger in 2008 with the health care segment of Misys increased Allscripts' reach to one-third of all actively practicing physicians in the United States. This was a second bet-the-company decision, which included a shared leadership model and ceding majority ownership for a period. Glen's view was that his job was at risk, but the merger would put the company on the map permanently, which was the most important thing he could do as a leader. That tipping point decision paved the way for the much larger and more challenging merger with Eclipsys in 2010, creating a $1.3 billion enterprise. The idea was to combine Eclipsys's strength in acute care with Allscripts' strength in ambulatory care.

The merger with Eclipsys woke up the market, and Glen had seized the historic opportunity for medical information technology to play a leading role in the transformation of health care. Bold changes were imperative, driven by revolutionary innovations in medicine and digital technologies as well as the American Recovery and Reinvestment Act of 2009 that provided $30 billion for medical providers to make meaningful use of EHR. Allscripts' merger with Eclipsys assured its role as an innovation leader.

As noted earlier, the merger was larger, bolder, and different from the other mergers he had successfully led. With Eclipsys, Glen learned that every merger has its own pulse, and what worked before did not work this time. This was partly because of a split board that tied his hands relative to some key decisions. A major delay in product launches promised to customers and disappointing first quarter 2012 performance provoked a power struggle in the boardroom. Despite Glen's swift measures to stabilize the conflict, politically divided camps continued to hamper integration and sales.

The boardroom politics were new to Glen, who had a career of supportive boards focused on company growth. The boardroom antics spurred a much-publicized shareholder action from one large shareholder. Although Glen successfully managed through that, he ultimately concluded that the next big thing couldn't be accomplished without a fully supportive board. He announced his resignation on December 19, 2012.

During the 15 years that Glen led Allscripts, other opportunities had beckoned to the serial entrepreneur who loves the intensity of start-ups, but he focused on the intensity of continuous growth of Allscripts in a fast-changing market. His commitment was to take Allscripts and EHR to a certain point where he could leave a strong company with a well-defined market in someone else's hands, and know that his leadership had made a sustainable difference in improving health care. Although he made his letting go decision under intense pressure, the industry and Allscripts were at the inflection point Glen had helped make possible as the 2009 stimulus package pushed EHR through the health care system. Getting to this stage made it easier for Glen to let go, knowing he had done what he set out to do; it was time for new experiences.

He moved on to cofound 7wire Ventures, which invests in innovations for health care, education, and energy. Glen's letting go of Allscripts was a recommitment to his passion as a serial entrepreneur and innovator to address a variety of opportunities.

WHAT MATTERS TO GLEN TULLMAN

Glen's Playbook

"In many respects, leadership is the opposite of management. Management is about keeping things consistent, keeping the trains running on time. Leadership is about disruption and change."

Relishing the CEO's responsibility to stay several steps ahead, Glen knows that a large part of his job is, first, to help customers, employees, and investors cross the bridge from today to a tomorrow they cannot envision and, second, to manage its risks. He learned to live with the onslaught of misunderstandings, skepticism, and criticism, especially from the short-term focus of the financial community. You see this in Allscripts' long-term stock performance when declines followed announcements of strategic changes, and several months later its stock steadily rose to new highs. He says:

> We have this dichotomy of the market wanting focus on this quarter's performance and a leader's job requiring strategic decisions. My job is to address business strategy, basic operation of the business, and where the market is going. I have to manage not just for today but also for where the company should be two or three years from today.
>
> One of the things that a CEO is paid to do, to steal a line from Wayne Gretzky, is skate to where the puck is going to be, not to where it is. All you can really do is have your internal compass for knowing. Are we doing the right things? Are we making the right decisions? Do we have the right metrics to help us achieve our goals and are we comfortable with them? I think first and foremost it's about having something you believe in if you want to do great things. So part of my job is to create the vision that people can get behind and believe in and know is real and authentic. At Allscripts, we were saving lives, making health care safer, and people could see it happening every day. It was important work and all of our people could make a difference. That's what makes all the long hours and tough assignments worth it.

As he explains his growth strategies—from small physician practices to large practices (they have more money), then back to small practices (half of the physicians in the United States were at that time in practices of 10 or fewer physicians), and then to hospitals (where the most urgent and critical medical decisions are made)—the logic is so clear that you wonder what doubts investors and analysts could have had.

Glen understands all too well the paradox entrepreneurial leaders always face: that business agility arises from the willingness to experiment whereas leadership effectiveness requires unwavering conviction. Too often bosses hand down decisions that may be intentional experimentation, but they appear to staff as weak leaders without vision and strategic focus. Or we see the opposite situation, when bosses overrely on numbers and ignore the need for good judgment and conviction, but they appear as strong leaders able to make decisions. Or bosses can ignore disappointing numbers when pride of ownership makes them defend their decision. In all cases, it takes critical judgment to interpret the numbers, to see the story they tell, and to assess the risks. Vision and fortitude involve knowing short-term declines are often necessary to build long-term strength, and short-term strength can belie long-term weakness. Glen has learned when to change course and when to stay the course from what he calls "failed experiments."

> There are times you just know, "I'm going to stick this one out," and other times, "We need to abandon." But it can be very tough to know—I think this is what makes people say that you can't be taught to be an entrepreneur.
>
> One of the most agonizing lessons for an entrepreneur comes down to having an idea you may have fallen in love with, but the facts don't support it. You have to be "crack-able"; you have to have a strong enough core but a soft shell so you can say, "We tried it, and we gave it our best shot. It didn't work, now let's try something else. Let's move on." You have to not have it tied up with your ego, not have so much pride of ownership that no matter the costs, I'm going to prove I'm right.

It's common knowledge that many CEOs, in the face of almost indisputable evidence that a project or idea does not work, actually double down if they are personally invested in it or if it was their idea. You have to surround yourself with a strong team who can save you from yourself every so often. That kind of honesty is not all that common for those who report to CEOs. Glen managed to find that team.

Glen avoids the challenge of intractable teams and organizations stuck in insular habits and turf wars by letting people know that full responsibility for outcomes rests squarely on his shoulders. Holding himself accountable gives him laser focus on the goal and builds trust with his team. He gathers information and opinions not to find the path of consensus or least resistance but to examine his perspective and thought process critically. He then takes unambiguous ownership of the decision, backs it with conviction, and sees his decision through to some measurable outcome that drives further decisions. It's not complicated but it takes clear acceptance of leadership responsibility for the decision and its consequences.

I always take responsibility for decisions so I have to make the final call, but I get a tremendous amount of feedback from my team and as many people as I can. Sometimes the decision I make goes against conventional wisdom or in another direction from the opinions I've gathered. I always explain to my team that I've listened to them and considered their input. It doesn't mean that I necessarily agree with them. It means that I value their input and it weighs heavily. I take the rest of my experience and the market conditions and I make the call. Fortunately, most of those calls have been the right calls, and that earns you respect and the right to do that again. But to be clear, you are only as good as your last decision, especially when you are public.

People are willing to believe if they see you believe. Early in my career, a boss said to me, "You need to tell your team to do this." I said, "I don't believe in it, so I can't tell them." He said, "But if you tell them, they'll do it." And I said, "But they'll do it because they know I would never tell them to do something I wouldn't do myself or that I didn't believe in." It took him a minute, and then he understood.

Glen's Playbook

"I think sometimes you're driven to get somewhere for one reason, and when you get there, you've changed and your goals have changed."

Although Glen is clearly self-assured, humbling experiences make him an ordinary guy who has extraordinary goals. Time is his most precious resource, yet he isn't so hurried that self-importance and stress get the better of him; actually, he has that friendly look that can get anyone needing help to pick him out of a crowd as the one to ask.

His passionate drive has roots in his early family life. His mother fortified her six children with curiosity and independence. She also instilled a deep sense of personal responsibility to contribute to society; all six are entrepreneurial, mostly in education or health care. At the same time, her attempt to instill humility by comparing and downplaying the siblings' accomplishments ended up cultivating keen competition.

> There was a tremendous competitive drive in the family that my mother pretty ruthlessly encouraged. It was very tough to be good enough. I always laugh about the time there was an article in *Time* magazine on Allscripts with a photo of me. My mother said, "It was nice you were in *Time* magazine. Your brother has never been in *Time*"—she was sending a message to him—"On the other hand, it's not like you were on the cover."
>
> It's a subtle message, over and over again: You might think you're good, but you're not that good; you can do better. Good enough never was at our house!

From his father, a salesperson of women's apparel, Glen learned the importance of making people feel they are on your team. He has an important memory of his father often using the payphone to handle business when the family ate out. "He was always in touch, way before cell phones. At his funeral, there were people from the factory floor, from sales, people who he mentored, and his customers. I heard stories about his help, encouragement, and generosity. Every story was fundamentally the same: He cared about us."

From this early family life Glen developed the entrepreneurial spirit of experimenting, making things happen, and caring. Thriving on competition became a well-honed skill, thanks to his mother but also to the impact of his parents' rancorous divorce when he was in high school. Having to pay his own way through college made him want to prove that he was as good as his wealthy classmates.

> I'm sure there's a psychological element to what drives me. My parents had gone through a very messy divorce when I was in high school. My father said, "You're on your own." I knew if it

was going to be, it was up to me. There was no safety net. In fact, I was resentful. There was some sense of aloneness and having to prove myself. That was furthered by my experience at Bucknell University. There were many very wealthy kids who had money and resources, things I didn't have. I was just determined to demonstrate that I was that good. I had a chip on my shoulder. I probably still do.

I think that's a very real, direct and honest answer. That was what drove me for a long time. An absolute fear of failure was also a driver. We spent $35 million on a business called Late Nite Magic—magic was a hobby that my brother and I loved—and it didn't work. That happens. But it wasn't a failure; it was a lesson about having the right partners and that easy money never is. There was, and is today, a willingness to go to extremes to win, as long as winning is legal and ethical.

At some point, some combination of success and failure helped him make the shift from being driven by the past to become driven by the future: first to provide for his family, and once he did that, to make systemic change for an important purpose.

I was very driven to be successful to provide for my family. When you've done that, then there's a different set of drivers. That came after we sold Enterprise Systems, where I was CEO before going to Allscripts. After selling Enterprise, it became about what do I *want* to do. Financially I could do anything. I became driven by changing things on a larger scale to make a greater impact. I wanted to make a difference on things that matter, like health and education.

Allscripts gave Glen the platform to make a greater impact. Once his impact on EHR and health care gained real momentum, an important driver became his impact as a leader on how people learned and grew at Allscripts. Culture became very important, both to support growth and to build a company that, in his words, he and others would be proud of.

As a leader you have a responsibility. You are changing people's lives. Part of how I measure my own success is how our people do and what they learn from the focus, the intensity, and the honesty in our business. One of our great success stories is a pizza delivery guy who we thought had a terrific service attitude, so we hired him. He rose to become head of customer service. I said to him, "You really have to get your college degree," not realizing that he didn't have his high school degree. So, he got his GED and college degree. And then he said, "I don't understand these numbers." He went on to get his CPA [certified public accountant] and MBA [master of business administration] from the University of Chicago. At one point, he went out on his own to prove he could. I recruited him back. He's an amazing man. To watch this person develop and become a serious business executive is an amazing thing.

The interesting thing is that it's not about what we did for him, but what he did for us. He showed us (and every employee) what was possible with commitment and sheer work. He showed us the impact we could have on our people if we had the right culture. And he showed me in particular how good it felt to help others succeed.

Glen's Playbook

"I want people who tried things and failed at things because that's where learning occurs."

Glen's education and career took him in many directions (which we'll come back to later), yet with hindsight, it all comes together as if it were a deliberate plan. Even at 54 years old, he is more akin to younger generations in finding unconventional experiences more gratifying and thriving on multitasking. He is not impressed by years of experience on linear career paths. Nor is he enamored with steady and reliable performance results. But that pizza delivery guy who always gave exceptional customer service and tackled self-development out of personal responsibility to the opportunity given him inspired Glen's imagination. He enjoys discovering people with probing curiosity and relentless initiative and keeping them challenged.

> Some people come in and say they are qualified for a job here because they have 20 years of experience. So I say, "Well, that depends. I'm looking for people with experiences, who tried things and failed at things because that's where learning occurs. But 20 years doing the same thing isn't really valuable or interesting to me."
>
> I look for people who strive for excellence at something—it can be playing a musical instrument, sports, or chess—so they know that feeling. I look for people who have won something because once you taste that feeling of excellence, of being the best, of working hard to a goal and often, but not always, of winning, it's easier to harness that kind of drive for other endeavors. I look for people who understand that inner power and have been able to transfer that to other experiences. Passionate people want to work with other passionate people. In fact, they can't understand how someone would not be passionate.

He knows firsthand how diverse experiences enrich and differentiate one's perspective in ways that can't be anticipated and simply come from exposure to a variety of jobs. Glen's early experiences included factories, government, an entrepreneurial small business, and a Rotary Club fellowship to study anthropology at Oxford University.

During his high school and early college years, Glen worked on the loading docks of a unionized glass plant in New Jersey. While a junior at Bucknell University, he applied for a Truman Scholarship, submitting an essay in favor of Proposition 103 for cutting back government. That led to a job offer from the US Office of Management and Budget. "I went in more liberal than I came out. I came out a Democrat from a social standpoint but more conservative from an economic standpoint, believing that the more done by the private sector, appropriately regulated and managed, the better. But as we've clearly seen, there has to be a meeting in the middle. Government of extremes doesn't work well (or at all)."

After graduation, he worked for a small alternative energy company, Energy Utilization Systems, near Pittsburgh, doing a little bit of everything and learning not to take himself too seriously. He left the company to accept a Rotary Foundation Fellowship, studying social anthropology at Oxford University with the commitment to speak at Rotary Club events. He traveled extensively to small Rotary Clubs all over England, immersing himself in the culture and honing his listening, speaking, and selling skills. At Oxford, he piqued his professors' curiosity over his unique access to, and understanding of, the closed culture of the Pennsylvania Amish. He had been one of the few people to be accepted into their community and had unique insights into how their culture drove their decisions, something that would come in handy later as he managed businesses.

What seems from the outside like a meandering path prepared him to lead with a broad perspective and keen eye for opportunities. Enjoying new and different challenges, Glen made pivotal decisions in his 15 years at Allscripts that put him on a continuous learning curve, with spikes of steep learning every two or three years that helped him grow as a leader.

Glen's Playbook

"Often people ask me, when is enough, enough? It's not about the money. It's about making a difference—it's about changing people's lives for the better and providing opportunities for them to grow in sustainable ways."

His diverse experiences shaped him into a humanist with an orientation that says it has to be about sustainability. It's not about charity; it's about building good businesses that make money while doing good. Glen has an intensely competitive drive and an equally intense concern for improving the world. At Glen's core, passion and responsibility are the same. In whatever he does, the responsibility to make a difference sustains his passion, and his passion for improving how things work lightens the weight of responsibility.

There's something in the Jewish faith called *Tikun Olam* that is a responsibility of repairing the world. That was very much drilled into us by our mother. It's not enough just to do well yourself; there's a responsibility to others. There is a burden to not sit back but to take action. That really defines who I am.

One of my favorite quotes by John F. Kennedy sums it up well: "We go forward asking His blessing and His help but knowing that here on earth, God's work must truly be our own." We all know what we should do, but we often get distracted and don't do it. My mother had the attitude you can do anything you want; you just have to do it. I give my mother a lot of credit for never saying no to anything we wanted to do. At best she would use distraction but *no* didn't exist. When I think of some of the things I did when I was young, I really question whether I would let my own kids do those things.

Around the age of 10, Glen made leather wristbands, watchbands, and belts and traveled from New Jersey into New York City to sell them. At 12 years old, he built a solar hot water heater and drilled a hole in the roof. "The solar water heater worked for a while; the hole in the roof, which became a leak, lasted forever. I'm sure the owners of that house are still dealing with that leak." About 25 years later, Glen founded, with his partner, Pete Kadens, SoCore Energy, which created a simpler and more cost-effective way to install solar panels on commercial buildings. That business was recently sold to Edison Ventures, parent to Southern California Edison, in a very favorable transaction for Glen and his investors.

Early independence seems to have raised an entrepreneur. He sprints through everyday experiences with an eye toward improving something— whether he's in traffic jams or a doctor's office, on airplanes or the phone—because Glen loves seeing things work the way they *should*. His focus, however, is on areas that align with his humanist values where he can make a real difference. Throw into the mix his equally strong belief in free market dynamics and the drive to excel, and you have a hard-driving business leader grounded in a genuine desire to help people.

If you look at the big problems, they are health care, education, and energy. These are the areas I really want to focus on with new technologies for new solutions. We have to use technology with intention and design.

At a certain point you understand that if you're good at something, it becomes about making a difference, being significant, to use the title of the book, *From Success to Significance*, by Augie Nieto, a very close friend and founder of Life Fitness. I think that's what we all want, to make a difference in doing something that we find meaningful.

For me, what makes the effort worth the investment of time and energy is seeing your product working, being the best at what you do, and having people say, "Thank you for doing what you're doing." And, ultimately, it's about growing people. It's gratifying when people say, "I never thought I could do it or *we* could do it. I thought you were crazy. People said we couldn't do it. You pushed us and we did it."

When asked by family and friends why he lives in the same small house that preceded wealth, he answers that his family—wife and three children—wanted to be within yelling distance rather than to have to go look for each other. A big house, in his real answer, would have sent the wrong message to his kids and other people. What message does he want his children to get? Success is about using your talents and resources to make a difference. Also, be driven by your passion, not by money. The money will come if you love what you do and are truly committed to it.

Glen's Playbook

"I've often said that being an entrepreneur is a way of being; you can't turn it on and off."

Dissecting Glen's skills and style would miss the elemental power of his leadership: He understands that the responsibility of the leader is to lead. It's a truism but the real purpose leaders are supposed to serve is obfuscated by the short-term focus of financial markets and simplistic leadership competency definitions and measures of organizations. Along the leadership journey, Glen—and all the leaders this book profiles—internalizes leadership as a way of being. Although they have human flaws like everyone, they understand the difference between *doing* leadership as a career builder and *being a leader* as accountability to self and a responsibility to others.

He also understands that when he eschews the processes corporate structures require, he intensifies the accountability entrepreneurial innovations require, which explains the profound commitment many entrepreneurial leaders make to see their ideas become real. So, although many would say Glen is a workaholic, Glen would say he is an entrepreneur.

> Many people say they take their work home. You never hear this from people who are passionate about their work because it's not work; it's part of their being, of who they are.
>
> I was on a panel of entrepreneurs advising a group at Northwestern University about what we learned in business and being entrepreneurs. Each of these very successful entrepreneurs, without exception, said you need work-life balance. I don't think any of these panelists had work-life balance when they built their businesses. Work-life balance comes after a time of working with no balance in your life until a measure of success is achieved.

The notion of work-life balance measures balance in terms of how we allocate time between work and other life activities, each in its own compartment vying for a share of time fixed at 168 hours in a week. The way Glen sees it, the clock does not measure what he puts into work and family or his effectiveness, and his activities don't separate in neat compartments of work and nonwork. Glen plays a strong role in the values his kids learn and addresses the more challenging day-to-day routines of family life by being fully engaged when he is with them. He learned a new term from his culture and talent leader at Allscripts. She called it work-life flexibility; it's the ability to do it all on your own schedule. Go to your kid's football game or performance and later work through your e-mail.

> One of the values I've had is to invest a tremendous amount in my kids to have open minds. I have the goal of taking them to every continent. Kids are growing up in a flat world where everyone is connected, so they have to be comfortable anywhere in

the world. And we want to teach them to go out and try things, get comfortable with learning from mistakes.

With today's pervasiveness of technology, the challenge is making sure you're really present when you're with your children. Where I live, I see half of the parents walking around with headphones on a conference call while watching their kids' game—and I've done that, too. I'd love to say I've figured it out. Being present wherever I am—that is a very tough thing to do. Over the years, I've done anything I could to get back from road trips for their events, including flying in for their event and then flying back out. These are things that I constantly work on.

He understands that as Allscripts matured so did his people. The young company was filled with young people, who, without constraints on their energy and time, could give singular focus to their work. As the company matured, so did its employees as they shifted priorities to include family and personal goals.

We all go through different stages. That's a reality. When you're young, you can work 24/7, you can be totally passionate about your work and you can put that ahead of money and security. It gets more complicated when you have employees with responsibilities other than business. When the company gets older, you have to face some sense of rationality. You also have to deal with the fact that as you get larger, 100 percent of your people can't be at the same level of passion. I tell people that there *are* trade-offs. There are events I want to be at and I can't be at if I'm doing this job. That's a choice but it's not a choice for everybody.

Glen's Playbook

"Sometimes I hear people say, 'Don't take it personally.' Are you kidding? Want to build a great business? Make it personal."

Delivering the best product possible became a personal goal as well as a business goal after poignant experiences with his two sons. They gave Glen a father's clarity about doing the right thing first and figuring out how to make it work for the business second.

Earlier in Glen's career when he was CEO at Enterprise Systems, his oldest son had sinus surgery. The father was allowed to go in the operating room and place the mask on his son to put him to sleep for the surgery.

My son looked up and saw one of our monitors labeled Enterprise Systems and said, "Look, Dad, that's your company." I looked up and saw an old version of our software. That's when I understood what quality control really meant—when your son or daughter or mother or father is on the operating table—that's when I understood that things really matter.

When I went back to the office, I said I don't want any parent and any child to be in an operating room without the best software we have to offer. That's when we changed the way we did upgrades to deliver them for free.

A few years later when Glen was at Allscripts, he found out that his youngest son, diagnosed with juvenile diabetes, had missed a clinical trial.

I asked the physician, who was clearly one of the top physicians in endocrinology in the state, "How could you have possibly missed this clinical trial?" She replied, "Glen, there are so many different clinical trials, with so many inclusion and exclusion criteria, that it's impossible to remember. You would need a computer to keep track of all of that." So we began to build that into our software, connecting information about clinical trials and patient diagnosis and treatment.

No parent and no child should ever miss an opportunity for better care because our physicians don't have the best information. I intend to fix that, but I know we are not there yet. We've laid the foundation, and the best is yet to come.

These things are very, very personal and that helps drive my passion. We say, "People don't care how much you know until they know how much you care." One of the secrets of being an entrepreneur is that entrepreneurs care. I say to people, "I can almost guarantee you that you'll have problems with our software; that's software. But I can also guarantee that no one will care more, or work harder to fix it, than we will."

GLEN'S PIVOTAL DECISIONS

Pivot Point: Launching Decision

"Sometimes, you don't know exactly where experiences are going to take you."

Glen's passion seems to have found him more than he found it. Actually, his passion was not for software itself but for change and how software enables improving how we do things. A chance encounter with a few Amish in a buggy turned into a serendipitous lesson about change. Ironically, understanding a culture opposed to change and technology helped him lead change and technology.

It all started with a phone call for help during one winter snowfall when Glen was a student at Bucknell University in central Pennsylvania. A professor had a heart attack, and his wife asked Glen to take care of their farm while they were stuck in the city.

When someone calls and asks for help, you go. So I went and arrived at this mile-and-a-half-long driveway, just a shovel and me. I dug a path and got to the top of the hill. All of a sudden, a buggy with Amish people pulls up. They had heard that I had come to help, and it's very Amish to help your neighbors. The next day they arrived with pies and food, and they invited me to ride in their buggies to their homes.

The more time I spent with the Amish, the more fascinated I became with them. Later, they invited me back, giving me amazing access to their community and answering my endless questions.

Many people thought the Amish were two-faced. They would use a phone, but they wouldn't own one. They would take a ride in a car, but not own one. I came to understand what it really was about: They were very, very careful in managing their culture. They used to say about the TV, "The devil often comes dressed as an angel." The elders explained, "TV will teach our kids; *we* want to teach our kids. In a buggy, we know our kids can only get 10 to 15 farms from home, and those farms are *our* farms, so they're safe." I watched this community split, when entire families moved, over a decision as to whether they could own portable chainsaws. The elders said, "We'd rather have one and force people to share it and work together."

The year he spent with the Amish gave him an understanding that change must be addressed in the context of the cultural values with insight into the cultural meanings of how things are and how things could be. As the saying goes, "Culture eats strategy." At Allscripts that culture encompassed long-held conventions and legacy systems in the medical community as well as the relationship Americans have with their health and doctors.

Returning from Oxford in 1983 with a job offer from Digital Equipment, he was urged by his mother first to visit his older brother, who had just become a father in Chicago. Glen went to Chicago to meet his niece to make his mother happy, or, at least, that's what he thought he was doing.

In Chicago, his brother had arranged interviews for Glen with the board of directors of the company he'd started in 1980, Certified Collateral Corporation (which later became CCC Information Services), which developed software to vertically integrate auto insurance claims. Members of the board advised Glen to try out the job and get to know better his brother, who was 14 years older. They said that he could leave if he didn't like it but to try it. Glen tried it.

I took a very winding, circuitous path, so for many, many years, my mother asked, "When will you hold a steady job?" When I came back from Oxford, she wanted to make sure I was going to have a steady job.

How I got into this, some of it is starting down a path and some of it is good fortune. Sometimes you don't know where experiences will take you. In some respect, things just happened. But things happen to those who are ready and seek opportunity.

As Glen watched his brother's amazing capacity to learn rapidly and his endless energy, he handled increasing responsibilities for areas for which his brother did not have the patience or disposition. With complementary skills, the brothers grew CCC and changed the service industry for auto insurance claims.

> With CCC's success, I began to realize the power of software. I began to see software more and more as an approach to change. It's not about being a software expert—it's about change. It's about making things better; it's about transformation.

CCC was sold in 1989 in a go private transaction, and while his brother moved on, Glen stayed as president and chief operating officer (COO). After 10 years at CCC and at 35 years old, Glen evaluated his options. He could stay until he eventually moved into the CEO position, or he could test his wings.

Glen moved on to test his wings as CEO of Enterprise Systems, a hospital information management company. Three years later, after leading the IPO and secondary offerings, he sold Enterprise Systems to HBO & Company (which McKesson owns today) in a $250 million stock swap. With Enterprise Systems being *his* success, "It became about two things. One, I realized I love the creative process of leading and building businesses. Second, I realized the power in changing things for the better on a broader scale."

For people of all ages stymied by how to find or renew their passion, Glen's story points out that the answer is not in pondering the question but in trying out different projects and environments. Glen discovered his passion—distinct from various serious interests—by doing, by trying, and by nurturing an emergent passion until mastery. Joining CCC gave him focus. It was a decision to develop as an entrepreneur, and in software he found his tool for improving things.

During the 1990s, he could have taken these skills anywhere, but health care captured his imagination for the systemic impact he could make. Shortly after selling Enterprise Systems, Glen became CEO of Allscripts, a troubled 10-year-old company that was both a repackager of medications and a specialty pharmacy benefit manager (PBM). Before long, Glen had sold the PBM, the only profitable part of the business, and having burned the ships behind him, embarked on finding a better, safer way for physicians to write paper prescriptions. Electronic prescribing was going to go mainstream. For Glen it was a decision to make a bigger impact on health care. It was 1997 and the Internet was a vortex of change and entrepreneurship.

Pivot Point: Turning Point Decision

> "We were betting the company on a vision for the future that we had to get right. There was no plan B."

In the beginning, it looked like Glen's job at Allscripts was to repeat what he did at Enterprise Systems. It was during the tech boom when entrepreneurs were supposed to have an exit strategy guide their operating strategy. In this business environment, Glen's first two years at Allscripts were spent preparing for an IPO. On its first day on NASDAQ (July 26, 1999), the stock closed at $16. In less than eight months, it soared with the expanding dot-com bubble, reaching $89 on March 9, 2000.

After we took the company public, the stock zoomed up and was worth more than $3 billion, and we hadn't really done anything. This was during the dot-com boom and within six months, 10 other companies were launched that did exactly what we did and they were giving away software while we were selling it.

After the burst of the dot-com bubble, with Allscripts' stock at a low of $1.60 on August 14, 2002, and desperate *"to get it right,"* Glen talked to customers.

We reached out and listened to our customers, who are physicians, and they said, "First of all, we don't want 10 different devices: one for prescribing, one for capturing charges, one for dictation; we want one device that does it all." So we realized that prescribing alone wasn't going to cut it.

Second, there's something called a practice management system; that's when you check in with your physician's office to do scheduling and registration, insurance information, and such.

Physicians said, "You have to link into our practice management system because we don't want to have to reenter all that data."

The third thing they said is, "We just don't have the money or the technology skills to implement this."

We realized we have a big problem here: We have customers without money, we have competitors who give it away free, and we're not sure we have the right product.

Crisis of survival gave Glen clarity to focus on Allscripts' most important asset—its public stock—to expand its product line and sell to large physician practices that had money and training for technology.

There were many times when we had to bet the company. There's a great quote, something like, "An entrepreneur can keep two completely opposite ideas in their mind and not be insane." On one level you're saying to people, "Go forth, go forth"; on another level you're saying, "If we fail, what are we going to do?" This is the conversation you have with yourself; this is how you live—it's a very tough thing to do.

We spent almost $300 million in stock to acquire a company from IDX, the leader in practice management for large physician practices. What we really bought was a 10-year, exclusive relationship with them to be their electronic health record provider. It was a total change in market from the smallest offices to the largest offices.

It was a big bet. The equity market didn't understand it. We moved forward and became the leader in sales in the large physician group market, the doctors who set the trend and had the money. People now look back and realize that was a turning point.

Allscripts clawed its way above $15 a share in mid-2005. However, the company was still operating in a marketplace skeptical about the role of EHR in health care. With complex and intricate interdependencies across diverse medical personnel in diverse medical settings and locations, EHR was encumbered with patient privacy issues and slow user adoption rates compared with other major professional sectors' use of electronic records.

Strategic growth had to be guided by a compelling strategic vision, which Glen treated as his number one responsibility. The core of his vision was to harness the power of technology for improving medical outcomes and not just for operational efficiencies. He evolved his vision as Allscripts, technology, and the marketplace advanced. Achieving the vision evolved from e-prescribing to software integration for physician practices, then to connectivity across the health care continuum, and ultimately to help steer public policy standards.

Sometimes, realistically, the path that you start on as an entrepreneurial business isn't where you end up. That's why when you're a venture investor, you always bet on people rather than an idea—because that idea might get transformed. We started off with one idea at Allscripts and it's been transitioned a number of times. We kind of sculpted that to what worked, what the market needed and what made sense.

I used to hear, "Physicians don't like technology, and they don't want to change." And yet, I see physicians using MRIs [magnetic resonance imaging] and all kinds of technology. Give them technology that makes their lives easier, that wows them, and they'll use it. Figuring out the human relationship with software is the tough part and always wins the day.

While we knew we were in the huge marketplace of health care, we never knew how broad an impact we could have. One day we woke up to the reality that our software touched 30 million Americans with these systems that didn't exist before Allscripts developed them. With our merger with Misys, we touched 100 million Americans. Our products were saving lives.

According to his own definitions—management is about keeping things consistent; leadership is about disruption and change—Glen became a true leader when he pulled Allscripts out of near oblivion to its turning point. At CCC and Enterprise Systems, he had managed operations and a product line of software as efficiency tools. At Allscripts, he turned crisis into the opportunity to give doctors a tool for improving patient care. With this shift, Glen made himself accountable for making an impact on the quality of American health care, which was in need of insightful and innovative solutions.

Pivot Point: Tipping Point Decision

"Ultimately, a good leader builds a company that he or she can leave and will outlast them."

On February 1, 2007, Allscripts' stock closed at $30.99, a solid reversal from the low of $1.60 five years prior. His transformation strategy had worked, allowing Glen to focus on strategic growth. With the company reaching 50 percent penetration of the large physician groups, Glen contemplated what was next. The financial market, he knew, would soon ask, "How much more can you grow?"

He kept one eye on Wall Street's expectations for growth and the other eye on the health care industry's need for information systems to talk with each other. EHR were residing in isolated databases, preventing doctors and patients from grasping the whole picture, which often incurred unnecessary costs for tests and treatments. The question, Glen pondered, was not in terms of how to grow but rather how to touch more American lives. This was what energized him, getting the market to a tipping point for reaching universal adoption of EHR across the health care spectrum.

Glen analyzed what had worked so well in turning around the company and what could have worked better. He had leveraged Allscripts' core competency in EHR in a partnership with the leader in practice management software. Glen knew that companies in practice management— which is working with people who handle registering, scheduling, and billing—had not been able *to crack the code* on EHR—which is everything relating to medical practitioners' delivery of patient care.

> Companies that have practice management DNA can tell the staff what system to use and what to do. When you grow up like we did in electronic health records, your DNA relates to physicians and convincing them on what to do because you can't tell them what to do. It's very hard to transition from one to the other.
>
> So we had taken our electronic health record business and partnered with IDX, the largest and most successful company at practice management for large groups of over 200 physicians.

We had six years of uninterrupted sales growth. That was great, but I was restless to move on to our next stage. I knew we could do more and have a more significant impact. Since half of the physicians in the United States are in practices of 10 physicians or less, I asked, "Who is the leader in practice management for small practices like IDX was for large practices?" That was Misys.

The first discussions with the health care segment of Misys, an English banking concern who had acquired a successful US practice management company, Medic, but had little idea how to manage it, took place almost two years before the merger was completed in late 2008. In the first meeting with Mike Lawrie, who was the newly appointed CEO of Misys and a 27-year veteran of IBM, the two CEOs agreed that the perfect marriage of Allscripts and IDX was a little bit imperfect because IDX and Allscripts had continued to operate as two companies. They brainstormed the idea of putting Misys and Allscripts together as one company. In a meeting a year later, the two CEOs worked out an atypical financial scenario to create a merger that increased Allscripts' reach to nearly one-third of all physicians in the United States.

They wanted us to run the combined company, so we actually merged their assets into our publicly held company. But they also wanted an opportunity to enjoy the upside, which we couldn't pay up front. So they said, "We will pay your shareholders what is effectively a dividend of $5 per share, totaling $330 million. Your shareholders get to keep their shares, and we end up with a higher percentage of the company."

Fortunately, Mike and I had a very good relationship and a shared vision. And we also both had a lot to win, but also to lose, so we both understood the importance of our relationship. One of the beauties of this transaction was that we had clients who were already using both systems together. One of the analysts said, "I'm amazed no one thought of this before." But, at first, there was a lot of pressure on our stock.

Fully recognizing that most mergers fail to deliver strategic gains and build greater value, Glen understood the scrutiny of whether he could execute on this promising concept. Before shareholders approved the deal, the two CEOs were well into preparations for combining into one company the two operations that included Allscripts' home office in Chicago and Misys's home office in London, as well as facilities in North Carolina, Texas, and Bangalore, India.

Mike and I agreed on our guiding principles: Begin with the clients and focus on results. Number one priority was to be one company and act like one company, everything from technology systems to facilities to organization structure. Number two priority was to know our go-forward strategies.

The strategy that has always been successful for us is to make it very clear up front that it's not one company over the other that wins; it's the best people, the best products, and the best process. There's room for everyone who is a performer; if you're a top performer, you'll have more opportunities.

We interviewed the top 60 people, 30 from Allscripts and 30 from Misys. This was a bit controversial; people said, "So am I interviewing for my own job?" The easy answer is, "No, no, you're not." The real answer is, "You always are interviewing for your own job." That's not comforting, but that's the reality.

This process is uncomfortable for a period of time. Yogi Berra said, "The secret to managing is keeping the people who hate you away from those who are undecided." So I spent a lot of time with people and wanted to err on the side of overcommunicating with the big middle portion of people who were trying to figure it out.

They identified 13 operating teams, composed of people from both organizations as well as a third party to help manage the process. They made a list of decisions that were made, decisions that needed to be made, and open topics. They focused the teams only on the decisions they needed to make, posing a number of questions for the teams to debate. Every two weeks the groups gave progress reports to Glen and Mike. When the groups couldn't make a decision, the two CEOs made it.

In the execution piece, you have to make decisions and move on. You have to be very clear about what those decisions are and that's not going to change. When we announced the transaction, I announced to both groups that all of our people in North

Carolina would move into the Misys facility in North Carolina on day 1. That was a very important symbol to say we are going to be one company. We don't need a team to discuss it. We've outgrown our building even though we own it; they have space. It makes sense; I want one company and I want it day 1.

Our teams came back and said, "It may take time, and we need to figure out furniture, we need to redesign." I said, "The day after day 1, our people will be sitting in their facility. If they have desks, that would be wonderful; if they have phones, that would be wonderful—but they will be there." Some people pushed back, "What if we lose some good people because they have to commute further?" I said, "There are people who have good reasons for not wanting the longer commute, but you can't build a company and a transaction off of those people."

We told people we have to keep our eyes focused on why we're doing this. I was at one of the leading hospitals in the world and they said, "We do a MRI here and one of our specialists across the street does a MRI, and the two systems can't talk. If our systems can just talk and exchange information with patient permission, we can save thousands of dollars, give better care, and deliver it faster." The merger of Allscripts and Misys meant we could connect all these physicians and have their systems talk to each other, and we could touch one out of every three physicians in the U.S. and 100 million Americans. That had never been done before.

Allscripts' stock increased from $9.75 on March 18, 2008, when the merger was announced, to $22.38 on April 12, 2010—not bad in a bear market that was still ensnared in the economic collapse of 2008. This worked out the way mergers always promise but rarely fulfill. It delivered strategic benefits to customers, created real value, and rewarded shareholders of both companies. Glen built a company that could outlast him.

Pivot Point: Recommitment Decision

"We have made the investments to enable us to lead the industry. We can execute better than we have, and we will."

Although Glen could have celebrated the successful merger with Misys and growth in market capitalization by slackening his hard-driving pace, he did the opposite. In 2010, Allscripts stood at the door of opportunity presented by the American Recovery and Reinvestment Act of 2009 (ARRA), the stimulus package that was signed into law by President Barack Obama that provided $30 billion in federal funding to encourage meaningful use of EHR. It was the stimulus for the next merger, Allscripts' boldest and biggest that would create a $1.3 billion enterprise and help clients access ARRA funds more effectively.

This was implicitly Glen's decision of recommitment to Allscripts. The expeditious and smooth integration with Misys gave Glen and stakeholders the confidence to move forward with the blockbuster merger with Eclipsys. When it was announced on June 9, 2010, and closed on September 1, 2010, Glen relished the challenge of merging Allscripts' strength in physician offices and post-acute-care settings with Eclipsys's leadership in hospitals. This connected the whole spectrum of medical treatment settings where medical decisions and coordination between clinicians are most necessary. Glen was in the home stretch to see his vision become reality.

Glen understood that Eclipsys was troubled but thought the combined strengths of Allscripts and Eclipsys would give the new company the chance to take part in what Glen described as "the single fastest transformation of an industry that we have ever seen." And this merger would lead that transformation. Glen, CEO of the combined company, presided over the NASDAQ opening bell on September 1, 2010, to celebrate the closing of the deal. He acknowledged that this integration would be complex in bringing together different customers, different products, different DNA, and different cultures. But with both companies using Microsoft's .NET platform and open architecture, there was confidence in delivering integration very quickly.

Eighteen months into the merger, there were delays in new products and software glitches as well as hurdles integrating sales and client service into one organization. Conflict brewed in the boardroom.

On April 26, 2012, Allscripts announced first-quarter revenues increased 9 percent but net earnings fell 50 percent. Prior to that earnings call, the board voted to support Glen's leadership, but three dissident members, including the chairman, left in protest. On that earnings call, Glen announced their departure. At the same time, an activist shareholder that owned about 5 percent of Allscripts immediately called for the board to ask Glen to step down. Allscripts' stock dropped 36 percent by the end of the trading day. Some reported the turmoil as a clash of cultures and possibly a silver lining for Glen to lead unencumbered by dissension.

Glen knew what he had to do: Lead decisively with total focus on solutions. The next business day, Monday, April 30, he announced that the board of directors elected a chairman, Dennis Chookaszian, who had been a director since September 2010, when the merger was completed. Chookaszian was a known leader with a big task. The board also authorized an additional $200 million stock repurchase program. A week later, Allscripts announced a board-approved stockholder rights plan, sometimes referred to as a poison pill, to enable "all stockholders to realize the long-term value of their investment in the company and protect them from unfair or coercive takeover attempts." The following week, Allscripts announced the appointment of two new directors to the board. One was Paul Black, the former COO of Cerner Corporation, a major health care information technology company, whom Glen had been in discussions with for almost a year. Ultimately, the new directors were uncomfortable with where the company stood.

Pivot Point: Letting Go Decision

"At the end of the day, you run that marathon alone."

The continuing hostile environment threw Allscripts' staff and customers into an anxious wait-and-see mode, further eroding productivity and sales. Allscripts' competitors were able to exploit the situation and gain customers. At the end of 2012, Glen decided it was time to let go. He announced his resignation on December 19, 2012, which was immediately followed by Allscripts' announcement of a new CEO.

In a comment he made years before the Eclipsys deal, Glen was almost prescient about how quickly there can be a reversal of fortunes. Although he didn't expect a reversal, he also wasn't afraid of it. And true to his worldview that the best teacher is experiences, his statement was about the journey that never ends because there are always new lessons that contain new possibilities if you keep learning: "I think good companies are tested constantly. It's an unfortunate part of life but it also makes life interesting."

Glen's story, with uncommon extremes, demonstrates the importance of taking a long-term perspective of leadership and success. He came to a decision point that demonstrates the responsibility of a leader to let go when conditions favor passing the torch. Glen concluded that without the right conditions, he couldn't execute the strategy he thought was best for the company. By stepping down at 54 years old, Glen made a decision of recommitment—to the company for what he believed was best for it; and to himself, to begin again with what he loved—building new companies that could make a difference.

This decision point in some ways is the ultimate test on the leadership journey. Passing the torch with intention—without making it about one's own ego needs—eludes many even when they can point to a succession plan. For Glen, he had the honesty and self-awareness to face a truth no leader wants to confront: The company he led so successfully and built was ready for a change in leadership. Glen made the decision feeling both dejected and liberated. He comments, "It would have been very easy to stay but I was ready to move on. There were conditions under which I would have stayed but those were not met, so it made sense to embrace uncertainty and stay with my principles rather than compromise. The company was ready and could absorb the change."

This makes Glen's letting go decision one of leadership. It dramatizes the truth of the leadership journey and the time to move on: Crossing a goal line does not mark completion, nor does encountering a pivotal obstacle. Neither diminishes the leader's achievements or takes away from the leader he or she was and still is. Real leaders survive because they keep moving forward. Being a serial entrepreneur, Glen made a seamless transition to 7wire Ventures, where Lee Shapiro, his long-time business partner and former Allscripts president, joined him.

The importance of the five decisions on the leadership journey is that they define leaders' agendas as well as challenge them to evolve and grow while being true to their personal values. As Allscripts grew into a large corporation, Glen thought about the challenge to sustain the entrepreneurial culture of passion and agility that he thrives on and that fits his personal values. Just before closing the merger with Misys, Glen pensively commented on the biggest trade-off he had made: Commitment to finish what he set out to do at Allscripts meant having to resist the tug of attractive new business ventures and adventures. Five years before his resignation, he gave an uncanny description of what was in store in the next five years.

> Ultimately, a good leader builds a company that he or she can leave and it can outlast them. With that said, you have to get it to that point. Allscripts has a tremendous amount to do. I came here with a goal to make a difference in health care in this country. We haven't yet had the impact I want to have, so there's a lot more to do.
>
> As I've gone through the years, my head of sales retired, my CFO [chief financial officer] retired, my COO retired. Some of our top people get recruited away. I've brought in new people, but in some respects, you own the brand, so to speak. Other people can move and leave and you can't because it's your company and your vision. So, at the end of the day, you run that marathon alone.
>
> My thesis paper at Oxford was titled, "No Thank You's." The Amish never said thank you because thank you is a way of saying, "We're done, I'm finished, and I'm done paying you back." They wanted to say, "You're never done, you're never done giving, and you're never done paying back."

THE LEADER'S LEGACY

In the process of struggling to survive, Allscripts under Glen's leadership began a journey that helped transform health care in the digital age. On that journey, Glen transformed—from a young man determined to prove himself—into a visionary determined to improve the health care system. Although personal needs drove his goals as he established his career, success gave him freedom to work for new and bigger goals. Those goals empowered customers—who are physicians, nurses, all the people who work in medical settings, and ultimately, patients—with more and better information to make better medical decisions.

Glen's story is about access to great possibilities when you keep learning and experimenting. His emphasis on the value of different experiences is not about impulsive activities and job-hopping; it is about catching the big opportunities that one can't see when one sticks within a comfort zone or sticks with a preconceived plan. He regularly drives change that challenges him to keep learning and experimenting. He made visionary decisions and opportunistic deals and optimized every resource. He earned respect and trust as a successful entrepreneur who could lead mergers, a large public corporation, and an industry.

His launching point decision, to join his brother's young software company instead of a large, successful computer hardware corporation, became his serendipitous start to using software as a way to make systemic change for a need as big as health care. His turning point decision to reinvent Allscripts when there seemed to be little to salvage launched a new vision that continually adapted to the fast-changing environment of technology, health care, and business. In his tipping point decision to build one network as broad as health care itself, Glen steered the industry to a patient-centered and user-based model for EHR. And his recommitment decision helped the industry reach an inflection point in the digital age. In letting go, Glen passed the torch when he believed he could no longer execute on his vision but with the knowledge that the company had grown to the point that it could survive the change.

Letting go on Glen's journey also encompasses a recommitment to his passion for serial entrepreneurialism. It also demonstrates that the five pivotal decisions do not have to be linear, nor do they have to be single occurrences. In moving on to 7wire Ventures, Glen may experience a new tipping point. His narrative at the end of his career could recount his experience in two career cycles or change what I have presented here. When the entirety of his leadership results are known, 7wire Ventures may be the tipping point that made a bigger impact than the expansion of Allscripts. As with all the leaders profiled in this book, Glen never allowed circumstantial pressures get the better of him. He held on to, and exercised, his personal power in good times and bad.

A leader with a vision and a vital personal stake in improving medical outcomes championed the work of improving health care for all Americans. The hallmark of Glen's leadership is this passion—an authentic part of his core identity and values as well as a principled ambition to make a significant impact. You find yourself wanting him to succeed in whatever he pursues.

CHAPTER 4

TEAM

John W. Rogers, Jr.

Founder, Chairman, and CEO of Ariel Investments LLC

WHY YOU SHOULD KNOW HIM AND ABOUT HIS WORK

John Rogers, founder of Ariel Investments LLC, parlayed $500,000 into $21 billion in only two decades after founding the firm in 1983. When only 24 years old, John raised the initial investment capital from family and friends. By the time he was 30, he grew managed assets to $1 billion. With disciplined focus on business fundamentals and strict adherence to John's investing principles, Ariel manages assets of individuals, corporations, university endowments, and public and private pension funds. Through 30 years of successes and setbacks—often dramatically outperforming major stock market indices but also taking a beating at the bottom of the Great Recession of 2008—Ariel Fund ranks in the top 20 percent for long-term performance since inception as of December 31, 2013. Although John's business success is measured by return on investment and net asset value, what defines John's leadership is his work for diversity and for financial literacy that were breakthroughs in the mutual fund industry. Ariel was, in 1983, the first minority-owned mutual fund company and ever since has been amongst the largest.

Success came early, yet was built on a solid foundation since 12-year-old John started getting dividend stocks from his father for birthdays and Christmas instead of games and clothes. By the time he was 24 years old, John had already studied annual reports for 12 years, investing wages from part-time jobs and developing the skills of a disciplined and principled investor, when most people are only balancing their checkbooks. Because of his own early hands-on learning, John is genuinely dedicated to developing the financial literacy of African Americans and youth. In 1996, he established the Ariel Community Academy for kindergarten through eighth grade on Chicago's South Side.

An active civic leader, John received the 2008 Woodrow Wilson Award honoring alumni of Princeton University who embody the ideals in President Wilson's speech, "Princeton in the Nation's Service." President Barack Obama appointed him in 2010 to serve as chairman of the President's Advisory Council on Financial Capability. He served as president of the Chicago Park District Board in the 1990s and on the Millennium Park Committee that secured generous business support for constructing one of the most innovative urban parks in the world, which revitalized downtown Chicago. An ardently loyal alumnus of the University of Chicago Laboratory Schools, he is its chairman of the board. The Economic Club of Chicago, a prestigious group of business leaders, elected John its chairman 2009–2011. He also serves on the board of directors of McDonald's and Exelon and is a past director of Aon.

Taking a team view of every community of which he is a part, John defines leadership as being a good teammate who helps others succeed—a lesson from playing on Princeton's basketball team that had a profound impact. Building his Ariel team took more than careful selection. Coaching them and together tackling challenges and pulling ahead from setbacks forged time-tested trust. John covers this team's back and they have his back; together they brought Ariel to its tipping point of success in about its twentieth year in business. The extraordinary performance-driven growth of Ariel and its leaders makes this the most important stage of John's leadership journey. It helped him wield influence in his uncompromising passion to make diversity flourish in the mutual fund industry that has had low representation of minority business leaders as well as minority investors. This drives him to build a company of diversity that will last into the next generation, no matter the challenges.

Crushing challenges quickly followed the firm's cresting growth in 2004. Hit with the double whammy of underperformance during the

2006 oil crisis, followed by the 2008 Great Recession that started in the fall of 2007, Ariel suffered a dramatic outflow of pension plans. The Dow Jones Industrial Average (DJIA) would not reach its prerecession level until March 2013. By year-end 2009 Ariel Funds were outperforming again, and in 2012, the *Wall Street Journal* named Ariel's flagship fund, Ariel Fund, with a one-year total return of 35.5 percent, a category king in midcap value. The Ariel Fund had gained 386.24 percent as of December 31, 2013 from the recession low. Ariel's road to recovery continues with managed assets in excess of $8.7 billion as of January 31, 2014.

Although by nature he likes orderly routine, and by conviction he stays the course, John's staunch recommitment to building a company that lasts into the next generation has taken him in new directions. Having consistently led Ariel out of downturns to new heights, John this time had more to lose and so more to win back. As he keeps working on fund performance to rank as a top-performing fund manager, John is determined to show the same unflagging drive and unflinching discipline that built Ariel.

As he diversifies Ariel's fund offerings, he has expanded his team with studied caution, taking time to see if they have the courage of conviction that Ariel's investing principles require. Perhaps that is because John's own experience makes him acutely aware that you can't judge a book by its cover. John's mild-mannered demeanor obscures the hard-driving competitor who always plays to win and his reticent composure belies his powerful influence. Between the restrained covers of John's book is a story about bold decisions and goals pursued with prodigious energy and commitment. John's story is inspiring for everyone who, on his or her own path, rebuffs our cultural attraction to showmanship and notoriety.

WHAT MATTERS TO JOHN ROGERS

John's Playbook

"I became a true believer in looking out for your teammates."

Most noteworthy about his wide-ranging accomplishments is that John creates power and wields influence by being an unselfish teammate. Taking a team view of every community of which he is a part, John contributes as a good teammate who helps others succeed. Once he is on your team—and you are on his—he is a true believer and steadfast teammate. A *true believer* to John is loaded with meaning—character, principles, conviction, a credo for living, and fulfilling individual talents at the same time you have the team's back. In fact, chief true believer would be an apt title for John in all his commitments. In business, civic affairs, and friendship, he is first and foremost a true believer in the virtuous cycle created by good teammates generating good outcomes and how mutual gain can gather momentum for stunning results.

In one demonstration of his team perspective, John tells his story with an autobiographical voice that is less about self and more about all the people who shaped him and his aspirations. His industry mentors have been constant role models. His heroes, African American pioneering leaders, were neighbors in Hyde Park, the storied environs of the University of Chicago. And there is the single greatest teacher who defined the leader John became: his basketball coach at Princeton University, Pete Carril.

John discovered the singular power that comes from being an unselfish teammate in one life-changing week during his junior year at Princeton University, where he majored in economics. A shooting guard on Princeton's basketball team, John had played a mere four minutes going into the season's last four games. Then at halftime against Columbia University, to his bewilderment, Coach Carril put him in the game. By the end of that defining week, John turned from an unknown benchwarmer to an acclaimed most valuable player. The next year he was captain of the team.

> Junior year I had been on the bench. I was just happy to get on the team. At the Columbia game, Coach Carril got mad at the starting guard and at halftime says, "You start in the second half; take off your warm-ups." Take off my warm-ups? It was incomprehensible. So I played. I was diving all over the place. The next weekend, I scored 14 points against Yale, then 20 points against Brown. We won those games. The next year I got to be captain and play against really great teams at Michigan State, the defending national champions, and Duke. It was a special experience.

As he recounted the story, John had a distant gaze as he was transported back to that transformative weekend. His real triumph in those winning games was losing his selfhood to *team-hood*, playing as Coach Carril had drilled into him: *"Help your teammates be successful, and you'll be successful, too."* It was a different John from the high school athlete on the Illinois Class A All-State Hall of Fame basketball team.

I was the kind of basketball player in high school who let people know how good I was. But when I got to Princeton, Coach Carril drilled into us how that was totally inappropriate. You're part of the team, and it's not about you. There's no place for selfishness. As long as you think about your teammates first, good things will happen to the team and to you, too.

This is how John would work, play, and live from that point forward.

I became a true believer in looking out for your teammates. When I got the Woodrow Wilson Award at Princeton in 2008, I told Coach Carril he was the best teacher I've ever had. Sometimes you do what your parents or teachers say because you have no other choice; other times you become a true disciple of what's being drilled into you. I became a true disciple.

I took what Coach Carril taught us about teamwork in basketball and found a natural fit with the community of business leaders in Chicago. It's a unique community where the CEOs [chief executive officers] are so involved in coming together to help, whether it's Chicago's Olympic bid, or Millennium Park, or renovating Orchestra Hall. There's a real urban league and a real spirit of cooperation and teamwork. So, I decided that I am a part of the Princeton team, part of the Chicago team, and part of the African American team.

John engages beyond the call of duty with his teammates in Ariel, civic affairs, education, and politics. "I think that's what good leaders do, show up and be there for people—not show up just because you're going to get your picture in the papers." Our interview on one Saturday morning at Ariel's office—which is open on Saturdays with a receptionist working—catches John between speaking to master of business administration students at the University of Chicago and attending a basketball game at the Ariel Community Academy. He is particularly thoughtful about personal touches that support students of the Ariel Community Academy and the Lab School.

> When Warren Buffett was here, I had an idea the day before. There's a contest, Money Smart Kid of the Year, that's really hard to win and only one kid wins each year. The contest has been running for only five years and we have two kids from Ariel Academy who won the prestigious award. We invited these two kids to our office to meet Warren Buffett. They got their pictures taken with him, and he signed their pictures.

Being a good teammate suits John's natural inclination and competitive drive to focus his time on people and activities where he can make the biggest difference. He does that the way he covers the basketball court: Don't hog the ball, take care of teammates, and concentrate on the game. Although he seeks purposeful publicity for Ariel, he regards self-promoting as grandstanding and a waste of everyone's time. He relies on performance-based honors, such as being selected for *Time*'s 1994 list of "50 For the Future: America's most promising leaders age 40 and under" when he was 36 years old.

> I'm very reluctant to take over the room. I'm happy to sit on the sidelines and observe, not force myself into the conversation. It's a combination of things from people who have influenced my life. My father was that way. He saw himself as someone who had overcome many obstacles. I think he was influenced by growing up with both of his parents dead by the time he was 12 and then living with a kindly uncle and not having a lot of money. So he wasn't that impressed with himself. He instilled that in me—you're not a big deal, so get over it. Treat everybody the same. You don't have to be the star.

John's stories about being a good teammate are better than fiction. Here's one of several examples. John played basketball at Princeton with Craig Robinson, brother of Michelle Robinson. John got to know Michelle, who later married Barack Obama. Craig, Barack, and John played basketball together. John was a tireless supporter of Obama in his 2004 US Senate race, as well as his 2008 presidential campaign and 2012 reelection campaign. Ariel's offices were used for prepping the candidate for the 2008 presidential debates and served as the temporary transition headquarters for president-elect Obama and vice president-elect Joe Biden.

> I played basketball with Obama on Election Day 2008. I try to think of the terms to describe how good he is—so calm, deliberative, doesn't get rattled even when the stress and strain build—exactly what this country needs at this time. I get rattled sometimes with the ups and downs of the market, the stresses and strains of the schedule. That's where I can do better.

Are national affairs in John's future? Without hesitation, he replies with a grin, "I'm a Chicago guy. I'll visit the White House but always come back home to Chicago."

John's Playbook

"Live up to your commitments."

John habitually works seven days a week to fulfill his commitments, including catching up with staff during weekends, attending sports games at the Ariel Community Academy and the Lab School, and supporting community organizations and candidates for local and national elected offices. His only pure leisure time, which he guards, is for his only child, Victoria, and for playing three-on-three basketball and in tournaments. A side note worth mentioning—which says a great deal about John's skills and competitive drive—is the game of one-on-one at a Michael Jordan fantasy basketball camp where John beat the basketball legend.

> My father drilled into me, "Always live up to your commitments," and [stressed] how critical that is for success in life. He had an extraordinary background and personality. He was in

the first group of African American fighter pilots and was a member of the legendary 99th Pursuit Squadron of the Tuskegee Airmen. He flew more than 120 combat missions in Europe during World War II. He went to a teachers' college on the GI Bill and wanted to go to the University of Chicago Law School, which wouldn't let him in at first. He went back and met with them wearing his Army captain's uniform. He graduated in 1948. He became a judge in 1977 and served on the bench for 21 years. I have strong values because I have a dad as strong as he was and still is in his 90s. [John W. Rogers, Sr. died at 95 years old on January 21, 2014.]

Maybe I ended up absorbing the profound influence of someone like Coach Carril because of the values my father had set up originally. Maybe I was looking for a straight shooter who believes in teamwork.

I tell young people that whatever promises you make, work hard to keep them. If you do that, you will be such a rare commodity that people will give you more and more responsibility. Some of these things build on themselves.

John has set his own list of firsts for an African American as he built Ariel into the largest minority-owned mutual fund firm in the United States. In the same way his parents broke through race barriers, John steps up to increasing responsibilities and lives up to those commitments with no excuses. He understands that trust works reciprocally: "When you get involved, you have to believe you will be treated fairly."

To live up to his many commitments, John keeps highly disciplined work habits. Number one in his daily priorities is talking with clients, but a close second is voracious reading and research. And he works out six days a week.

I'm very disciplined and consistent, for good or bad. I plan my week in advance; I know what I'll be doing during business hours; I know what I'm going to read and when I'm going to work out. I have everything pretty orderly, which made my ex-wife a little uncomfortable. I plan my days so I can use my time very effectively, including getting from place to place. And I don't have an e-mail address because that can use up to 4 hours in a day when so much of what's in an inbox is nonessential.

If an important job isn't done when it needs to be done, I give the offenders a hard time. I try to keep my calm, though, especially about the markets—when it collapsed, I tried to calm everyone down.

Has this supercharged executive been able to live up to his family commitments? It's a clear yes as a father. He has always made time for his daughter. A small but important demonstration of that came when she called during one of our interviews, and he took her call without cutting her short, even though he refrained from taking a call from a member of his management team. John admits with amusement that he has given stocks to his daughter in the same way his father gave stocks to him, but she "couldn't care less." Her passion is art history, her major at Yale University.

> My daughter has always been a priority just as my parents made me their priority. With my daughter, in her whole 18 years before going away to college, I may have missed one small event. I was at every Ice Capades and theatrical performance she was in. I've never had to regret being so busy that I missed a lot with my kid.
>
> But my ex-wife, Desiree, would say it's not appropriate to have so much focus and efficiency; she wanted me to be more spontaneous. So I guess I've sacrificed in that way; it's a trade-off that I've made. With that said, I think there is a challenge for modern dual-working couples over whose priorities are first.
>
> It's complicated and tough. I now see many women leaders with their spouse taking more of a support role. It's not a sexist thing; you just can't have two people going full force all the time.

During his 10-year marriage (1988 to 1998) to Desiree, she was director of the Illinois Lottery and vice president of corporate communications at Peoples Energy. (In November 2008, Desiree was selected White House social secretary by President Obama; she stepped down in March 2009.) John's wife in his next marriage, Sharon, left a marketing career to go to law school and became assistant US attorney.

His above-and-beyond engagement in work and public service is more than a commitment for John; it's a lifestyle picked up from his parents, John W. Rogers, Sr., and Jewel Stratford Lafontant. His father, a juvenile court judge in Illinois, kept him down-to-earth with local community work on Chicago's South Side. His mother, a prominent attorney in business and government, gave him enormous exposure to the world beyond Chicago. The first African American woman to receive a degree from the University of Chicago Law School in 1946, she became the first African American woman to be assistant US attorney in Illinois in 1955. She was US representative to the United Nations in 1972, was the first female deputy solicitor general in the Justice Department in 1973, and was appointed US ambassador-at-large of refugee affairs in 1989 until 1993. She also was the first African American woman on several corporate boards of major companies.

> I watched my mom and dad working and doing stuff on the weekends—my dad putting leaflets under doors when he was second ward precinct captain. He just wasn't sitting around the house and garden. My mom wasn't either. So I grew up with the sense that you're always out getting something done.
>
> But I don't think my father ever missed a basketball game of mine. I always knew they were there for me.
>
> My mother would take me everywhere—going to the Justice Department as a kid, Saudi Arabia when she was on the board for Mobil—that exposure was very helpful, seeing as much as I did as a kid. I learned from having a strong mother a respect for women; it's extraordinarily important in my values. In our firm, two of the top four leaders are women—Mellody Hobson and Merrillyn Kosier.

John was three when his parents divorced. He had to adapt to their very different lifestyles as he was shuttled between their homes every week. And, as an only child, he took the role of trying to make both of them happy.

> Every weekend my father picked me up on Saturday afternoon and dropped me off at school Monday morning, like clockwork. I lived two totally different lives. My mom had a nice corner

house in Hyde Park with a Cadillac in the heated garage; my father had a studio apartment near Michael Reese Hospital with a Pontiac in the outdoor parking lot. My parents had totally different parenting styles and values. It probably had to have some profound impact on me. I wanted everybody to be happy. Some people say that's my main weakness as a leader— I want everybody to be happy.

I felt fortunate to have such a successful mom and dad. I was also fortunate to have accomplishments in areas that had nothing to do with my parents' prominence as attorneys, which probably helped give me confidence that I could tackle just about anything I wanted. It was fortuitous that my skills are separate and distinct from theirs.

His success with an early start has some critics pointing to privilege or affirmative action. Leave no doubt that although his mother helped open some of the early doors of opportunity, John put himself at those doors with a series of well-timed and well-executed bold decisions. In an industry that lives and dies by performance numbers, and notoriously lacked diversity, he had to deliver by the sweat of his own brow. With confidence in his research and stock-picking skills, John lived up to his commitments to investors.

John's Playbook

"What I'm most proud of at Ariel is that it's a grand experiment to create a group of business leaders on the strength of diversity."

Like all the leaders in this book, John's personal measure of success transcends money. Of course he knows that he is in the business of making money, making lots of money for investors. But ask John what makes him most proud, and his answer reveals the leader who is much more than a money manager in an industry that has a daily published scorecard. He could be most proud of the 30-year firm history; of the 27-year history of his flagship mutual fund, Ariel Fund, which placed in the top 20 percent of mutual funds as of December 31, 2013 (as measured by the Lipper Diversified Equity Universe); of starting the first African American-owned mutual fund company; or of being mutual fund comanager of the year when he was only 30 years old. These are proud achievements, but John gets the most satisfaction from the emergence of "high-wattage leaders at Ariel, smart people who succeed by helping their teammates succeed."

> Ariel is an accumulation of lots of decisions and events. It's always a work in progress. What I'm most proud of at Ariel is that it's a grand experiment to create a group of business leaders. I'm really proud of the talent and diversity of our team, unprecedented in the mutual fund industry. I'm also proud of the brand. The Ariel brand stands for patience, diversity, and looking out for your teammates, whether that's the team at Ariel or outside of our office.
>
> We want to continue to celebrate that diversity and encourage people to be their own person and let their personality shine. We're always looking for ways to support individuals to achieve their goals. We have people at Ariel who moonlight as musicians and TV personalities. Since the beginning I encouraged that; the firm will always support people to have outside activities, especially civic affairs. And I always remind people that great success comes from thinking of others first.

Cultivating a culture of leadership in and out of the office for his team revolves mainly around John as a role model and coach. Long before coaching became popular as a business practice, John took what he learned about coaching on the basketball court to the office. People who take to John's coaching learn the nuances of managing and leading effectively at Ariel. The few individuals who get defensive and resist John's coaching usually don't last long at the firm. Although he would like to be better at handling uncoachable people, he also knows that he can't really help them.

> My critics would say I need to be willing to make more people uncomfortable. I don't want to hurt their feelings, so I'm not as direct as I could be. For example, I gave feedback to one guy on

how he could do something better, and he got all defensive. So I just stopped giving him feedback. He ended up leaving the firm.

I could have been more direct with him. With that said, Coach Carril told us, "If you have a knack for something, I can help you get better at it; if you don't have a knack for it, I'm not going to be able to help you." The best people are coachable, and with them I am very direct. And I am direct about speaking out for fairness and inclusion.

With parent-like pride John calls out teammates whom he mentored and coached and who have bound onto the national stage. Mellody Hobson first worked at Ariel as an intern upon graduation from Princeton in 1991 and became Ariel's president in 2000. She has become a high-profile leader in her own right as a regular financial contributor on ABC TV's *Good Morning America* from 2001 to August 2012, analyst and financial contributor to *CBS News* since early 2013, and appointee in 2012 to the new 21-person panel of the Securities and Exchange Commission on investor concerns. Another leader is Arne Duncan, whom John hired to work on the Ariel Education Initiative and who went on to become secretary of education in the Obama administration. Their stories show the powerful outcomes of being good teammates.

> I met Mellody when I was a volunteer recruiting minority students for Princeton. While at Princeton, she was one of our interns. After graduating, she came to work here. She became president of Ariel. So I ended up helping Princeton, Mellody and Ariel. There's more. Mellody worked on Bill Bradley's campaign to win the 2000 Democratic presidential nomination, where she met Howard Schultz, the CEO of Starbucks, who later recruited her for the boards of Starbucks and DreamWorks. She is now chairman of the board of DreamWorks Animation. She helped the Bradley team, and it was very good for her, too.
>
> Coach Carril was right.
>
> Arne Duncan is another great example. When he got back from playing professional basketball in Australia, he was trying to figure out what to do next. I knew he had a love for helping kids, so we created a position for Arne to run our Ariel foundation

and coordinate our community efforts. His sister also worked for the foundation and the three of us participated in the "I Have A Dream" program. It inspired us to create Ariel Community Academy at 46th and Greenwood, which opened in September 1996 with 400 students. We're using one of the values my dad taught me; we give them real dollars to invest to teach financial literacy.

After seven years, I said, "Arne, you're such a superstar; this is too limiting for you. You should go see what it's like inside government and see if you can make a difference there." He got a job running the Chicago magnet school program and then became deputy chief of staff for Paul Vallas when he was superintendent of Chicago Public Schools. When Paul decided he wanted to run for governor of Illinois in the 2002 election, Mayor Richard Daley put Arne at 36 years old in charge of the nation's third-largest school system. And in 2009, President Obama appointed him US Secretary of Education. Those were proud moments in my life. I used to mentor him; now he's the one mentoring me. He knows me really well, so he knows how to help me be better. So it was good for Arne, good for Chicago, good for the country and good for me.

The multiplier effect of being a good teammate gives John a larger purpose for Ariel's success. In an industry with a history of exclusivity and reputation for greed, John wants to prove that a different kind of firm—one that celebrates diversity and teammates and social responsibility—can succeed. "All of this adds up to a leadership model at Ariel that people don't expect."

John's Playbook

"People know because of performance."

John grew up in the midst of highly accomplished people in Chicago's Hyde Park, the distinctive integrated community of the

University of Chicago. These pioneering leaders shaped his aspirations and ignited his passion.

With historical segregation in Chicago, on the South Side was a small social circle of African American doctors, lawyers, and business leaders. I went to school with their kids. I had the opportunity to know these people and think that maybe doing something important was possible for me, too. They were my heroes.

Thirty years ago, Chicago was a Mecca for African American entrepreneurs. You could ride down the Dan Ryan Expressway and see George Johnson of Johnson Products. You could visit John Johnson at Johnson Publishing on Michigan Avenue. There was Ed Gardner of Soft Sheen, Tom Burrell of Burrell Advertising, Stu Collins and Jacoby Dickens of Seaway National Bank, and Al Boute of Independence Bank. They were great institutions that were African American owned and run by these larger-than-life people. That had an impact on my thoughts of being an entrepreneur.

Years later when John started Ariel, a big influence was a keynote speech at Harvard given by John Johnson. Young John Rogers was serving on the panel for Harvard Business School's Black Alumni Weekend.

Mr. Johnson spoke so eloquently about his experience. He said, "If you are successful at what you do, you don't have to tell people how successful you are." When he was starting *Ebony* and *Jet* and was so desperate to make sales and get a bank relationship and get a printer to print his magazines, he had a terrible time getting people to take him seriously. He said it was amazing how once the business started to take off, all the people he was desperate to go see all started coming to see him. "Mr. Johnson, can I be your banker? Mr. Johnson, can I print your magazine?" He said, "I didn't have to tell people; they knew we were doing a great job and the word spread." Michael Jordan doesn't have to tell people he's a great basketball player. People know because of performance.

I was on a panel the other day. A guy in the back of the room got up and gave a 5-minute speech about his firm and what a pioneer he was. He couldn't just sit in the room, he had to get up and let everyone know how successful he was. That was the opposite of what Mr. Johnson taught me when I was 28.

Another major influence was the University of Chicago Lab School, where John went to high school. There he learned to trust and respect people from all walks of life. John remembers the principal saying that his job was to help create an environment for kids to learn, and that occurs in an environment of trust rather than of rules. This would become the central tenet of John's leadership and parenting.

The principal said that the Lab School works because we trust the Lab students so much they ultimately don't betray that trust. I became a true believer in the idea if you trust people and treat people of all religions, races, and sexes with respect, they will treat you with respect.

He also calls out Edgar "Ned" Jannotta, managing partner from 1977 to 1995 of William Blair & Company, the regional investment bank based in Chicago, where John began his investing career. John regards Ned, who is William Blair's current chairman, "the Michael Jordan of business leaders."

Making and taking opportunities to learn firsthand from great leaders has always been John's success strategy. His advice to young people is to get jobs that give them proximity to top decision makers and creative leaders so that they can directly observe and learn from them. Even today, he describes serving on boards with respected leaders as the best place "to talk with people who are making decisions in all of the world's economies. There's no better place than those forums to help you better understand what's working, what's not working and can't work."

JOHN'S PIVOTAL DECISIONS

Pivot Point: Launching Decision

"What I do is who I am."

I can still remember looking out the window of the plane coming back to Chicago after graduation, deciding that what I learned from Coach Carril is how I want to live my life. I started this firm believing that it's all about being a good teammate.

John knew he would start an investment firm. His father's gifts of $200 in Commonwealth Edison, $200 in First Chicago Bank (now part of JPMorgan Chase Bank) eventually grew to be $500 of dividend-paying stocks. By high school, John was picking and buying stocks with money earned from selling hot dogs and Cokes at Comiskey Park and Wrigley Field, ballparks of Chicago's two rival baseball teams. While an economics major at Princeton, he won $8,600 on the television game show *Wheel of Fortune* and invested it in stocks.

The early lesson in investing was his father's gift, but it was John's passion that turned a prudent lesson into his life's work. Investment newsletters and quarterly reports stimulated the teenager's curiosity about how a company builds value and when its investors make or lose money. After school he would stop by the office of his father's stockbroker, Stacy Adams, just to sit with him and watch the stock ticker tape.

My father tried to get me interested in a lot of different things. The stock market is the one that stuck. I always loved to read and gather information—I read the newspaper every day even as a kid—so I think there's something about the stock market being such an information-based profession that was just a fit for me.

There's the thrill of discovering some hidden jewel before everybody else does. It's exhilarating. And I'm very competitive. This is kind of a big game of picking stocks against the best stock pickers in the world with a scorecard every day. There's something in the competitive terms that I enjoy and plotting strategy to come up with the game plan to win.

Coaching basketball was the only other career John had considered. Choosing business, he applies all that he learned from basketball—teamwork, discipline, competition, perseverance, and winning a *good* game—to his life and work. Knowing there are no shortcuts to improving skills and playing as a team, he observes other leaders the same way he studies basketball players. John seeks out and learns from leaders with well-honed skills and an appreciation for a *good* game. The athlete and teammate in John sees no great victory in winning an ugly game. He embraces perseverance and constant improvement as the way to win. This makes John a reliable teammate and formidable competitor.

Rejected after graduation by Merrill Lynch, his first choice, John was the first African American hired by William Blair. He soon relished working at the regional firm where he got to interact with everyone, including the top leaders. From the beginning, John didn't depend just on the firm's research. By doing his own research, including getting on the plane to meet people, he was building the experience that would be vital to starting his own firm.

> I learned a lot at William Blair. It has an extraordinarily strong and focused culture about doing the right thing for the customer. Treat customers well and good things happen to your business. Ned Jannotta, a quintessential business leader, was an important influence. Wherever he is, he makes a difference. I watched how Ned navigated through his meetings, speaking to something you can react to and if he sees something out of kilter he gently guides it back in the right direction. His judgment is so extraordinary and at the same time he epitomizes teamwork. I still am learning from Ned.

John left William Blair to start Ariel in 1983. Even with his early interest and training in stocks, what made John think at the age of 24 with only two-and-a-half years of formal work experience that he could start his own money management firm?

> I was especially influenced by a couple of terrific family friends who were pioneers and giants, John Johnson and George Johnson. Both had started young and both had singular focus when they started. George built Johnson Products into the first African American company on a major stock exchange. John Johnson built Johnson Publishing into the largest African American business in the country. He started it with a $500 loan secured by his mother's furniture and made *Ebony* into an extraordinary success and brand.
>
> The real inspiration for me was that they were able to pioneer in fields they were passionate about. I had this passion for

the stock market and thought maybe I can do something similar in financial services. I found excuses to see John Johnson and get advice along the way.

And I tied what I learned from Coach Carril to how I wanted to live my life when I moved back to Chicago after Princeton. I started the firm believing that all of this is about helping your teammates succeed and together you can do great things. My goal from the beginning was to build a company that would last into the next generation. To do that, I knew we had to out-perform and give our clients good service.

John started Ariel by raising $180,000 from family and friends to open an office, hire one employee, and have a small budget for research, travel, and marketing. By the end of that first year, he raised $500,000 of investment capital. The following year, Ariel won its first million-dollar institutional account from the city of Chicago.

I went to individuals and asked them for $20,000 to put in what we called the Ariel Fund, which we set up legally as a partnership in 1983. I went to see every friend, family member, and former client from my stockbroker days. In this way we had a real live pool that allowed us to create a track record when you don't have any money to manage and no one is going to give you serious money. I didn't ask for $100,000; I asked for $20,000.

It worked out. I just thought it was such a compelling idea that I felt confident asking people to invest. I didn't have a lot of angst around it. I was confident in my ability to pick stocks well and take good care of customers. Right off the bat our perfor-mance was good.

Why would prosperous people hear a pitch from, let alone trust, a 24-year-old with no track record to manage their money? To have a per-formance story, John started a monthly newsletter, *The Patient Investor*. He figured that as a young investor needing credibility, he would empha-size stable long-term return on investment. He laid out the rationale for stock picks before there was a real mutual fund, with detailed discussion about his thoughts about the stock market, best stock ideas, and how they performed. The newsletter established the theme of patient investing, and the Ariel brand, at a time the industry lacked transparency, in disclosing what they did and how they did it. By creating a performance scorecard that explained the rigorous research and thoughtfulness of stock picks, John built the partnership account into a real mutual fund at the end of 1986.

He also made sure he was not trying to do everything and hired a professional marketer when he couldn't really afford to. They worked hard to be noticed by the financial media. His first big break was appearing on *Wall Street Week* with Lou Rukeyser. John recalls, "I was very young and he was really nice to me."

Conventional wisdom would have kept John in his good job at William Blair for at least several more years of training. Instead, John at 24 years old, made the bold decision with calm confidence to start his own firm, a decision that soon proved to have launched more than a company. What happened next made what appeared to be a risky move of an impatient young man a perfectly timed decision of an astute investor.

Pivot Point: Turning Point Decision

"We avoided the glamorous small stocks that soar and then plunge."

On October 19, 1987, stock markets around the world crashed. The DJIA shed 508 points (22.6 percent), the largest one-day percentage decline in the Dow's history. And it was John's big break.

The market crash, known as Black Monday, rewarded John's patient and disciplined approach to value investing. John focuses on small and midsize basic businesses, conducts rigorous research and analysis, and finds companies holding a promise that has gone unnoticed and therefore is undervalued. By definition these stocks aren't on the same ride as the general market—they aren't on the same ride up, so they don't take the same ride down. These out-of-favor stocks make the investor not only wait several years but also sit out of short-term buy opportunities. Good value investors eventually are amply rewarded. On Black Monday John earned his stripes.

Only in its fourth quarter of existence on Black Monday, Ariel Fund ranked in the year's top 10 performers, finishing 1987 up 11.4 percent when the Russell 2000 Index was down 8.77 percent. The following year, the fund gained 39.93 percent, substantially outperforming every major index. Ariel had benefited in two ways—avoiding the battering other mutual funds took from Black Monday and actualizing gains from operating improvements of its undervalued holdings.

Also, if John had not succeeded in raising enough money to start the first Ariel Fund in 1986, Black Monday in the following year would have impeded the fledgling firm's ability to attract investment capital. Instead, the market crash greatly accelerated Ariel's success.

It was like John's turning point on Princeton's basketball team. Seemingly from nowhere comes a star. At 30 years old, John was selected the 1988 mutual fund comanager of the year by the popular magazine *Sylvia Porter's Personal Finance*. In 1989, John was on *Crain's Chicago Business* first 40 under 40 roster along with Oprah Winfrey. John was 31 years old and Oprah, 35 years old.

At the start of 1988, Ariel had a team of nine managing more than 28 pension-fund accounts totaling $196.4 million. The following year, Ariel crossed the threshold of $1 billion in assets under management, including the addition of a new fund for midsized companies, Ariel Appreciation Fund. This early and dramatic success validated Ariel as the patient investor. It became much more than a positioning strategy as John embraced value investing as a true believer, marking a decisive turning point.

Black Monday was a perfect time for value investing. For example, Ariel snapped up the stock of hotel and casino company Caesar's World at $17 per share, which grew 80 percent by July 1992. Although at times emotion rules the market, John believes the common sense of value investing prevails. He buys low undervalued stocks; these companies fix their problems and increase their value. Meanwhile, hot stocks he avoided succumb to market corrections, and he can snap them up at bargain prices. It simply makes sense to John but it takes rigorous investing principles, thorough research, and nerves of steel with uncommon patience.

> When I started investing, I read more and more about John Templeton and Warren Buffett, people who truly stand firmly against the tide. It spoke to me; it just made sense to me. As the years moved on, I read about behavioral finance which says to get above average returns you have to buy what the average

person doesn't buy. It's just common sense. I was a true believer before behavioral finance became popular.

Stock picking the behavioral finance way plays to John's well-honed skills for prodigious research and vigilant analysis of the sectors and prospective companies in which to invest. But how John gets stellar returns is in the art of investing. He discerns which management teams lead as true believers of their businesses.

When I talk with management teams, I try to read whether people are true believers and have a well-integrated plan that is logical. I'm looking for people who are straight shooters. A lot of people talk a good game, but you can tell they don't really believe. Discerning that is more art than science. We sought experts in the field of constructing questions to help us develop ways to identify true believers.

As the market recovered from Black Monday, the industry also changed. Ariel's first 10 years outperformed major indices and developed a strong presence in the market of defined-benefit plans, which are set up to pay an expected fixed annual retirement income, with the employer making investment decisions. Beginning in the early 1990s, however, growth was in defined-contribution plans of 401(k) accounts, which are based on set contributions by employers and employees into the employee's pension account, with the employee making investment decisions. The number of American workers able to participate in 401(k) plans rose from 7 million in 1983 to more than 48 million by 1991. To grab this market, San Francisco–based Charles Schwab & Co. pioneered in 1992 the mutual fund supermarket, giving individual investors the ability to buy, sell, or switch between a range of inside and outside funds with no sales loads or transaction fees. Fidelity Investments soon followed Schwab's lead.

By mid-1994, Schwab and Fidelity were taking in billions in outside fund assets as the national discount brokerages raced to start their own mutual fund supermarkets. The simultaneous growth of the Internet accelerated and amplified these industry-changing trends. In 1995, the number of people in the United States using the Internet had grown to about 20 million and was growing 100 percent each year.

In this environment that changed the equities market forever, John decided to join the fund networks in the fall of 1994. For John and Ariel, joining the networks would give Ariel shelf space, so to speak, in front of a far larger market of shoppers than was possible through traditional channels. By charging 25 to 35 basis points against a fund's assets in the network, the new third-party channels handled marketing and servicing. But it also meant ending well-established partnerships with investment advisors, such as the Calvert Group based in Bethesda, Maryland. The real cost to Ariel was giving up relationships with many direct shareholders.

Another tidal shift in uncharted waters during the early 1990s was the remarkable growth of semiconductors and the proliferation of technologies, which would gain wild momentum as investors showed unbridled enthusiasm for anything to do with the Internet. Emotion took over the market. Meanwhile, the rest of the equities market struggled. It was in this struggling market that Ariel Fund was invested, the unglamorous stocks.

The rise of the supermarket in investing was like what had taken place in the retail industry; volume and one-stop shopping replaced service and relationships. Investors could choose from 5,200 stock and bond funds. On top of that, Ariel was getting low returns from unglamorous stocks in the face of booming technology stocks. Against these competitive forces, John's decision to participate in the networks brought on the first major test of his leadership.

The 36-year-old founder's first brush with the possibility of failure brought into sharp focus his commitment to build a company that is more than just about quarterly performance. John remained focused on the long-term horizon of patient investing while he evaluated Ariel's position in the transforming marketplace. He raised more capital. He targeted growth in the defined contribution plans of 401(k)s. Realizing that he couldn't be everywhere, he established a more formal leadership team for the 10-year-old company. According to John, he and his team then simply worked harder on every aspect of the business. And the true believer knew the market would once again reward patient investing.

It was a brutal, brutal time. We lost about half of the assets. That was a major test. We were only 10 years old. We raised extra capital to make sure we had some cushion. We worked extra hard, touched base more frequently with management of our portfolio companies. The experience also helped me define my responsibility as a leader to work on our leadership team. We turned things around and came back stronger than ever.

This turning point stage began with stellar performance in a devastated market and ended with a test of John's strategic leadership. Emerging from Black Monday with early proof of his investment philosophy and principles, he didn't doubt himself as an investment officer when facing Ariel's first crisis. Instead he turned his attention to making infrastructure improvements for Ariel to be more responsive and adaptable to the transformed marketplace. By steering the young firm through this crisis, all the while explaining why it was important for investors to work with Ariel, he actually laid the groundwork for reaping the rewards of contrarian investing when the Internet bubble burst.

Pivot Point: Tipping Point Decision

"Ariel is an accumulation of lots of decisions and events. It's always a work in progress. What I'm most proud of at Ariel is that it's a grand experiment to create a group of business leaders."

During the mid-1990s the equities market kept driving up stock prices of technology and Internet companies, peaking in 1997 through 2000. This period of the Internet bubble—a market euphoria described by Federal Reserve chairman Alan Greenspan as "irrational exuberance"—saw tech stocks trade at irrational multiples, including start-ups with virtually no sales.

Staying on the contrarian path throughout this period, John warned there would be a market correction. Meantime, he continued to build his leadership team as Ariel worked its way back from its 1994 crisis. It turned out that Ariel was poised for a tipping point that exceeded his own expectations.

When the new economy crashed fast and hard, the Nasdaq Composite, which listed many dot-com stocks, lost 78 percent of its value from the peak on March 11, 2000, to the bottom on October 9,

2002. The DJIA ended 2001 down 11.88 percent and 2002 down another 22.1 percent. In this devastated market, the Ariel Fund shone like a beacon, ending 2001 up 14.21 percent and 2002 down slightly by 5.18 percent. Just as Black Monday proved the wisdom of John's highly disciplined investing principles, the dot-com bust proved that long-term performance wins over short-term infatuations.

Ariel entered the new millennium with $3.7 billion in total assets under management. After the technology bubble burst in early 2001, Ariel's assets soared 66 percent to $10.3 billion between June 2001 and June 2002, then more than doubled to $21.4 billion by year-end 2004.

> Our growth took off after the burst of the dot-com bubble. We stayed true to our investment philosophy during the Internet bubble. So we were poised to benefit from the market correction. Also, we had been so clear about our perspective and point of view that when we were sort of vindicated by the market correction, people thought, *Geez, these people said early on they thought the Internet bubble was going to burst*. It actually burst, validating this idea that Ariel is a firm that stays the course, doesn't meander around, and doesn't get swept up in groupthink of chasing hot stocks.
>
> The second thing is that our team was growing more experienced and stronger. So, all of a sudden, I think people were saying here is a firm with terrific performance and terrific people leading key areas of the business. So they felt confident and comfortable giving us more money to manage.

In 1999, he had named Peter Thompson head of institutional marketing and client services and Merrillyn Kosier head of mutual fund marketing and investor services. The following year, John turned operating responsibilities over to Mellody Hobson and made her president of Ariel. She was 30 years old but John had mentored her since her first day at Ariel in 1991. He knew she had the leadership skills to run the business—client service, marketing, brand building, operating financials, compliance, and technology—and the "sparkling personality to be the face of Ariel." This she literally became when she was selected in 2000 to be a regular financial contributor of financial advice for ABC TV's *Good Morning America*. The expanded leadership team helped

John right the ship after Ariel's 1994 crisis, and by 2001 the firm could catch the trade winds in its sails.

Although Ariel's success as an investment firm is measured by financial performance, developing "high-wattage leaders at Ariel, smart people who succeed by helping their teammates succeed" is John's own measure of his success as a leader. Giving equal weight to both, John handles investments as the firm's lifeblood and the leadership culture as the firm's nerve center.

Because of the rapid information exchange around the world now, things get telescoped into shorter periods. The cycles that used to take three to four years to play out now can play out in one to two years. So, we think focus is really important. In the management of the firm, everybody can't try to do a little bit of everything. We've split up the responsibilities here. That frees me up to think about the markets. I have a call this morning with the CEO of a company we invested in that's not been performing well. Eight o'clock last night I was having drinks with the CEO of one of our major holdings. So that's what I do day to day: talk on the phone and meet with management teams of the companies we are invested in.

I always try to find game-changing leaders for our organization so that the team is a composite of different skill sets. As I get to know people, I've looked for different components to the team and people I could possibly recruit into the organization.

In addition to a rich composite of skill sets, we want people who are truly selfless in their thinking about what's best for the organization and what's best for their teammates. Part of that is treating people the way you want to be treated. And we want people committed to working hard. Everybody at Ariel who has been here for one year is a shareholder in the company. I want everyone to feel they're an owner.

With a team of high-performance leaders in place, John stepped up and out as a leading voice of increasing diversity in the mutual fund industry. In 1999, Ariel had joined with Charles Schwab in conducting a study that found prosperous African Americans were averaging a little more than half the savings in 401(k) plans of whites with comparable incomes. Supported by data, John and Ariel became leading advocates for raising African Americans' savings so that they too could participate in the boom in mutual funds.

As with most tipping points, John's was a confluence of events, some planned and others not, that intersected at a special point in time. The tech bust in 2001 created an opportunistic moment John fully leveraged to attract money, support his teammates as they flourished, and take a leadership stance on the social responsibility of business. What happened next also took a special confluence of events.

Pivot Point: Recommitment Decision

"I believe so strongly in staying the course and not succumbing to fear and groupthink that I am not going to be shaken out."

Ariel had prospered through 25 years of bull and bear markets, emerging from underperforming years stronger than ever. The firm had benefited from market collapses. However, the Great Recession of 2007–2008 was different. This time, Ariel was caught in the crosshairs of the broken financial industry and economy. There was panic set off by rumors that the government would seize major banks.

After Ariel's stellar year in 2004, the perfect economic storm was gathering. The energy crisis ran up the price of a barrel of crude oil from $60 in August 2005 to $147 in July 2008. The bull market since October 2002 peaked in October 2007 and quickly turned when there were signs of major troubles. Then, in 2008, questionable mortgage-backed securities dramatically imploded. Ariel's assets under management dropped from its high of $21.4 billion in 2004 to $16 billion in 2007, then nosedived to its low of $3 billion in March 2009. Ariel had its first layoff in its 25-year history.

During the years the price of oil surged, Ariel's large investments in consumer goods companies saw lower profits as they encountered sharply higher shipping costs. Ariel was vulnerable by the second half of 2008 when high-risk, mortgage-backed securities brought down financial giants in rapid succession. The market went into a panic as billions of dollars were pulled out of mutual funds and equities, including Ariel.

John was shaken but was "not going to be shaken out." Even as investors pulled out money at the worst time of the plunging DJIA, John adhered to a disciplined and steadfast course. Midyear 2007, John told a reporter, "There can be periods when we wildly outperform our benchmarks and periods when we underperform our benchmarks. We need to be patient throughout the cycle." By the second quarter of 2009, Ariel was outperforming the major indices—but the damage was done.

> It was the most difficult time we've had. I think the lesson is to never take anything for granted. Things can shift and change quickly. Prepare for the worst because it really can happen. Warren Buffett was in our office in 2008, and he talked about how it was one of the toughest years he's seen in his career. He says value investing is like an inoculation; it either takes or it doesn't.
>
> It can be a lonely job in terms of the decisions you have to make, when people want to go with the past and you know that's not what to do. We worked hard at explaining this: If your stocks go down, don't sell into the fear; if other stocks go up, don't buy into the greed, as Warren Buffett wrote during the market turmoil. We made the case to investors that this is the worst time to fire us because our stocks were selling at bargain prices. If they had fired us before the downturn, they would have been geniuses. But the worst thing was to fire us at the low.

It deeply frustrated John that he couldn't persuade more people to stay the course. It didn't make sense to him that investors who lost billions of dollars on the way down decided to lose again by missing the way back up. He believes that he needs to improve at getting people to see that he has the requisite stamina, performance-tested conviction, and competitive skills to consistently deliver long-term performance. But perhaps he also needs to teach investors his secret to having a stomach of steel for the wild ride.

> The best advice I got was reading about Warren Buffett and Charlie Munger's belief in staying within your circle of

competence. Second, once you have a strategy and philosophy you have to stick with it when it's extraordinarily uncomfortable to do. When it's most painful, you've got to stay the course. It's so easy to say and it's so hard to do.

I believe so strongly in staying the course and not succumbing to fear and groupthink that I was not going to be shaken out.

As of year-end 2010, Ariel Fund gained a cumulative 215.06 percent since the bottom of March 9, 2009, and Ariel Appreciation Fund gained a cumulative 170.06 percent. By early 2013, Ariel was recognized as one of the mutual fund companies beating the bull market that began in March 2009. Over this period, Ariel Fund gained a cumulative 236 percent, ranking ninth in its category, and Ariel Appreciation Fund gained a cumulative 199 percent. Managed assets have grown steadily: $3 billion in 2009 to $4 billion in 2011 to $8.4 billion as of January 31, 2014.

John fully appreciates that it takes a certain kind of person to be a leader in value investing. When selecting his leaders, he looks for the independent thinker who is comfortable taking a contrarian position.

I've been promoting some people here to have a greater leadership role in portfolio management because I've seen them battle tested through the financial crisis. The fact that we went through that trial by fire that was so debilitating, so difficult, you really did see which people had the conviction to want to buy more of a stock that had just been totally crushed. It's hard to come in and recommend buying more of a stock that was $25 and down to $4. And we had several of those situations during the financial crisis. We saw which people were willing to do that and which waivered with a let's-wait-and-see position.

Because of how they responded during tough times, we want to give some people leadership roles in portfolio management and steer others to roles in gathering facts and information but not in decision-making portfolio management roles. Not everyone has the constitution to be contrarian.

With that said, I think it's healthy to have people with different perspectives. I do love having the give and take and the pressure. Part of my job as the leader is to cultivate an environment where people push each other and challenge each other. It's also a big part of my job to discern which people are consumed with the short-term noise, and I'm here to remind people to not let that impact their decision. We are going to always be the firm that looks out over the horizon, willing to look past where the short-term problems happen to be.

As Ariel's chief investment officer, John focuses on problems of execution rather than experimenting with investment principles or second-guessing his acumen. First, he improved Ariel's balance sheet analysis. Second, he targeted shifting the mix of business to increase assets under management in mutual funds and be less dependent on institutional funds. Third, he added new funds to take advantage of more opportunities. And he continued to build his leadership team.

The financial crisis of 2008 and early 2009 taught us that we had to be stronger in our balance sheet analysis. We thought we were good at it; we thought we had the appropriate level of margin of safety, but we learned the hard way during that financial crisis that catastrophic scenarios can happen. Charlie Bobrinskoy, our director of research, led a very robust in-depth analysis that culminated in very significant improvements in our balance sheet analysis.

Now we have our own proprietary debt ratings that we create internally and Charlie is our quality control guru to make sure that all of our analysts have to justify the quality of the balance sheets of the companies we own. It's a very rigorous disciplined improvement that came out of the crisis.

In the first half of 2008, John changed the name from Ariel Capital Management to Ariel Investments. The old name positioned the firm as primarily an institutional money manager, and the new name signaled the shift to treat as equally important the no-load funds it manages and markets to retail customers. John was protecting Ariel from ever again being so vulnerable to decisions of institutional benefits managers and committees that involve hundreds of millions. In 2013, approximately two-thirds of assets under management were through mutual funds and one-third institutional. He also added funds to capitalize on more opportunities.

When money starts flowing back into mutual funds, it comes back fast. And you don't have that risk of a big pension fund taking several hundred million dollars out in a moment. It's better to be more diversified.

We are also way more diversified in our funds than we were in 2008. Our new microcap value fund is doing very well. Our international and global funds, which we started at year-end 2011, have the capacity to be a big part of our business. Our new small-cap deep-value Ariel Discovery Fund has gotten off to a good start. And we brought on new teammates to help us be more effective. We have substantially more arrows in our quiver than we had before, so I think that is going to serve us well to get bigger and better.

Since 2009, John has been logging more miles meeting with corporate pension plan managers and asset managers. He attends more investing conferences and takes more interviews with journalists and business reporters. He has decided to do the uncomfortable—tell his story to more people. John would rather read business journals, talk with customers, or play basketball than put himself in the spotlight. But he has embraced the need as Ariel's chief investment officer and founder to establish Ariel's brand reputation in a changing marketplace.

A boost to morale at Ariel during its most punishing year of asset management was that it coincidentally also was one of the most rewarding years of Ariel's civic leadership. Participating up close in Obama's historic 2008 victory and Chicago's thriving urban renewal gave John and his team the boost they needed to carry on through the protracted time of uncertainty and instability of the economy and financial markets. Will Ariel reach again its apex of $21.4 billion in 2004?

There was a nice feature in USA Today [January 8, 2013] on Ariel hitting on all cylinders and having taken the "bull by the horns" since the market bottom in 2009. Our first goal is to get to $10 billion. Then to $15 billion, and work our way back to the $20 billion range. It will take time but we think those goals are certainly achievable.

We want to prove that this unique firm of extraordinarily talented and diverse people who have an enormous amount of commitment to our community here in Chicago can ultimately build an extraordinarily top-performing money management and mutual fund company.

This is by far the most diverse mutual fund company in the country's history. There's never been a firm like ours that has really been successful in money management and mutual funds. It wouldn't be magical if we didn't have this uniqueness of diverse people committed to helping others and to excellence in the overall performance that we deliver to our customers. That's my passion; my reason for being here is to prove that model can work.

Pivot Point: Letting Go Decision

"I want them to make their own independent decisions on the portfolios they oversee, and not wait to see what I'm thinking or try to please me in some way."

John is determined to steer Ariel into the future for other generations to build on its diversity, leadership, and success. He knows that he is fortunate to have time—today only in his mid-50s—when others, such as Bill Miller of Legg Mason, faced the most challenging years near the end of their illustrious careers.

People get so caught up with short-term performance numbers. People should try to understand the character of the leadership team behind the long-term track record. It would be different if you were a one-hit wonder with two good years and that was it.

A few years back I was in a board meeting and the 401(k) plan of this corporation had money in the Legg Mason mutual funds managed by Bill Miller, who has demonstrated throughout most of his 35-year career excellent performance over the long run. One of the board members brought up that Bill Miller was having several bad years. Then someone said they knew a consultant from a large benefits firm that could help determine whether we should keep Bill Miller. I said, "How can this consultant be one-tenth as smart as Bill Miller and have one-tenth of his experience?" It's like if the general manager of the Bears hired me to pick the quarterback—I only watch and throw a football. It doesn't make sense.

As long as market challenges make sense, John has the confidence and fortitude—and a large dose of sheer competitiveness—to do what it takes to continue building Ariel for the next generation. What doesn't make sense unsettles John. Buy low and sell high makes sense; selling low into the fear and buying high into the run-up doesn't make sense. Respecting expertise developed over a long-term record of accomplishment makes sense; acting on advice not battle tested doesn't make sense. There's a hint that John has contemplated the possibility of market dynamics changing so fundamentally that it won't make sense to him. That day hasn't come.

In a sense, the improvements John has led for each recovery, especially for the current comeback from the Great Recession, involved significant letting go of control by the founder. John has progressively built up his leadership team, helped it shine, and handed over big areas of responsibility. Although he will continue as chief investment officer for a long time yet, he has now changed that role from sitting at the head of a table to having a seat at a big round table.

> Being chief investment officer will continue to be the most important role that I play here. The most important difference will be that I am now part of the mosaic of portfolio managers. It used to be I controlled almost all the product.
>
> As part of a broader group of leaders overseeing the funds, the most important change in my role is that I have to remind people that I want them to make their own independent decisions on the portfolios they oversee and not wait to see what I'm thinking or try to please me in some way by recommending a stock they think I might like or not selling something because they think I liked it years ago.
>
> My job is to constantly remind them to form their own independent views and perspectives, and to execute on those independent views as long as they're making decisions within the spirit of Ariel's core values and culture.

Buy cheap stocks and hold them for the long run. The turtle is still here.

At 55 years old, John is in midcareer and determined to leave a legacy of sustainable success. When we look at the octogenarians profiled in this book, we see them facing pivotal challenges in their mid-50s and emerging more successful than they ever had reason to expect. Bud Frankel and his cofounder ended their 20-year partnership that had deteriorated. Al Golin considered retiring to end bitter conflicts with new owners. At those points during their mid-50s, neither Bud nor Al had any idea of the success that lay ahead. The journey of these leaders show that decisions, not age, define their opportunities.

Those decisions are still ahead for John. We can be fairly certain that those decisions for John have to do with having a diverse team of strong and confident independent thinkers with the conviction, strength of stomach, and leadership to take determined steps down the lonely path apart from the crowd.

THE LEADER'S LEGACY

John confidently remains chief true believer in what Ariel stands for: Slow and steady wins the race. He is driven by the legacy most important to him—that is, the legacy of succeeding by helping others succeed through strength in diversity. Strong performance according to the stock market scorecard is the necessary metric to enable market success; his personal metric of enduring success is Ariel's leaders and their impact on the industry and community, especially around diversity and financial awareness.

The people I have worked hard to influence, I think, are going to go on as extraordinary leaders. The second thing I feel really good to be part of is the legacy around financial literacy, what we've done with the Ariel Community Academy and the work we're doing to expose the potential crisis in America where people of color won't be able to retire comfortably because they weren't familiar or comfortable with 401(k) plans and all of the decision making involved. I feel extraordinarily proud that we were the first to highlight this in a major way and develop an action program. In recognition of our Ariel Education Initiative, Ariel was named the 2008 recipient of the Mutual Fund Education Alliance Community Investment Award.

John seizes every opportunity to move forward greater participa tion of the underrepresented in financial management. Serving on the board of directors of McDonald's since 2003, John urged the company to better understand employee participation in its 401(k) program by conducting an in-depth analysis of its composition, contributions, and discrepancies between demographic segments. When the McDonald's 2004 study did in fact find significant discrepancies, especially low enrollment of low-income workers, the company worked with its employees on improvements that resulted in automatic enrollment and default employer contributions. This work inspired the landmark study by Ariel Education Initiative and Hewitt Associates, "401(k) Plans in Living Color: A Study of 401(k) Savings Disparities across Racial and Ethnic Groups," conducted in 2007 and published in July 2009. Government agencies, employers, and employees have adopted many of its recommendations. A follow-up study was released in early 2012.

And finally, I am proud we've built a money management firm that is all about excellence and performance, which at the same time believes that the way we get there is by creating a team of diverse individuals who care about others. Teamwork is not just about how you care about each other; it's also how you care about your community. That is a part of the culture of diversity we have worked hard to create. It's never been done before, at least in our industry.

John's journey demonstrates resolve, character, and intellect. But what gives it special resonance is the built-in tensions leaders have to reconcile as they try to be at once authentic, impactful, and understood by the public. This low-key leader outside of the office wants people to see how tough he can be in the office and on the basketball court. This good teammate is selflessly generous in helping others but also fiercely competitive—"I'm committed to win; that drives me every day." This quiet introvert speaks out as an extrovert when it comes to inclusion and fairness. John doesn't have it all figured out, but these tensions make him a leader you want to see succeed.

At a time when financial winners are acclaimed one year and investigated or convicted the next, John is an important reminder that it's worth losing some battles to win the war. John exemplifies the kind of leader we want our future leaders to regard as their hero.

We want to prove that bringing together people from diverse perspectives and different walks of life can be extraordinarily successful and at the same time are committed to helping others. I'm driven by the importance of this to work. It's such a unique model; it sets the right tone for how small businesses can make a difference. That's why it's really important for us to be successful.

CHAPTER 5

CULTURE

Al Golin

Founder and Chairman of GolinHarris

WHY YOU SHOULD KNOW HIM AND ABOUT HIS WORK

Al Golin, founder of GolinHarris, is recognized by *PRWeek* as one of the 100 most influential public relations people of the twentieth century. The GolinHarris of 2014 is a global public relations (PR) firm with 45 offices around the world and a client roster of blue-chip companies. Named large agency of the year by *PRWeek* in 2007 and 2010, GolinHarris was recognized for creativity, innovation, financial growth, and a reputation as one of the best agencies to work for in the industry. It won the Holmes Report 2013 Large Agency of the Year in the Americas, 2011 Best Large Agency to Work For, and the 101 Best and Brightest Companies to Work For.

One of the founding fathers of PR, Al wrote the book—figuratively and literally—on PR as an opportunity to gain the public trust. In 2005, the master of reputation management published a book, *Trust or Consequences: Build Trust Today or Lose Your Market Tomorrow*, to bring attention to "the most valuable asset anyone and any company can build." With case studies of how trust is won and lost, the book defines Al Golin's brand of PR and leadership: Never take people's trust for granted or knowingly risk losing it. Accepting an honorary PhD from DePaul University in 2012, Al told graduates of the College of Communication, "There is a positive connection between trust and results. It's not necessarily a short-term connection but one that reveals itself over time. Organizations that work hard at building strong relationships with employees, customers, peer organizations, the media, policy makers and their communities are the ones that last." The 2008 collapse of Lehman Brothers that exposed the catastrophic greed of Wall Street has made Al's message even more relevant.

GolinHarris could have been another good enough business—good enough to provide a very comfortable living for the founder, good enough to attract buyers, and good enough to fetch a selling price for the founder to walk away. Al did almost walk away after Shandwick International, a London-based PR agency, bought the firm in 1990. But from the start, the culture of GolinHarris was on a collision course with the culture of its British owners. In retrospect, this 10-year period of struggle that tested Al's leadership compelled him to achieve his real legacy of building a company to last. His decision to recommit to the business became the most important of all the decision points in Al's journey. It started as a decision to push his limits of endurance, if not to win, at least not to lose. It became a decision to grow as a leader.

Al emerged from each pivot point with more clarity about what the essence of the brand and economic value of GolinHarris was, what was worth fighting for, and what would make it sustainable. He accomplished this by avoiding the common problem of founders becoming obstacles to the growth of the company's future leaders and its business. Succession can be the toughest test of leadership, especially for founders. It took Al two tries; the first presented him with the most difficult decision of his career.

Al's meteoric rise in PR began when he made a cold call in 1957 to Ray Kroc, who had just begun building the McDonald's franchise in the Chicago area. A junior partner at Max Cooper & Associates when he landed the promising new account, Al was made a partner the following year, and the firm was renamed Cooper, Burns & Golin. In 1975, Al became the sole owner of Golin Communications. In 1981, he renamed the firm Golin/Harris Communications, to acknowledge the contributions of Tom Harris, a partner in the firm from 1978 to 1990. Owned by The Interpublic Group (IPG) since 1999, GolinHarris has thrived with Al transitioning from chief executive officer (CEO) to chairman and appointing Fred Cook CEO in 2002. In 2012, GolinHarris celebrated the 55th anniversary of its continuous relationship with McDonald's.

His journey was measured, steady, and financially conservative, the opposite of the path pursued by many of today's entrepreneurs and financiers, whose goals of speed and vast personal wealth can detract from building real economic value. Al's path produced a company with real sustainable value, a soul, and a moral compass. Al's story reminds us that his path of dependable and steady is a good choice, perhaps the better choice, for most people.

WHAT MATTERS TO AL GOLIN

Al's Playbook

"Devotion to your profession makes the difference. I happened to get into something I truly enjoy and am devoted to."

Al more than enjoys PR; it is a way of life for him. A news junkie who reads five newspapers every day, he can't enjoy vacations that last longer than three days because he feels cut off from the news. One might expect to see a legend in PR present a highly polished camera-ready image, but Al looks more like a slightly rumpled news reporter even though he is always well groomed. That could be because his clothes hang on his athletic frame, trim and fit from tennis and golf, or because his first dream career was to be a news broadcaster.

His straight talk and low-key presence give him instant credibility. A genuinely unassuming man, Al easily gains trust, even though he admits to being extremely competitive. He has a special air of being simultaneously open and closed—one approaches Al knowing that he is an engaging conversationalist, making points by telling stories, but also has little time or patience for banal talk.

He tells his own story not in terms of visionary ideas, bold plans, dramatic financial decisions, or brilliant strategies. Instead, Al talks about his success in terms of doing what he enjoys, working with people he likes, never being complacent—oh, and, making bad money decisions that ended up with mergers gone awry. His devotion to his profession helped him persist through that angst-filled 10-year period. It gave him the resolve to take a stand for what made the company worth his continuing commitment and the resilience to move forward with all his hard-learned lessons.

With more than 55 years in the PR business, he finally feels *"his turn"* at success has come. He's always enjoyed the PR business, but in recent years he has seen the full fruits of his devotion. At 84 years old and still an active chairman, Al more beams with pride than exercises his powerful influence in any overt display.

> I guess I must have been having fun all these years because I'm still at it and still enjoy it. I find it's a stimulating field I'm in. You have to be current to be good at it, and I've been a news junkie since I was a kid. So I think it was a natural business for me to go into, in the sense of being very interested in what's happening today.
>
> We're supposed to come to clients with ideas that will help sell their products or services, and in doing so, we should be good observers of what's going on out there. Being current and being with it means a lot of things. Today, there is such a sea change in the world with technology and everything else that's going on, you have to be curious and learn about the new. You have to be careful to not rely too much on your gut instinct about the way things have been and be very conscious of change and how things are today. It doesn't mean I have to like rap music, but I have to recognize its importance.

Al's Playbook

"I worked on the culture because that was the kind of company I wanted to run."

After 50-plus years of thousands of leadership decisions, Al hopes the one that was encoded in the company's DNA is his belief that people who enjoy their work have clients who enjoy working with them. He never needed financial proof that happy employees mean happy clients. It just made intuitive sense.

> I'm not a religious person by any means, but I think the Golden Rule is important. We like to treat people the way you'd like to

be treated. We put it in our credo and values statement, and everybody has all that and everybody sounds alike. But I think I've established a culture for our people to really enjoy coming to work. I feel sorry for people who say they hate Monday mornings. I know we all like Friday afternoons, but you can't hate Monday mornings.

It's been said there's a Midwestern work ethic, and I think that's really true. There's a low-key, real, authentic kind of feeling. We've tried to establish that in our culture, helping our people be the kind you want to be with. We try to hire people who take clients seriously but don't take themselves too seriously.

When we win new business, more often than not it's because of the chemistry factor. Every firm can tell you about their track record and case studies, but it's chemistry that wins the day. In the final analysis, culture makes the difference in retaining employees *and* clients.

Al's Playbook

"We should try to change things before we *have* to change it. Don't be complacent."

Counterbalancing Al's low-key style are self-assuredness and boundless energy for work, both born out of self-reliance developed in childhood because his father never fully engaged with his family or his work and had financial struggles.

His father, owner of a movie theater, lost the business in large part because he was out of touch with the changing world of television. He handled the daily basics of opening and closing the movie theater, not showing interest in much else. Al recalls going home after playing a citywide tennis tournament, and all his father said was, "You're late for dinner"—never asking his 13-year-old son how he did in the tournament.

My mother's family owned theaters and her brothers, who never let him forget this, gave him the opportunity of owning one. When the going got tough, he wasn't ready for it. When

television came in, things got bad in the movie industry and theaters started selling popcorn for additional income. My father
didn't want to have popcorn in his theater. He ended up losing
the business. Seeing my father worry about supporting his family in the later stages in his life left a deep impression.

I never wanted to ask my parents for money, so I guess I've
always been independent. Early on, I always had jobs—selling
fans to doctors' offices during the summers and all sorts of
things. Knowing that I could make money and never have to ask
anybody was its own reward. Later, witnessing what was going
on around my house, I didn't want to put any burden on my parents. I watched some of my friends go away to college and many
going to expensive schools. I worked my way through college
here in Chicago.

From his father's passivity, Al learned to never be complacent and
to be self-motivated. It doesn't take too much psychology to see that the
son's reaction to his father was to make it his business, literally and figuratively, to be curious, keep learning, and embrace change. By reading
five newspapers every day, Al stays in touch. By doing more than necessary for clients and employees, Al tries to fix things *before* they break. By
embracing change, Al's comfort zone never confines him.

Maybe my insecurity was a good force for success. It prevented
me from ever being complacent. I've always said that even if it's
not broke fix it. I think that is really the key philosophy I've lived
with: We should try to change things before we *have* to change it.
Part of not being complacent is not taking anyone or anything for
granted. And I always thought that doing things right when you
really can't afford to do them right will pay off in the long run.

Somebody will say, "You've had McDonald's for 50 years—
why do you have to worry about them? Why do you see or hear
something in the news and feel obligated to call someone about
it?" I don't know whether it's insecurity or just pride in what you
do; maybe it's a fine line. I like to be calm in my leadership but
there's a lot of turmoil on the inside.

My wife says to me, "Why do you get so excited about winning a new client at this stage in your life?" I tell her, "The day

I don't still get excited about it is the day I won't come in to the office anymore." Actually, under this humble Midwestern nice-guy thing, I have a very competitive edge. I really like to win.

Al's Playbook

"I think without trust there is nothing. If people don't have trust in a company or in a product, it's not going to make it."

Corporate scandals were not the inspiration for Al's book, *Trust or Consequences*, but they provided the push Al needed to write the book that was in him after 40 years of building the company's niche as trust strategists in the PR industry. The paramount importance of trust in business, Al proposes, warrants creation of a new role in corporations: chief trust officer.

> *Trust* is probably the most important word you can use in our business. Everything you do is to build trust. Things *do* break, and the people and companies who have trust are those who can fix it and recover.
> Clients essentially hire us for our judgment; they trust our judgment. Whether it's our judgment in telling them how they should react in a crisis or how to sell their products or services, we have to be a good judge of how people are going to react. If you're trying to help the company stock, you have to know how Wall Street will react; if it's a product, how the public will take to it.

Experience has fine-tuned Al's uncanny ability to know what PR can and cannot accomplish for a client and the ideas that will get the job done in a trustworthy way. He feels it in his gut. Although he treats other points of views with respect, Al's gut usually makes the call.

> When I've made a mistake in the past it's because of not following my gut—when I knew in my heart what was right but was talked out of it as a matter of expedience. You usually pay the

price. Someone once asked me, "What are you *most* proud of and what are you *least* proud of?" I said, "It's probably the same thing. I've been the least proud when I've been talked out of a good idea when I knew it *was* good, and I've been the most proud when I stuck to my guns and didn't listen to naysayers and followed my gut." It's the same deal.

A good example is when McDonald's was opening in Moscow in 1990 and we decided we wanted to have a big splash over there. So we came up with the idea that they should give the proceeds from the first day's sales to a local children's charity in Russia. The people over there said that's impossible. No private company ever does anything like that over here; the government takes care of everything. That's not part of the Russian culture.

We said, "Isn't it time that things change? First of all, the country is turning into a market economy, so why not throw out the rule book and do something that is going to be shocking, different, and exciting. If you want to play it safe, sure, we can do a lot of things and play it safe. But I think this thing is going to work because I think people are people, they have the same emotions, they have the same interest in children—I don't care where you are in the world."

We stuck to our guns. They did it. It proved to be a huge success. It endeared McDonald's not only to the Russian people but also with government officials. It opened up doors for them for additional real estate sites, things of that nature. So it was a very successful thing, but we could have been very easily talked out of it.

Trust is not just advice Al doles out to clients. When the firm was in danger of losing very good people made miserable by an unreasonable client, Al resigned the business because it was the right thing to do for his people.

It's as important to keep the trust and respect of your own people as that of your clients. Short-term financial decisions are usually the wrong decisions and come back to haunt you every time. In this case, it was a long-term decision and this sent a positive statement to our own people. People said, "This is the kind of company I want to stay with."

Al's Playbook

"I learned that you should deal with the people at the top because they often are more approachable."

In his first job after college as a field press representative covering the Midwest for Metro-Goldwyn-Mayer Studios (MGM), Al learned his first important career lesson. It was from none other than Clark Gable, whom Al was assigned to publicize. When they met for the first time, Al was struck by the respectful way the superstar treated autograph seekers in contrast with the haughtiness of a wannabe starlet nearby.

I first met Clark Gable at a train station; there were a bunch of autograph seekers around, and there was a young starlet who was arriving on the same train. She came over and said something to Clark Gable, like, "Isn't this a terrible part of what we have to put up with?" He looked at her and said, "Honey, when they stop asking, *that's* terrible. This is not terrible." It was a crazy little incident when I was 22 years old, meeting a superstar who gives everybody respect and some starlet you've never heard of before or since who gives everybody a hard time.

I've found that to be true in business life. Leaders can be themselves; they don't have anything to prove. They have the security and confidence in themselves to say what's real. The bigger they are in stature, the easier they are to deal with, the more reasonable they are, the more interested they are, and the more curious they are. There are middle managers who are so insecure that they are intent on showing everyone they meet who is boss.

This made a deep impression. Building relationships at the top became the foundation of Al's success in client service. Treating everyone with respect was also the core value he built into the company's culture. To this day, Al treats everyone with respect and humility, in and out of business circles.

AL'S PIVOTAL DECISIONS

Pivot Point: Launching Decision

"I think too many people can pontificate and tell you how they planned their life to the nth degree. I don't think that's true. I think things happen. However, you have to be willing to take advantage of a given situation and you have to be willing to take risks."

Some people insist that the path to success is having a plan with clear goals and specific action steps. Others insist that plans can be blinders, limiting one's ability to see opportunities and options in the wider vista and seize them at the right time.

Al insists that defining experiences in his career were unplanned—"Things happen," he says. For Al, it's all about turning situations to his advantage.

Enjoying the publicity end of the business at MGM but taking to heart advice from an older cousin that chances for real responsibilities and advancement are better at small companies, Al joined a small PR firm in Chicago in 1956. As a junior partner at Max Cooper & Associates, Al saw the opportunity to depend on himself to succeed.

That opportunity came when Al made a cold sales call one day in 1957. A friend working at a radio station told Al he had met Ray Kroc the day before and was impressed by what a super salesperson he was. In 1955, Ray had opened his first McDonald's in Des Plaines, Illinois, and by 1957 had opened about 10 more in the Chicago area. The friend suggested, "Why don't you call him? You may be getting in on the ground floor."

Al called Ray.

Well, you hear about ground-floor opportunities a lot. But I made the phone call. Ray had a small office in downtown Chicago for McDonald's System Inc. He said, "Come on over."

I said, "Now?"

He said, "Yes, now is fine."

So I went over to his office and after about a half hour he said, "Okay, you can start Monday." He calls in Harry Sonneborn, who was president of the company and the financial and real estate guy, as Ray wasn't very sophisticated about finances. He introduced me to Sonneborn. Ray said, "This young man"—I was young at the time—"is going to start Monday." Sonneborn hit the ceiling.

He said, "What are you paying him?"

Kroc said, "$500 a month."

Sonneborn said, "You and I can't even afford to draw salaries. What are they going to do for us?"

Kroc said, "I don't know, but I have a good feeling about it. I think that's what we need."

Ray was sort of the quintessential PR person's dream. He went along with everything. If you told him to go to Muncie, Indiana, for an interview the next day, he said, "Okay, what time do we leave?" He was very, very receptive to new ideas. For many years our activities were the only way McDonald's became known.

That cold call was the seminal event launching Al on the path of leadership. In the following 10 years, Al was Ray's trusted advisor for, what was at the time, the only marketing activity at the corporate level. McDonald's didn't have national television advertising until 1967. By that time, it had grown into a national chain of 967 restaurants.

After getting McDonald's as a promising client, Al became partner of the firm he had joined one year prior. The firm became Cooper, Burns & Golin. Max Cooper was the top banana, Ben Burns the writer, and Al Golin the client service person.

In 1957, no one could have predicted the phenomenon that McDonald's became. Getting McDonald's gave Al a leadership launching point because it was a rare opportunity to work closely with an entrepreneur who had big ideas and the experience at 55 years old to be both a creative and pragmatic leader.

The launching point actually consisted of several key decisions. The first key decision Al made was to "depend on himself for success," moving to a small company. The second key decision was to act on his friend's suggestion and pick up the phone. The third was Al's decision, learned from Clark Gable, not to be shy about approaching busy people at the top. In 1957, the age difference could have been intimidating for 28-year-old Al to advise 55-year-old Ray (who was 52 years old when he bought the rights from the McDonald brothers in 1954 and was 71 when he retired in 1973).

This series of three decisions put Al at that proverbial door on which opportunity knocked at that special time. If it hadn't been McDonald's, Al would surely have gotten other accounts and had a respectable career. But McDonald's was a client that challenged Al and was open to all his ideas. Ray Kroc, one of the great entrepreneurs and business leaders of the twentieth century, tapped Al's potential to lead among leaders. In just over 10 years (1957 to 1968), together they applied the power of PR in local communities to grow McDonald's into a household name with a thousand restaurants.

In the early days of our work for McDonald's, we were really writing the book on community involvement, trying to endear ourselves to the local community in ways that would be fairly inexpensive and give visibility to the local franchisees. We said, "If your product is not discernibly different than your competitors', people would rather do business with you if you're likeable and get involved in the community."

That whole concept was brand new. You might have heard a local bank sponsoring a Little League team or bowling team, but you never heard of a fledgling company like McDonald's, selling low-price food, doing all those things and a lot more. That confounded everybody. All the community involvement got the franchisees and McDonald's widely known. Despite the fact that they have become one of the largest advertisers in the world, they still believe as strongly today that community involvement is part and parcel of their culture.

Ray Kroc died in 1984. I worked with him for 26 years and knew him very well. In the early days, I used to go with him on interviews. A reporter once asked him, "How many of these are you going to open?" He said, "We're going to open a *thousand* of these someday." We'd go out later and he said, "Yeah, that'll be the day." Now they have over 33,000 around the world. When they opened the thousandth store in 1968, we had a big party.

Al and Ray were vital to each other's success. And they shared common styles and traits, or, it could be that their working relationship and long friendship had a symbiotic effect on both of them. Al's description of Ray could describe him: direct, no-nonsense, principled, and belief in doing things right just because it's right. For both Al and Ray, by doing things right, their businesses grew.

> I wrote a speech for him when he got some award. I gave Ray a line he did use a lot. "We had principles when we were *poor*. We sure still have them today when we are successful." When you think about it, it's very easy to have principles when you are rich. It's a lot easier to give a shirt off your back when you have *two* shirts. It's very difficult to have principles when you're poor and struggling. Everybody is looking for shortcuts when building a business. We've all been guilty of that to a certain extent.
>
> It's the company that succeeds that thinks bigger when they can't afford to think big. If you always think small, you're never going to get big. McDonald's thought big when they couldn't afford to think big, and that's one of their keys to success. They had training programs and they did all kinds of things nobody would have dreamt of for a fledgling company. They never had the attitude of "Take the money and run."

If you bought 100 shares of McDonald's stock in 1965 when it went public, your investment in 2011 would have turned into 74,000 shares, and the initial $2,100 you invested would be worth more than $7 million.

These activities defined McDonald's development as the world's largest restaurant chain and defined Al's development as a PR leader. Getting in on the ground floor with McDonald's and growing with the world's largest restaurant chain became the kind of job that makes the person. In working with and keeping pace with Ray and McDonald's, Al came up with ideas that were perfected over the years into his brand of PR: Build trust, use good judgment, and involve the community.

Al came up with the term *Trust Bank* in the early 1970s working on McDonald's. "McDonald's still uses the term Trust Bank today. They'll say, 'Well, we need more deposits in our Trust Bank.'" In 1992, McDonald's established the Al Golin Trust Bank Award. The annual award goes to a franchisee who excels at community involvement with employees or customers that furthered his or her local company. The goal for McDonald's to be the most trusted brand in the world has guided Jim Skinner, CEO of McDonald's from 2004 to 2012, and Don Thompson, his successor.

At the celebration of the fiftieth anniversary of the relationship, a McDonald's executive said to Al, "You always treated us like you *just* got us as a client." About his trusted relationship with five McDonald's CEOs over those years, Al says, "Never, ever, take anyone or any company for granted. When you start taking any relationship for granted, you've got a problem—whether it's with your client, your employee, your spouse, or your kid. You need to keep nurturing a relationship and keep it fresh. The trick is to continue to keep the excitement going and never rest on your laurels."

Pivot Point: Turning Point Decision

"I think that the job makes the person more often than the person makes the job."

There's no question that Al learned and grew as a PR leader from his work with Ray and McDonald's. But the quantum leap in his development as a business leader would occur when he became the sole owner of the firm. That decision in 1975 marked the turning point of Al's journey, from PR thought leader to business leader.

Al and Max Cooper were business partners for 18 years, most of that time with an unusual working arrangement. Getting in on the ground floor with McDonald's and becoming Ray's trusted advisor fueled growth of the PR firm but also took the firm's partners down a path of complex relationships and choices that inevitably posed a conflict of interest. For a while, Max wore two hats, serving as McDonald's marketing director and Al's partner in the PR business. (Ben Burns had left the partnership in 1965.) Making the relationships even more complex was the partners' purchase of a McDonald's franchise in Birmingham, Alabama, in the early 1970s.

"Things happen." While Max was out of town for six months at a time tending to these other interests, Al was the dedicated PR man running the firm. After about a year, Al decided he couldn't be both McDonald's

PR firm and franchisee. Not having the time to do both, Al was more interested in the PR work. So, he offered to sell his shares in the franchise to Max at a loss, which he did.

Max spent so much time away that the partnership in the PR firm became unworkable. Yet, both were reluctant to dissolve the partnership but for different reasons. Even though Al had run day-to-day operations and client service, Max was for Al a psychological safety net for the company's financial management and for a shared sense of responsibility. "Up to that point, I was assuming many of the responsibilities of being the leader but Cooper still had his name on the door; he was still around, and he was still the very strong financial person. I could come to him for advice on financial matters and things that I thought he had better knowledge of." For Max, the firm was an anchor for his diverse business interests and gave him a certain credibility.

At 46 years old, Al felt stirred to make a change. The status quo had to be challenged. Al decided he had to do something he never intended— go solo as owner and operator of the PR firm. As Max protested, Al became more resolute about what had to be done. They settled on the terms of the separation. Al bought Max's shares in the firm, renaming the company Golin Communications. Success, at first, was survival.

> I don't think I ever dreamt that I'd be growing a business as successful as it became. I still had some doubts about my leadership abilities even though I was doing it at the time. I guess I rose to the occasion. There was no turning back as to my full responsibility. It was a sink or swim kind of thing.
>
> I never thought of myself as a leader. I was always a good client person, a good people person internally, because I have innate skills in that area that served me well. And I was probably a good salesperson. I thought this was a great way to prove what I could do and I found myself doing everything, from worrying about making this company profitable to serving our clients well.

Al's decision to take solo responsibility for everything changed his outlook and decision making. Having full responsibility and accountability for revenue, profitability, and operating cash flow went against his happy-employees instincts, but he quickly learned to make the tough business decisions in a way that fit his values and desire to be a nice guy.

Muddling through cash flow crises, he learned that firing underperformers could be a principled way to be fair to everyone and actually motivate people. It was an opportunity to ask people to step up.

> When the cash flow was bad, I didn't want anyone to miss a paycheck. So I didn't take a paycheck for months at a time. I guess that's the definition of an entrepreneur—someone who is willing to do that sort of thing. I just made it work and knew that the cash flow would improve. I borrowed money and did whatever it took to keep it going.
>
> I still tried to retain my Mr. Nice Guy thing because that is sort of the way I had succeeded in this business. But I had to make tougher decisions.
>
> I had to make economic decisions and couldn't let my emotions get in the way of good sound business decisions. For example, if I liked a person here who I thought was not performing to the best of their ability, I used to give him some leeway. But when I took over sole responsibility of the firm, I realized that I couldn't do that anymore and had to be more black and white than all the gray areas I was living with. I terminated some people who weren't cutting their mustard.

It took him a few years to make Golin Communications *his* company and gain confidence in financial management. He had to change his practice of overservicing clients and balance client satisfaction with agency profitability. And since he had modeled overservicing clients at the firm, he had to not only change his own behaviors but also everyone else's.

> You can't stay in business without profits. I learned this very quickly after I took sole responsibility for this company. Then I had to impart that to our people. They were so conscious of serving the client properly that they overserviced them, and we couldn't make a profit on many accounts. They learned that from me because I was guilty for years of overservicing clients.
>
> So I had to sell them on you can't continue to do what you're doing. We did a minibusiness course on the real expenses of doing business—it's not just salaries—and we opened up our

financials to everybody. When I started out, everything was very secretive—you wouldn't want to let your people know if you're making money or not making money. Everything was very mysterious and close to the vest. We changed all that and enabled our people to understand this business.

This opened doors for our people for advancement. Even when people feel it's a great job or they're making a lot of money, they have to know the next step for them.

By becoming solo owner and leader of the enterprise, Al learned that his job was to create the conditions for all employees to do *their* jobs at contributing to the success of the whole enterprise. It was his turning point, changing his perspective and redefining his job. He learned that the leader's responsibility for the basic health of the company was not financial wizardry but rather empowering everyone to be an informed contributor to the greater good. And, when individuals don't live up to their responsibility to their colleagues, those people should be addressed with disciplined focus on the greater good. This was how Al internalized the lesson of balancing the profit factor and the human factor as compatible in his leadership philosophy. From this turning point, he gained confidence that he could, in skills and in philosophy, lead a company.

Some people say entrepreneurs aren't made; they're born. Well, I don't believe that. Some people have that innate ability, but I think that the job makes the person more often than the person makes the job. I think a lot of people have the latent potential, but it never comes out because they never have the right opportunity. Buying out Cooper's share of the PR business was my opportunity.

Today the firm has 45 offices around the world. Max Cooper today owns 40-some McDonald's. We both succeeded.

Pivot Point: Tipping Point Decision

"We had the reputation of, 'They're a great agency if you're McDonald's.' We felt pigeonholed. We felt we were a great agency for any client."

After the partners' split, Al was fully occupied running the agency and personally servicing clients, especially McDonald's. He had a growing concern that he wasn't devoting the time he should to developing new business. McDonald's accounted for 40 percent of the firm's revenue, which was not a healthy situation. "We took the easy way out because they grew so fast and we were doing so many things for them."

On Al's mind was, "Fix things before they break."

He was at the next decision point. He decided he needed to make a real effort to land new clients and build the firm's reputation beyond McDonald's. That effort would require hiring a top-tier PR professional with business development experience and contacts. Who that PR professional would be was another in the string of Al's fortuitous unplanned events. "Things happen." Al had met Tom Harris socially. Tom had been in the PR business a long time and had worked at three of the largest PR firms. He knew a lot of people. When Tom called one day in 1978 and said, "Let's talk," Al was ready.

> I brought in Tom Harris and said to him, 'Don't worry about McDonald's. The account is doing just fine. You should spend your time strictly on new business. Bringing in new business is your priority." And Tom succeeded in doing that.

Tom called on his contacts and opened doors. Al and Tom went into these pitch meetings together, highlighting their selling point that clients get attention at the top, which they would not get from a larger agency. They worked very effectively as a team, on PR as well as running the firm. Tom brought large-company experience and best practices, a serious business development discipline, and a performance management process. Al took care of brand stewardship and financial management. The company quickly expanded to 60 employees with offices in Chicago, San Francisco, and London. Al made Tom a partner and president, renaming the firm Golin/Harris Communications in 1981.

When Al had become the sole owner of the business in 1975, he had determined that he would shape the company's culture into the kind of company he wanted to run and an environment in which he personally liked to work. Tom was a natural fit, sharing Al's values and ethics. Al looked for people willing to go the extra mile, who respected the Golden Rule but also could make the tough decisions. He hired people he liked in his gut, *"people who you like going out and having a beer with."* Tom was Al's kind of folk.

Tom fondly recalls, "Basically we chose good people. People did not pull rank; they liked working together. It was natural. It wasn't that we preached our values as much as we lived them. We had a lot of fun. We didn't know how to be CEOs and presidents. We had lunch regularly with everybody. We took the work seriously but we didn't take ourselves too seriously. We seemed to do well with hiring people."

They made a few hiring mistakes. For Al, when you know in the gut a person isn't "our kind of folk," the only question is how much time and damage to allow before making the inevitable decision.

> A person in our office I didn't like and nobody liked handled a very important client. I felt the client valued this individual who was a key person on the business. When I let the person go because I couldn't take it any longer, I went to the client first and told him that. They said, "What took you so long? We thought you were protecting him to the point we weren't happy."

Al's brand of folksy and friendly style became the culture. In an industry fond of the polished and sophisticated corporate image, Al's brand of folksy was, and is, quite simply, authentic. We're not talking jeans and pool tables at the office, just a nonhierarchical camaraderie that fosters teamwork—the natural kind that doesn't have to be prescribed in performance measures. According to Al, "Most of the people love it and find the difference refreshing and enjoy it. That's the name of the game. It really does work for *us*. Hopefully long after I'm gone, this will be a key part of my legacy."

Al's decision to hire Tom to diversify the firm brought the momentum to get to the next level. More business and diverse clients increased revenue, which increased hiring, which expanded the firm's capabilities, which brought in more new business. McDonald's had taught Al the virtues of having larger and fewer clients. Focusing on long-term relationships with fewer companies, GolinHarris was able to build a portfolio of work that quickly established it as a leading firm for major corporations.

Al could have become complacent and remained content with a nice business centered on one high-growth, reliable client. His experience in PR and servicing McDonald's and in running the small business could have made him decide to stay focused on what he knew best. Instead, he decided to bring fresh thinking to the business—his own as well as of another PR professional. Having learned a lesson about partnerships that cease to work, Al's expression for guiding this partnership was, "One plus one makes three."

That tipping point decision enabled all the opportunities and accompanying challenges yet to come. It was a time of consolidation in the advertising and communications industry. The major advertising agencies were buying smaller agencies in PR, research, and marketing. When Chicago-based advertising agency Foote, Cone & Belding (FCB) made a surprise unsolicited offer to buy GolinHarris in 1985, Al was 56 years old and felt the need for financial security. Al and Tom decided to sell.

Pivot Point: Recommitment Decision

"When you know you're right, you have to stick to your guns and stay with it. Under new ownership again, I knew we [would] really have to stand up and be counted."

For four years under FCB's ownership, it was business as usual. Because of a potential conflict of interest, FCB sold GolinHarris in 1989 to Shandwick International, a British PR firm. IPG purchased Shandwick and GolinHarris 10 years later. During this 14-year period, Al had to learn a different kind of power. No longer having the power that comes with being the owner and boss—and now having a boss for the first time in 28 years—Al had to find a new leadership voice.

This period started on the wrong foot when Al realized shortly after selling to FCB that he had sold too early for too low a price, *"a bad money decision,"* he regretted. More of a problem was FCB selling GolinHarris to Shandwick. The British firm's elitist culture and derisive management style during that time nearly drove Al to quit. The kind of battles of egos and conflicting values Al experienced under Shandwick typically end with the voluntary or involuntary departure of the person in Al's shoes. Not only did Al survive, but he was also able to turn the dark age of his career into a renaissance. Let's take a close look at what happened.

> When I sold the business, it was too soon. I probably sold because of my basic insecurity. My father was a victim in his later years of losing his business—and I'm sure I was influenced by all that. FCB offered me a certain amount of money that would provide me with what I thought was lifelong security.
>
> FCB left us alone but when they were pitching to a competitor of one of our clients, they said, "Maybe we're better off splitting with you to protect you." I had no say in whom they were selling us to; I didn't own the place anymore. In 1989, FCB sold us to Shandwick—and it wasn't great news.

Shandwick's pompous style and focus only on profits irritated and angered Al and Tom, who took great pride in their PR work and the company's people-centered culture. Al and Tom liked the PR business; Shandwick didn't care enough to learn about their work. Al and Tom believed in delivering personal service to clients; Shandwick pushed relentlessly for more profits. Al and Tom believed in working in a democratic atmosphere; the elitist British owners referred to the rank and file as *underlings* and *the little people*. The folksy partners led by influence; Shandwick managed by decree. From the beginning, it was a bad match that only grew worse. Enjoyment of work stopped.

> Every month they sent in the CFO [chief financial officer], who was a character out of Charles Dickens. He would come in and speak to me in certain tones I had never heard before—no one has ever talked to me that way. I told him so, that I wasn't going to accept that kind of tone.
>
> He insisted on a huge profit margin, an amount I thought was out of line. I thought if we were to give him that percentage of our profits, we would destroy our service to our clients. Not only would this guy not buy that, his tone was so abrasive. He would come in for monthly visits, and the night before I would actually get sick thinking that I would have to face this character in the morning.

The cultures clashed so thoroughly that both Al and Tom concluded irreconcilable differences with the British owners left them with only one option: divorce. One year after Shandwick bought Golin/Harris Communications, Tom left the firm to consult and to teach in the graduate program at Northwestern University's Medill School of Journalism. He thought Al would be following closely behind him. Tom nostalgically reflects, "I thought Al and I had a marriage made in PR heaven. It was rare. We got along very well and complemented each other. If we didn't sell to FCB, which led to being sold to Shandwick, I'd probably still be there."

With 34 years in the business, Al considered retirement. He took a psychological assessment test to see if he could find some direction for trying something else in semiretirement. Lucky for Al, his test results indicated that he was doing what he should be doing and that he would not make a happy retiree. This gave him the stamina to endure his misery for a while longer.

This period of personal unhappiness crystallized for Al the central tenet of GolinHarris. "The DNA of this company is, 'Happy employees mean happy clients.' When Shandwick put pressure on me, I reacted to that pressure and I wasn't happy. You can't hide that kind of thing, and I would put undue pressure on people. I didn't like myself for what I was doing." Realizing that he had to change this negative cycle gave him the fortitude to decide when enough was enough.

> There was the final nail in the coffin. The CFO came into town for our monthly meeting. Arriving the evening before and staying at a downtown hotel, he was in the office at 9:00 to see me. That morning was one of the worst blizzards in Chicago history. We had closed the office. I drove from the suburbs to the office downtown, risking my life to meet with him. When I got there about 10:15, he said something like, "This is unacceptable to keep me waiting this long." I told him to look out the window, that the storm and driving conditions were unacceptable to almost everybody in Chicago.
>
> That was the proverbial straw that broke my back. I asked for a meeting in London with the CEO and told him that I couldn't continue this way. If this fellow continued as the CFO, I'm gone. I did not get an answer immediately. A few weeks later, the CFO was gone.

I knew we were dealing from a position of strength. If we were a dying brand and losing clients, I couldn't have afforded to take the stand I took. They had bought our brand because our brand had value. When Shandwick first acquired us, a couple of our long-term clients wanted to meet them and explain to them that they bought GolinHarris as their agency; they did not buy another agency, and unless that continued along those lines, they would leave. The clients wanted to do that; I didn't ask them to do that. They were concerned about the changeover, as they should have been. So Shandwick did realize if they rocked this boat, they would lose some key clients.

Things were better with the CFO leaving, not great, but at least this guy was gone. We went along because the CEO realized how serious I was. I toughed it out because this was sort of my baby, and I didn't want to buckle under. I stuck to my guns and fought like hell to keep what we had and not succumb to their culture.

You have to take a stand. I saw our whole culture going down the tubes and losing clients and employees. I said, "This is not what we bargained for. Our culture is respect for our own people; clients would always come first but our people came as a pretty close second. Unless we have happy people, we aren't going to have many clients." It was that simple. Fortunately they realized that this made our business go and they backed off.

He emerged from the 10-year battle with Shandwick a stronger leader with more clarity about his business goals and life goals. His resolve also had been reinforced by the tests that showed conclusively that in no way should he retire or be doing anything else. In the final analysis, having to make the conscious decision not to leave and to recommit to the business revitalized Al. He moved forward with battle-tested conviction about the purpose of his leadership.

Again, "Things happen," and lucky for Al, in 1999 Shandwick along with GolinHarris were acquired by IPG, one of the four largest global communications networks. IPG's belief in decentralized leadership and GolinHarris's brand equity gave Al the situation he could turn to his advantage.

A more seasoned and resolute leader now, Al was determined to apply his hard-learned lessons from his tumultuous years with

Shandwick. Under IPG ownership, Al focused his energies on taking GolinHarris where his clients were going—in 1999, globalization was clearly changing business dynamics. In retrospect, selling the company and the battles with Shandwick paved the way for the opportunity that lay ahead: becoming a global brand.

> After my experience with Shandwick, I realized that we had to be true to ourselves, that we couldn't ever be sublimated again. Under new ownership again, I knew we really have to stand up and be counted. I had the confidence that we were going to make this work to our advantage. In golf, if you think you're going to make the putt, more often than not, you do make the putt. If you don't think you're going to make the putt, you're not going to make it. Shandwick was a wake-up call.

With commitment and confidence to turn the acquisition by IPG to his advantage, Al moved forward with focus on what really mattered to him as his legacy. He turned over the CEO position to his handpicked successor and became chairman, changing his role from making operating decisions to capitalizing on IPG's support and resources to make the GolinHarris brand and culture consistent across the globe.

> We had to be competitive with bigger agencies for the bigger clients so, by this time, we had to have coverage around the world. IPG helped us open offices in Beijing, Shanghai, Sydney, Brussels, and Paris. They gave us almost instant identity, offices, and staff to serve our clients in those major markets.
>
> The key was for us to impart the GolinHarris culture in all those countries. I think we have succeeded with all due modesty. When I go to London, Beijing, or Hong Kong, the people there may look a little different but they are the same kind of culture. They are the kind of people you like to be with, they are fun, and they are creative. The success of our global expansion was our emphasis on cultural fit. Our CEO, Fred Cook, was responsible for this effort. Fred went into these markets and met with as many people as he could to try to get a feel for how those people would adapt to our culture—whether they are our kind of folk. We brought them to Chicago and continue to do that on a regular basis. They spend time here working with our people

in Chicago headquarters and get to know the key people well, not just the people who are working on the clients they may be involved with, but other people in the organization as well.

We do several things to build on our culture of respect and camaraderie, which emanates from our home office in Chicago and out to our offices around the world. We try to make brainstorm sessions entertaining. We give junior and senior people the same kind of recognition for their contributions. We do a quarterly competition on the most innovative things we discovered during that quarter. We try to recognize people for internal things. Everybody likes recognition—we try to live by that on a regular basis.

Fortunately, IPG has been very supportive, and tries to help us without imposing their will on us. I think they recognize the value of our brand because we fight like crazy to retain our culture and we've been successful enough where they don't want to tamper with it. The value of our name is important enough that they would not want to merge us with some other entity, as we represent such great brands like McDonald's, Toyota, Dow Chemical, Nintendo, Johnson & Johnson, and many others.

Without the good, the bad, and the ugly during those years under Shandwick, Al may not have invested so much of himself in the revitalization of GolinHarris under yet another owner. The decision to recommit was all part of the journey that brought him to the real prize: knowing he kept trying to the best of his ability and it paid off. Al's experience gives a perspective we need to think more about when facing our own career moments of seemingly endless misery, when we think life is too short to spend it this way. In Al's story, life is too short to walk away from what really matters. Conflict pushed him to have clear conviction about what really matters to him, making his recommitment the most important pivotal decision whereby his leadership and company flourished.

Pivot Point: Letting Go Decision

"Even if my judgment was better, there are times when you have to know when to hold them and when to fold them, and I didn't know when to fold them at certain times. I think that's a lesson that helped me turn over the reins to certain people."

The transition of power to the current CEO, Fred Cook, has been gradual and subtle. Although this has worked exceptionally well, it would not work for everyone.

Fred, appointed CEO in 2002, replaced Al's first successor who did not work out. So, the second time, both Al and Fred made it their joint goal and responsibility to succeed in the succession process.

At first, Al went with the person he thought was the obvious best choice. He was excellent with clients, loyal with 25 years of service, and a trusted friend, but he couldn't make the tough decisions in running the company. After a couple of years, Al decided he had to tell his good friend he was not making it as CEO. Not a sentimental guy, he still considers this decision as the most difficult of his career.

We all hate to make certain kinds of decisions, including me. Telling one of your key people, especially the CEO, that they're not working out and having them leave the company is a very tough decision. Of course, you do it as respectfully as possible. As difficult as it was, I think for the good of the company and for your own sake, a strong leader has to make those kinds of decisions.

The person to whom I first turned it over was probably a result of his longevity and my loyalty to him. He was a great client person, a great people person, and a good friend—but probably too nice a guy. Being a nice person and a good leader is a very delicate combination. A mistake some people make is thinking that a good leader has got to be a killer. But it's also true that a nice person can be a good manager but not necessarily a leader. Fortunately, our first CEO who succeeded me ended up just fine. His many talents, including good judgment, people skills and the like enabled him to land a top agency spot—and now as a successful consultant on his own.

My attitude has always been, never mistake kindness for weakness. But our first CEO couldn't make the tough decisions that had to be made. At that time, we had the wrong people on the corporate side. I felt those people were hurting our image with our own people. Our first CEO did not want to make that kind of decision.

With the next CEO I picked, these decisions were made. We terminated three key people. It improved the morale of our people; morale went sky-high because those were not the kind of people we said we were. It all did work out for the best. Also we had a few offices that weren't performing; we had to cut our losses and eliminate those offices.

When the buck stops with you, you have to make those decisions, or else you abdicate your leadership role. You have to look at the broader picture than those individuals; you have to look at the company as a whole. It's not fair for the other people in the company who are working hard and seeing certain people get away with things. It's not fair to *the individual* to be kept in a spot where they're not performing. Not making these decisions to be humane is false humanity. It wasn't fair to him or our company to keep it going. Those kinds of decisions are really healthy decisions to make. Nonetheless, it created a lot of angst for me.

Fred Cook was my personal pick, and he has really proven to be an outstanding CEO. We had brought in Fred from our LA office, where he successfully ran that operation, and we recognized his potential. He was a little tougher than his predecessor while still retaining the culture. He was not a killer by any means, but tougher in the decision-making process. Fred has absorbed our culture for over 20 years, lives the style and values of GolinHarris and he has tremendous leadership qualities.

Fred has successfully led GolinHarris for 12 years, with Al actively engaged as chairman, because they both understand, trust, and respect each other's sense of responsibility for the company and for personal fulfillment. Fred runs the business; Al leads by example, making the holistic impact that only the founder can make. Fred operates with accountability and responsibility for executive decisions; Al operates with influence and personal pride in the success of the leadership team and company. Fred made the global expansion work, while Al "provided spiritual guidance for how we join as one company and one culture."

It works, Fred explains, because,

Al is like a moral compass for us. He embodies in one person what our company is all about. He leads by example. It makes it easy to sustain the culture because he's here. His presence is the beacon. He rarely tells anybody what to do. He'll give his advice—but you sort of know already what he thinks is the right thing to do based on his leading by example. He's very support-ive of change, much more open to change than a lot of other senior management in the company. For our fiftieth anniversary, I suggested that we talk about the future rather than our past. Al was very supportive of that. My hope is I'm so in tune with what he stands for that I and the other senior leaders will be able to keep it going.

For Al, it works because he knows that the right leaders are in place and that they have demonstrated abilities that surpass his in many ways, especially in terms of the radically changing world that technology and globalization brought on. Al understands that his role now is to give spir-itual guidance, not directive decisions.

If you don't find the right people to replace you, then you're a bad businessperson. I've been smart enough to find people who could do things better than I could do. I've also tried to be care-ful in selecting people who have the same kind of ethics that I have for our top executive roles.

I recently attended an annual meeting of our key manag-ers and rising stars from offices around the world. There were about 130 people at this meeting, and I couldn't have been more pleased when I looked around and heard them get up and speak. I can't tell you how happy it makes me feel this will be carried on long after I'm gone.

So, has Al really let go? He still goes to the office every day, although he now allows himself a couple of winter months in Scottsdale, Arizona. He claims to have learned his lesson on letting go in recent years when he received some feedback.

I had people tell me that I would sometimes come into a situa-tion involving the client, and I would make changes at the last minute after they had knocked themselves out and done every-thing that they thought was right. I would shake things up to a point where they would be very unhappy that I came in late in the game and didn't have all the details. I was kind of shocked to hear this feedback because you never see yourself. As nice a guy as I think I've been, I guess I wasn't always.

It was a good wake-up call for me. It told me a little bit about my style of management that I needed to change. I always thought that my judgment was better than anyone else, and it may not have been. If they make a mistake, they make a mistake. And you have to realize that not only are there people who can do it as well as you; they can do it better than you.

When we landed Aon as a new account, and someone on their board said to me, "You ought to be personally involved," I said, "That's flattering, but we have people who are better than me."

In recent years, Fred has been more assertive in making his own mark. Al appreciates the deference Fred gives him when he invokes the founder's beliefs, such as, "Al always says, 'Fix it before it breaks.'" In 2011, Fred launched a new methodology and way of organizing the firm for servicing clients. There are now high-level meetings to which Al is not invited. He says, "I admit, sometimes, my feelings are hurt to not be included. But I have to step back and say this is Fred's ball game now and I'm not going to try to usurp his authority and power."

Truth is Al continues to go to the office because he wants to. He knows he doesn't need to. It's his lifestyle decision, not a leadership decision.

THE LEADER'S LEGACY

Through all the changing partnerships and owners, remaining GolinHarris in name and culture is quite a feat. For Al, the culture of the company was the real asset he built and fought for and what he hopes will be his enduring legacy. If his entrepreneurship had focused on maximizing profits and a windfall upon selling, his bad money decisions would have been major mistakes. But his focus was to do right by clients and employees, enjoy working while keeping his insecurities at bay, and make enough money to have financial security. He focused wholeheartedly on building trust in business. So in the final analysis, Al's bad money decisions were exactly the right decisions. They were trade-offs for the real prize at the end of the 55-plus-year journey.

It proves that the culture we fought to maintain built our reputation. When I sold to FCB, we had about 60 people; now about 600. A good culture retains clients and employees. I made the culture a priority because I wanted the kind of company I want to run, and it turned out to be good for retention and good for business. You do good things, and they're also good for business.

It's a great kick to travel around the world and see my name on the door in places like Shanghai, Beijing, Taipei, and Tokyo. I'd be lying if I didn't say I enjoy that. Also, to think that there is a legacy afterward of an organization that has your ethics and values with your name on it. Will it last forever? I don't know. Maybe they'll take the name off one of these days. But so far, I think it has real equity. That's the kind of thing that is certainly meaningful—to have built something that does have some lasting elements to it.

Al's focus was never the money, anyway. It was on building a company that embodies solid values of authenticity, humility, and pride in always giving one's best work. As he puts it, he wanted to build a company where he enjoys working. As for the role of money, Al wanted enough for financial freedom to have choices and not lose a business, as his father had—no more and no less.

I think success isn't really about money per se because I could have made better financial decisions if money was my only interest. I think that money should not be the ultimate goal. It's a by-product of what you do; it's not the end product.

I'm not belittling money; it's important to have financial security. I have a son who says to me, "I'm not like you; I've never been motivated by money."

I say, "That's fine." But I think without money, you're in jail. You don't have the freedom that comes with having choices. You have to have enough of it at least to give you the choices you want. I think that's important in life. It's not a matter of what you buy, the latest toy or new car; it's just the idea that you can make choices. That's everything.

GolinHarris and Al succeeded for many reasons; the one that matters most is that Al never stopped growing as a leader. His launching point in securing McDonald's business provided financial success to have the choices that make a leader. His turning point as CEO was creating the conditions for people to succeed and be empowered with tools to manage financial performance. His tipping point in diversifying the client portfolio started the momentum that turned the firm into a true global brand 20 years later. His recommitment point clarified his leadership priority for the culture to win and retain clients and talent, making the company sustainable. Finally, at his letting go point, Al was able to trust someone else's gut. He had fulfilled his leadership responsibilities.

If Al had retired upon selling his company when he was 56, 60, or even 65 years old, he would have missed the supreme satisfaction he enjoys at 84, knowing that GolinHarris has enduring value, thriving in the technological transformation and globalization of the twenty-first century. Until the last few years, his job simply wasn't done. His so-called mistakes gave him the persistence to learn and lead the firm through changes in ownership, the business environment, the world, and his own leadership development.

"Things happen." Through the good and the bad, he tried to build real value and tried to turn given events to his advantage. By never believing that he masterminded his success, Al trusted his gut and his values. It worked for Al better than any plan for success could.

CHAPTER 6

PASSION

Dale Dawson

Founder and CEO of Bridge2Rwanda

WHY YOU SHOULD KNOW HIM AND ABOUT HIS WORK

Dale Dawson founded Bridge2Rwanda in a career transformation that the younger, ambitious financial executive would have dismissed as implausible. Nothing in Dale's successful 25-year career in business predicted a future in addressing poverty, and certainly not in Africa. Yet, with Bridge2Rwanda, he is hitting his stride, advancing economic development in Rwanda and reconnecting with his passion for provocative challenges while integrating work, family, and community in a way he couldn't in his for-profit career. Dale is on the advisory council of Rwanda's President, Paul Kagame, and on the boards of Rwanda's largest microfinance bank, Urwego Opportunity Bank, and US-based nonprofit organizations Halftime and Edify.

In his climb to success in the for-profit world, Dale had everything he thought he wanted. He wanted the challenge of continuous learning, and his pivotal decisions propelled him forward on steep learning curves. He wanted to be a world-class professional businessperson, and his career path enabled mastery of valuable skills. He wanted financial success, and his risk taking amply rewarded him. His career started at KPMG in auditing, and an early offer to join the firm's acclaimed tax accounting practice in Dallas launched Dale on the fast track. He made partner at 30 years old, and, two years later, became national director of the insurance practice. At age 33, he jumped at the offer to build an investment advisory unit at Stephens Inc., the Arkansas firm behind Walmart's initial public offering (IPO). Seven years later, he wanted to put his advice to work and own a business and bought TruckPro, a retail truck parts business serving America's South and Midwest. Turning around the company to profitable growth, he sold it to AutoZone in 1998. At 46 years old, Dale was financially set for life. Invited back to Stephens to find his next TruckPro, Dale returned but his passion didn't.

After a few years of neither finding nor knowing what he wanted for his next challenge, he was desperate to feel again the passion that had been the source of his energy, discipline, and courage for big challenges. That his passion might not return haunted him. He was too young to retire and too confused to be complacent with his financial success. At 51 years old, he decided to make the ultimate deal of his deal-making career: To get his passion back, he would leave Stephens, even though he did not know what he wanted, and surrender to divine guidance.

Having always worked in professions and organizations that had clear career paths, clear criteria for advancement, and clear destinations, Dale now chose to go down a path with neither guideposts nor a map. Odd encounters and strange coincidences began to form a theme—nonprofit, poverty, Rwanda. They challenged what he had always believed—that poor people had made bad choices and that creating wealth and serving social missions were incompatible.

While attending a conference of Opportunity International, a 501(c)(3) nonprofit, all that Dale had learned and done suddenly came together in a moment of grace. It inspired what became Bridge2Rwanda. Dale learned about poor people who have ambitions but no opportunities. He learned about how social entrepreneurship applies business practices to addressing social problems. By letting go of his definitions of success, his eyes opened to see an entirely different perspective and world. Not only did his energy and passion return, but he also came to see the impact he still could make. Dale found himself leading more naturally and making a real difference in many lives and a country. His story shows that letting go is ultimately a liberating decision.

WHAT MATTERS TO DALE DAWSON

Dale's Playbook

"I equate passion with energy. It is what drives me and energizes me.
I have found that I cannot create energy if it is not there."

Passion, in Dale's experience, is far more than a nice-to-have career consideration. It gets him out of bed and to the office every morning. It gives him the curiosity to learn and the discipline to master a skill and subject. It inspires his vision of the future. It enables him to mobilize others to do something beyond the ordinary.

In my experience, concentration and energy is how passion manifests itself. When I am passionate, I will get lost in my work. Hours go by and nothing is tedious; I sustain a high energy level and sharp attention span. The wind is at my back.

When that passion goes away, I find myself going to the office because I think I need to be there but I don't really care what's going on. My mind is not engaged in learning or tackling a challenge. I go through the motions but I'm completely confused.

Although many people can lose their passion and unwittingly settle into inertia, Dale is the first to realize when, having done all he can, he no longer can connect with his role and he needs to make a change. So the overarching theme of Dale's story is that he made himself responsible for doing what he had to do to connect deeply with his work and growth. When there wasn't anything more he wanted to achieve in a job or company, it was time to move on.

The understanding of passion itself was Dale's transformative career experience. Until his mid-40s, passion was in the striving and achieving. With achievement of the goals he set as a young man—financial security and success as a business owner—he found himself without energy and direction to move on to anything in the world he knew—not as a result of adversity, but because he lost passion for the work it offered. He says,

> How much more perfect could life have been than to stay at Stephens? When I returned there after selling TruckPro, I was in a position to take all my experience and apply it to making lots of money and growing those around me. But the challenge of running an investment bank no longer engaged me.

Knowing he was lost without passion, he came to see passion as a divine gift that is not his to control. This insight had a profound effect on the achievement-driven executive. Here was a successful executive who believed that achievement comes from self-determination and being in control, and he had to let go of his beliefs and control.

> Passion is something that someone turns on and off in me. Everything I have ever done where I was happy was when I was completely committed to the idea, "That's what I want to be, that's what I want to learn and that's what I want to be best at."
>
> If passion gives me the energy to do something, I came to the conclusion that it is God given. And when my passion was switched off, I realized at 51 that it would no longer just be my definition of what I wanted. How I define success today is to be what I am called to do, totally surrendered and totally committed.

He unwittingly started down this new path when introduced by a mutual friend to Bishop John Rucyahana, who was in the United States to raise money for building Sonrise High School in Rwanda. Before the serendipitous meeting, which I will discuss in detail later in this chapter, Dale was far removed from global poverty and social causes. But he could not ignore—in fact, he was inspired by—Bishop John's passion for his work in Rwanda. This triggered a chain of events that escalated his search for renewal and the decision a year later to leave Stephens without knowing what his next move was.

> Meeting Bishop John Rucyahana of Rwanda was divine intervention. Through him I saw that business could address global poverty and that I was equipped to help. Once I realized this, the passion came back.

Dale's Playbook

"It is instinctive to me to be a lifetime learner. I see challenges as opportunities to learn or change myself."

Dale doesn't know why he is so driven to learn, nor does he evangelize the virtues of continuous learning; he just knows that he has both succeeded because of it as well as lost his direction when there wasn't more he could learn from a job to develop into a businessperson of distinctive professional excellence.

It is all about giving and you have to have something to give. Ideally, you want to master a skill that is your strength and you can use to channel your passion. And whether you want to be a teacher, writer, salesperson, businessperson, or whatever suits your strengths, you have to have an overriding passion for professional excellence and invest time developing the skill, talent, and profession. Then you have something to give and make a real impact.

The drive for new challenges and continuous improvement had propelled his father's career. From him Dale learned that even when you are ahead of all your competitors, you keep improving. It was more than a strong work ethic or entrepreneurial ingenuity. "Growing up dirt-poor in Texas created this intense drive in my dad that was almost inhuman. There was nothing that was going to stand in the way of his improving."

Dale also learned from his father's example that once something ignites the drive to be relentless, it becomes the central organizing principle around which everything else finds a place, or does not. Dale's drive was ignited at the University of Texas at Dallas by rich students with little substance yet plenty of arrogant entitlement that they flaunted.

There's a lot of show in Dallas—looking like you are successful. Since my time at University of Texas, I had this burning desire to prove that results will win out over the show in the end. And so I worked 24/7 from college to really 45 to 46 years old to put up the results to prove that. You just put blinders on and something inside drives you and you don't even know why. That's what I saw in my Dad—that's the way I felt I was like into my late 40s. That's what I saw in Paul Kagame the first time we met in Rwanda.

Dale learned from his father that career decisions revolve around one central question: "Will you make money at things you are excited and challenged by or will you make money at things you are bored by?" The family moved 10 times in 20 years as his father went after new and bigger challenges, in the first 10 years as an independent business owner and the subsequent 10 years as an executive at Borden Dairy Company.

Whenever he got a new challenge, the family would just pack up and move to the next place. We were very conscious of the fact that he wanted new challenges. And so I grew up with this attitude that in our house you would leave friends, pack up and go to the next place, because the next challenge, the next opportunity was worth it.

There was never a question that money didn't motivate me. The question was when to move on once you got to a point when you also want more challenge and learning. You can always make money; you don't do things *just* to make money.

His father had started college but didn't finish, working as a milkman to put his wife through college. She got her accounting degree at Texas Tech University in 1950. In early 1952, when Dale was born, his 22-year-old father could not get Borden to give him a supervisory position over workers who were older returning war veterans; instead they asked him to open an independent distributorship in a small town 85 miles from Lubbock, Texas.

I grew up thinking my dad was the hardest-working man in Snyder, Texas. He worked six days a week and got up at three every morning. He knew everybody in town. He delivered milk to almost every home, every grocery store, every restaurant, and every school in the town of about 13,000 people. Everybody knew Bob Dawson and everybody knew Bob Dawson's three sons. Before very long, my dad had half a dozen trucks and people working for him. Helpers were young teenage guys—they called them swampers—this was the 1950s; they all looked like Elvis Presley. As a young kid, I got to hang out with them, ride in their cars and go to the Dairy Queen.

My mom ran the business. Mom was always running a 10-key adding machine as long as I could remember. For two days every month, the whole house became an accounting office. All the route drivers would bring their information to the house and Mom would manage all of this and generate bills for everybody in town.

I loved that family business and that sense of knowing what was going on and always looking for business opportunities. We delivered milk, we washed trucks, and we stocked the grocery store cases. We had an icehouse and sold ice to the roughneck crews that worked on the oil rigs and to the cattle ranchers. It was a great life. It established in me the values of hard work and respecting people of all economic levels and ethnicities.

When I was 10 years old, Dad declared that he was selling milk to every single person in Snyder, Texas, and there wasn't any more challenge to that. The people at Borden said they wanted him to move and launch home delivery service in Houston. I remember Dad coming home and saying, "There's a million people in Houston. Can you imagine building milk routes for a million people?" And so we packed up and moved to Houston. Dad became a Borden employee; Mom never worked again outside the home. It was okay, but I really missed that family business.

I saw in the first 10 years of my life that not only was an integrated life doable, but it was the most attractive way to live. I loved that life. It shaped me.

Dale never stopped wanting a family business where work and family and community blended seamlessly, but first he wanted to prove himself as a highly paid professional working with the best professionals. After proving himself, Dale would come full circle back to the ideals shaped by growing up in Snyder, Texas.

Unlike the other leaders in this book, Dale did not have a single expansive, long-term vision that became his life's work. He would intensely focus on fulfilling his vision for each new role, and once fulfilled, he evaluated where he was and what he needed to learn to be that excellent business professional he envisioned. Later, he came to appreciate the idea of a passion so enduring that it becomes his life's work.

There is real power in doing a self-assessment. It is a continuous evaluation of what works and what doesn't, then making decisions for building on your strengths and compensating for your shortcomings. This cycle of constant assessment and adaptation evolves into a management and leadership style, and takes you on a journey that ultimately is of self-discovery.

Dale's Playbook

"The goal is to find that which you are called to serve and to somehow craft a life around that playing to your professional strengths and talents, and somehow structured in some way where you can make enough money to support your family."

Dale got his first defining career insight as he chose his college major: There's a strong competitive advantage in developing the skills and strengths that come easily. He got his second defining career insight at 50 years old: Professional and personal renewal can come in unexpected ways if you let go of assumptions that hinder more creative use of natural aptitudes and learned skills.

At the time of his first insight in 1971, Dale was a hippie more inclined toward the liberal arts than business. In fact, during the turbulent protests of the late 1960s he saw business as bloodsucking leeches. At the University of Texas, he floated between majors ranging from history to psychology to religion. Then, in his sophomore year, a trifling incident lit the fire of ambition, setting him on the business path he had vilified.

I was sitting at the fraternity house and a couple of fraternity guys walked up with a couple of really attractive sorority girls. These guys were complaining they didn't know how they would ever get through their accounting courses and that their wealthy fathers, who were real estate developers in Dallas, expected them to join the business. So they were going to be really rich and really successful if they could get through accounting at the University of Texas.

I sat there thinking these guys are as dumb as a box of rocks and if I apply myself, I could run a race through and around them so fast without even trying. It was something about not working hard enough to get what you want that didn't make any sense to me, particularly when they are so stupid and thought they were so much better. Within a day or two, I transferred into the business school.

I found business, accounting, and finance were easy for me—I hadn't thought of those things as being particularly academically challenging. But I realized maybe the right career path for me was to play to that which came naturally. When I got into a group of people equally talented at those things, then there was the competitiveness of wanting to be the best.

In his senior year, he learned about public accounting on a student field trip to Houston. A partner at one of the firms told the students they could make $100,000 by the time they were in their early 30s. On the spot, Dale decided to get a master's degree in public accounting and aim for a job at one of the best firms. When he graduated, he had offers from seven of the prestigious Big Eight accounting firms.

He launched his career with sensible decisions—develop skills where he had natural talents, get a high-paying job in public accounting, learn business skills from a top tier company, and be able to take care of a family. It wasn't living his dream, but it prepared for his ultimate goal.

I never wanted to be an accountant, and certainly not an auditor; I wanted to be a businessman. But I was also very aware that you needed to pay your dues to learn basic skills and understand business. KPMG offered a great salary and terrific training.

One of the things I learned from my parents is that you rise to the level of the people you surround yourself with. And it's hard to be a lot better than the people around you. So, you give yourself an enormous advantage if you find people who are the best at what they do and you work alongside them. It's like catching the wind behind your sails.

At KPMG it really was about associating with people who are world-class. I just bore down and tried to be as good as everybody around me.

In college he wrestled with the choice between working for the church, like his grandparents, or going into business, like his parents. Dale couldn't overlook his father's cardinal rule that a man should take care of his family's needs first. Dale's father was the son of a cowboy who was a Pentecostal minister. Working since he was eight years old, he gave his mother his earnings and greatly resented that it was spent on feeding itinerant preachers who slept in his bed. He hated being poor. He was determined that whatever it took and however hard he had to work, life was going to be different. "Family first" was a commandment that kept Dale focused.

The truth is, when I left Stephens at 50 years old to figure out what purpose I could serve, I had almost nothing to lose, which I consider to be not particularly courageous. That's why I have enormous admiration for millennials who say they're ready to move to Africa and they trust it will work out. There's the big question of, What are you going to do to support yourself and the family you're going to have? They want it all—to be professionally excellent, to create wealth, and to have a positive social impact. I think that is wonderful.

That third piece wasn't any part of my experience as a young person. I wanted to be professionally excellent and create wealth, period. I thought giving back would be peripheral—I'd write a check or sit on a board. I don't know how the millennials are going to do it, but I'm happy to spend the rest of my life being an encourager, a coach, and an adviser to help them.

His transformative insight in midlife, that his business skills could help address poverty, was the missing piece of a puzzle that made his life story more than the sum of its parts. Suddenly, he saw that the entrepreneurial spirit shaped by his parents and the skills he learned and honed at KPMG, Stephens, and TruckPro had prepared him for this mission.

I started with clear goals for mastering business skills. For a long time, I had lots of skills to master in analyzing companies, dealing with people, making a sale, understanding how things really work. One of the blessings of passion is the drive that gives you the discipline to devote the time and effort to get to mastery.

The challenge then becomes: Are you able to use those skills more creatively and push yourself beyond what you have mastered? And the second challenge is whether you do it

I can now look back and see that all of the roles in my for-profit career helped me master the skills of an activator—evaluate a situation, assess the opportunity and challenges, identify what needs to be done, and make an action plan and mobilize people to go do it. I'm the guy who always says, "Okay, now that we figured that out, what actions do we take that accomplish something?"

And I'm a maximizer of potential. I'm drawn to the exceptional person who needs an opportunity to become educated and trained and a great entrepreneurial professional. I have very little interest in getting people to average.

At the outset of his involvement in Rwanda, it took a few years for Dale to learn how to transfer those skills he developed in for-profit situations to not-for-profit environments. He wanted to produce the outcomes he had at Stephens and TruckPro: Help people get started so that they can take something to a much higher level past Dale's work. "I want that now for the whole country of Rwanda. My challenge now is to create opportunity and accelerate the progress of the most promising talent so that it will create a tide that raises all boats. That's the hope and that's what energizes me."

Dale's Playbook

"If you get the right people in the right spots and you give them a clear vision and the latitude to use their own strengths, you can accomplish more than you ever imagined."

Somebody said that a meeting with Dale is like experiencing a drive-by shooting. "It's intense and exciting and things are going to happen and then I move on. They're kind of left with whatever they learned and whatever they remember, but it's not necessarily going to be much follow-up from me."

Even though Dale says he wants to improve on this front—"When you're the leader, most people expect that you're not a one-day event"— his leadership strategy has always been to create an environment where people can figure out on their own what they need to do. Of all his business deals and achievements, Dale is most proud that the people he trained flourished after he left. As he admits, it wasn't from his high-touch way with people; it was from setting up the infrastructure that enabled them to succeed. His leadership flowed from his vision of what the business should really care about doing well, developing the tools for measuring performance in those areas, and finding and training the people who can deliver those results. The leadership challenge, for Dale, was to refine those metrics and the team constantly so that people could focus on the few things that really drive success. This, Dale believes, is what builds a company's culture.

> At TruckPro, I figured out that if I have the right leaders with the right focus at a store, then everybody at the store was happy. These are the people who ultimately shape the culture and the organization's performance. My role as a change agent was to build into operations a way to identify exceptional people, to make them better and promote them up in the organization. The right focus and the right metrics do that.

He turned around TruckPro in six years. Reaching a point where he couldn't figure out how to continue growth, Dale sold it to AutoZone. The much bigger company put more money into the operation while keeping the management team, processes, and financial systems Dale had built. In eight years, its profitability increased tenfold from when Dale sold. "And I was really moved by that—those same people who didn't know how to read a financial statement made it a much better and bigger company."

The same thing happened at Stephens. Dale built the investment advisory business from scratch, in seven years hiring and developing the hallmarks of professional service excellence. When he returned to Stephens seven years later, he found most of the young people he had hired were still there, and the firm was five times bigger in number of bankers and transactions. "The quality of their work just took my breath away. Of the things I'm most proud of in business, it was the fact that both of those businesses kept getting better because of the team we had assembled and the systems and the reporting measures."

At Bridge2Rwanda, Dale gets immense satisfaction in encouraging young people, just as ambitious, bright, and driven as the ones recruited into major corporations but who have the extra dimension of wanting their work to have a social mission. He proudly points to the example of a 27-year-old named Matt Smith.

Matt was the first young man who worked with us in Rwanda. He had a college business degree and had worked for a small finance company in Texas for a couple of years. He's as innately a smart businessperson as anybody I've ever worked with. And yet he took all of his savings and he moved to Africa because he felt called there.

He started out helping reorganize a little business making greeting cards that employed the teenage heads of child-led households in Rwanda. Matt came over when he was 25 years old and in six months helped reorganize it, made it much more efficient and effective. Those young people are making more money than they thought possible.

I met Matt when he was going to go home because he had run out of savings and I asked him if he wanted to stay and he said, "Absolutely."

I asked, "What do you want to do?"

He said, "I want to be an American doing business in Africa because I think I can make money, I think I can learn how to be a great businessperson, and I think businesses can create jobs and opportunity and help improve the prosperity in Africa."

And so, when we set up Bridge2Rwanda, he became our business manager. When our friend Scott Ford was interested in starting a business in Rwanda, we assigned Matt to work with him to help him look at the coffee business.

Scott bought the largest coffee mill in Rwanda and hired Matt away from us and made Matt general manager of the largest coffee exporting business in Kagali. So this is a 28-year-old young Texan committed to becoming an excellent businessperson and making a positive social impact in Rwanda. I'm interested in promoting and finding lots and lots of other millennials that will do something like that. I don't want them to compromise their professional development or their commitment to creation of wealth while making life better in the developing economies.

We are equally engaged in the development of the best and brightest Rwandans. That's why we have the Rwandan scholars program. It's absolutely critical that ultimately we leave a whole class of young Rwandans who are equally talented, equally committed to making money and building businesses, and equally sensitive to the community impact and social impact that they're having.

That's the movement I'd like to create.

DALE'S PIVOTAL DECISIONS

Pivot Point: Launching Decision

> "The question is, Are you in an environment where you can take skills you've mastered and elevate it to a much more creative application?"

Dale came out of the University of Texas with a bachelor's degree in business administration and master's degree in public accounting and job offers from firms where he could learn the skills to be "the guy who had the resources, the money, the professionalism, the skills to be—I used to refer to it as—a Texas wheeler-dealer." He joined KPMG because of its strong commitment to growth in Texas.

After about a year in KPMG's auditing department, Dale knew there wasn't much more to learn about auditing that could make him a wheeler-dealer. His hard work and intuitive grasp of business made him a quick study, catching notice from the firm's partners. An executive from KPMG's tax practice asked if Dale would be interested in moving to the tax department to work on mergers and acquisitions (M&A). The practice focused on the insurance industry in Dallas and had recently named a young fast-rising partner in his early 30s to run it.

The KPMG tax department in Dallas was one of the best and most profitable tax practices in banking and insurance. They were national partners who wrote books and addressed new tax laws. It was an offer to work with the best in the business.

Keeping his head down, Dale made partner when he was 30. Joining the tax practice launched him on the fast track and on a career trajectory that developed the business professional he aspired to be. It was a connection with the most ambitious people, making each other better and more ambitious.

KPMG's tax practice taught Dale what first-class professional excellence looks like and what the standards of excellence should be. That included communication skills he didn't expect to learn from accounting work but that became one of his most valuable skills.

I learned to speak and write when I was at KPMG. I had two unbelievably boring topics—tax and insurance companies. Even the people who worked on it didn't find it that interesting. And yet I really honed skills of standing in front of a group and capturing their attention and getting my message across. The same thing was true in writing. I used to write a lot of protests to the Internal Revenue Service where I'd have to explain some incredibly arcane part of the law and walk them through a thought process that persuaded them that my position was the right decision.

Another decision, although indirectly related to his job, had a significant impact on all of his subsequent pivotal decisions. When Dale and Judi, also a certified public accountant at KPMG, got engaged, one of them had to resign, according to the firm's policy. Because both had the goal of becoming entrepreneurs, they agreed that Dale, then 26 years old, was on the fast track and should stay at the firm while Judi got experience running a small business. She went to work as the comptroller for a local chain of lighting stores that imported ceiling fans. In a couple of years, she was running 20 stores. Judi and Dale decided to start their own business, just as Dale made partner at KPMG in 1982. Starting the business would teach him some of the most important lessons of his career.

During the week I was flying all over the country working with investment bankers and doing M&A deals in the insurance industry; then on the weekends I would fly to one of our stores in Texas or Colorado and I would literally sell fans and lighting on the showroom floor. On Sunday night, I'd fly out to where the next deal was.

About a year later, Walmart and Home Depot began selling ceiling fans, forcing Dale and Judi to sell a $300 product for $99. They tried competing on better service, but it led to impossibly low margins for a small business.

> I remember sitting with Judi soon after I started at Stephens and saying, "We need to get out." I remember agonizing with her over the decision. We had these huge dreams for this business; it never occurred to us that it wasn't going to be successful. It was the hardest decision we ever made because we didn't know if we were pulling the plug too soon, and we were capitulating when we were 33 years old, had no significant net worth and had a million dollars of debt between the banks and the vendors.
>
> We spent a year liquidating inventory and closing stores. We learned that we went into the world wanting to be entrepreneurs and we were really accountants and we had very little understanding of how to evaluate a business. We were so hungry to be entrepreneurs; we just wanted to do it and weren't even aware that it had a very low chance for success. Later at Stephens when we learned how to evaluate companies as investments, we wondered, "How could we have thought that was a good deal?" It was amazing we didn't end up in bankruptcy.

As he and Judi struggled with the retail business, he realized that to be a wheeler-dealer, he had to be smarter about understanding the difference between a solid business that's poorly managed and a bad business that no amount of good management can turn around.

Pivot Point: Turning Point Decision

"When we moved to Stephens in our early 30s, for the next five or six years our learning curve went straight up."

Straddling the corporate world doing M&A deals in insurance and the small retail business competing against Walmart, Dale sensed that what he still needed to learn about business wasn't going to happen in an accounting firm. He realized at KPMG that his value was in the technical and legal skills of tax law that really wasn't about building businesses.

They used to say that working at KPMG was like riding a whale—as long as you want to go in the same direction as the whale, it's a great ride. But don't kid yourself that the whale could care where you want to go. When you don't want to go in the same direction as the whale, your only choice is to get off because you're not going to influence the direction of the whale. I saw investment banking as the opportunity to become a businessperson in the fullness of the challenge.

He interviewed with several investment banks. Jack Stephens, founder of Stephens, called and told Dale he wanted to start an investment advisory practice for their clients, such as Walmart, Tyson Foods, and Alltel Wireless. His line to Dale was, "If you come over here to work with me and Warren [Jack's son and successor] to build this, we'll have a lot of fun and we'll make an ass pocket full of money." At 33 years old, Dale left KPMG in Dallas to build the new division at Stephens in Little Rock, Arkansas.

Dale's first lesson at Stephens was that investment bankers and accountants look at businesses in dramatically different ways. Accountants have expertise in a narrow area—of regulation, tax, financial, or auditing—and evaluate the company's financials according to generally accepted business standards and legal requirements. Investment bankers look at a business from the much wider perspective of, "Is this something you would want to put your capital into?" This angle involves much more than accounting considerations.

I was taking a crash course from Jack Stephens and Warren Stephens about understanding the valuation and sustainability of businesses. The first IPO Stephens ever did, and it was obviously the best, was Walmart. They also took Tyson Foods and Alltel public. Stephens was an incredible platform; it was a billionaire family with lots of contacts. But they didn't have an advisory service. That was the great opportunity at Stephens, to start a new business on top of this very established platform to advise people on how to evaluate businesses, buy and sell companies, raise capital for businesses and understand management. It was a platform for learning how to be a shrewd, smart investor and businessperson.

Jack Stephens was a great deal guy, a great investor, and wonderful networker—I learned a lot from Jack. I was also reading lots of annual reports from Warren Buffett at that time and learned from some of the best investors in the country about how to look at a company, what do you value, what is a franchise and brand, what is good management, what's not.

To take opportunistic advantage of the boom economy, Dale had to quickly apply everything he was learning about investment banking. Fortunately, KPMG had taught him world-class standards for building teams and processes. To build the investment advisory business at Stephens from the ground up, Dale had to think more broadly and holistically, and cast a vision for the entire practice. Tackling the challenge marked the turning point when the ambitious, hardworking executive understood that the vantage point of leading is different from managing, and the work of leading is fundamentally different from managing.

In the first several years we were very fortunate to do some very large transactions and advise companies on billion-dollar acquisitions. I was overseeing managers who were ambitious and hardworking. Instead of managing them, you have to inspire them; you have to make sure they understand the vision and they buy into it, and they understand your values. All of a sudden you're not so much managing managers as leading managers. You have to be in their head a lot more because you're cutting them a lot of slack to go do it their way.

At Stephens, Dale learned from people with ambitions for the extraordinary. He found refreshing the authenticity of business titans, such as Jack Stephens and Sam Walton, especially in contrast to the show in Dallas. To his surprise, in Arkansas he met businesspeople more successful than anyone he had met in Texas. At Stephens, Dale learned that to truly lead you have to have your own ideas and that authenticity distinguishes the inspired leader.

Jack Stephens had no desire to care about what anyone else thought yet he was very humble and gracious. I learned from him that I would be more successful and have more impact if I do things my own way. That shaped leadership for me. It was a privilege to work for Jack Stephens, one of the best business professionals and leaders.

Arkansas then was poor and yet there were these unique individuals who did everything the way they wanted—Sam Walton with Walmart, Joe Ford with Alltel, and Don Tyson of Tyson Foods. Association with those people showed me that aspiring to be the best at what you do is a reasonable goal.

Then, life changed. Dale had children, first a daughter named Katherine and 20 months later, a son named Jack. His values shifted as he discovered a whole new side to himself. "When Katherine was born, just sitting on the floor with her was the first time since college that I didn't feel guilty about doing nothing. It was something purely relational; there was no other purpose." A year after Jack's birth, Dale's father suddenly died from a heart attack. Dale felt the loss deeply. His father's death amplified the shifting of values and priorities that had begun with the birth of his children.

For the next year, I couldn't be alone without crying as I realized that my dad had shaped my values and attitudes and influenced me so entirely.

I started going back to church because Judi and I had both grown up in the church and we wanted Katherine to go. Listening to a sermon in church, I all of a sudden relaxed. I had been so narrowly focused for almost 20 years. It became a gradual shift over the next 10 years to a life that was much more about what really matters.

He decided that any business that could completely control all of his time and energy was no longer the life he wanted. He grew tired of the bonus cycle in investment banking that focused on 12 months of contributions to the firm's bonus pool, at the end of which the cycle starts all over again from zero. He wanted ownership of the companies he was investing in and to have hands-on responsibility for increasing their value. It was a desire to learn again.

> After seven years of doing deals and taking fees, I felt there wasn't anything more I wanted to learn about that business. Investment banking is all about keeping your capital engaged and getting returns. I wanted to learn how to be an active manager.
>
> I knew how to structure, and I knew how to value and how to put the money together. I could watch what was happening and know when was a good time to sell or buy or liquidate or refinance. What I didn't know was what it was like to be in the CEO [chief executive officer] role and actually drive the growth of the business.

Pivot Point: Tipping Point Decision

"When I went to TruckPro, I was expected to be the lead dog and set the standards for what we aspired to be."

At TruckPro Dale learned the accountability of ownership and much more. He had to turn around a company that was losing money and had a workforce and culture far different from the world of high finance. At KPMG and Stephens, ambitious, highly educated people surrounded him. At TruckPro, Dale had responsibility for moving an organization to do what its people were neither prepared nor wanting to do. Dale had to act boldly with no excuses and no safety net. Leading was more than getting a job done, and being a leader was more than a role. He discovered that absolute responsibility *is* personal.

> It definitely changes you when you, and only you, have ultimate responsibility 24/7 every day of the year. It's a test of fire involving every aspect of your personality, your drive, your intelligence, your persuasiveness, and your thoughtfulness. It's a totally creative experience, and the pressure forces you to respond and there's nobody else to lean on. It's an exciting time because you know you're going to be tested.

At Stephens I was leading a significant practice but it was still Warren Stephens and Jack Stephens's firm. When I went to TruckPro, I raised the money, I bought the company, I had financial partners who I met with once or twice a year. TruckPro was my deal, and that meant if it was going to fail—when I took it over it could have easily gone bankrupt—I was completely and fully responsible. I knew if I didn't do something dramatic, it would go down the tubes.

When I first took over the business, we closed businesses that were marginal. The most agonizing decisions are to throw in the towel on people or stores or lines of business. Those are painful decisions because they have an impact on people's lives but at the same time, I've learned that you actually do people a horrible disservice as a leader not to make a decision and move on. That pain will be followed by a better outcome for the people who stay and who leave.

It was a very humbling experience to realize that the only ways that the company is going to deliver the results you want is the willingness and drive of an awful lot of people to come along and share your goals and do their best to achieve them.

Dale brought the managers of TruckPro's 15 stores in for training in basic business skills, starting with reading a financial statement.

I had to get people to see the problem the way I saw the problem, which was, we're not making any money. I said, "I want you to get in my shoes and look at the company's performance based on a financial statement."

I showed them that even if we raised sales, we still wouldn't make a profit. And, if we don't make a profit, we won't be in business. So let's talk about what will get us a profit. We can cut expenses, raise prices, and cut staff. Let's talk about that because I don't know which staff to cut since we have to keep sales up, so we have to keep customer service up—but we've got to cut payroll by 20 percent.

By bringing them along in the decision-making process, they own the action that we're going to take and have vested interest in trying to make it work.

The financial management training taught that it was the responsibility of the managers to do the same thing with their teams that Dale was doing with them, that the managers would not have a successful store if they didn't build a team of people around them who shared their goals. Within six months to a year, Dale could rank the 15 managers by the results they delivered.

> You have to create an environment where people have an opportunity to show what they can do, starting with their attitude. And it is about getting them in the right spot. We had to figure out how to financially reward people if we take them out of the position where they're managers and let them do what they're really good at.
>
> It was about moving as fast as possible without flattening egos and creating fear in the organization. Lots of people thought I was too demanding, too hard driving, and raising expectations and standards way too high. So you look for those who respond and don't think that, and those became the people to whom I gave more responsibility and bigger territories.
>
> So the fact that more than half the people thought that we expected way too much could not be the deciding factor. You can't let a rebellion start, but the point is to find the leaders quickly.

Dale also made changes at the entry level, where almost everyone started out as a delivery driver. These drivers who walked in the door of the customer's business, delivered the parts, picked up the used parts, and signed paperwork were delivering the customer experience yet making minimum wage. Dale increased the pay from an average of $7 an hour to $10.

> The managers just went crazy and said, "You want us to make a profit and yet you're raising the minimum for these jobs." I stood firm. In most of these communities in the South and in the Midwest at that time, the difference between making $15,000 and $20,000 attracted a significantly more professionally oriented young person.
>
> And then we had to start a training program because these kids really wanted to learn. We found a manager who was particularly good at training young people, and he created books to

teach them parts, procedures and paperwork. And all of a sudden, the quality of our deliveries and customer service improved. We had fewer wrecks, fewer screwed up paper deals, we got inventories right, and we created the first rung of the ladder of a career. We got the kind of person who with investment of time and energy had important value to the organization.

By bringing management discipline to TruckPro, Dale grew the company from 15 stores to 43 and it became profitable. In the sixth year, he couldn't figure out how to make it grow anymore. AutoZone approached Dale with money and ideas. Dale sold. They kept every one of Dale's managers. In fact, eight years later, the company had kept the same top 25 managers and the financial reporting system, and the business was earning 10 times the net profits as when he sold it. The full accountability of owning a company on the verge of bankruptcy with a workforce that had little formal training, and turning it around by developing and nurturing that workforce, brought about a tipping point for Dale's leadership. He had created real value for working families as well as himself.

There were so many days you could watch somebody have an aha moment. It was so rewarding to see lights come on in their heads by giving them the power and the responsibility to creatively make something happen. There were some exceptional businesspeople in that core management team. Together, we got the job done.

The years running TruckPro had been a crucial experience: Dale started out eager to prove himself as a CEO and exited as a confident business leader. But as often happens in our careers, life itself can present the most important tests and teach us the most important lessons of humility and wisdom. Although self-assured by the results he achieved as CEO, Dale encountered a deep sense of vulnerability with his father's sudden death. In the tipping point of his career, instead of feeling successful he felt vulnerable, conscious that what matters most is not within our control and that leadership is, in large part, sheer discipline and stamina to fulfill responsibilities.

I had admired and respected and, in some way maybe, idolized CEOs my whole life. And so it was a chance to see if I was good enough. I came through the test realizing that there is vulnerability in life, that there are elements of life that are not controllable. And yet you realize that you can make a difference, and that what you're called to do is give everything you have to right the ship and accomplish the goals.

I realized that ultimately we aren't in control—there's always that stray bullet, that huge wave; there are always things out there that can happen to you and your family and your life that completely change the deal. And yet, with a full awareness of that vulnerability, the issue is can you surrender everything you've got to being a difference maker and living with that situation.

Pivot Point: Recommitment Decision

"It's a mystery to me why I am the way I am, why I have that drive. It may be a gift or a curse, but it's who I am."

After selling TruckPro at the end of 1998, Dale had financial security for life. For the first few months, he felt relief that he didn't have any responsibility for satisfying customers and the performance of all those employees. Then the reality quickly hit that he had nothing to organize his day. "It's a very big challenge when the day-to-day patterns of your life just end. I was 46 when that happened, and I liked the freedom to craft a life of what I want, but I still needed a passion to push myself into being productive."

In 1999 Dale rejoined Stephens. Initially, he was supposed to look for more deals, but four months later, the head of investment banking left. Jack Stephens asked Dale to run it. That was at the beginning of 2000, right at the peak of the tech bubble. That bubble soon burst. For the first year, Dale cleaned up Stephens's investment portfolio. A couple of years later, he didn't feel challenged to learn anything new.

Stephens was a wonderful place; it was financially rewarding, and I liked the people. Yet something just gnawed at me. That I was settling for a life that wasn't driving the best out of me and that I any longer found challenging and exciting.

It's a mystery to me why I am the way I am, why I have that drive. It may be a gift or a curse, but it's who I am. I don't know why at 50, when I had this very comfortable life, that it wasn't enough. Maybe it was my dad dying early—he retired at 60, played golf every day for two years and then died on his sixty-third birthday from a heart attack. So when I hit 50, 63 didn't look that far away.

It was a time of self-assessment and reevaluation. "I started thinking, 'How do you measure a successful life?'"

During this time, Dale and Judi agreed to host a dinner at their house to help Bishop John raise money for building a high school. It was for orphans of Rwanda's 1994 genocide who were graduating from Sonrise Primary School, a boarding school Bishop John had opened in 2001, and for students whose parents could pay.

When I met Bishop John in late 2002, I had been in this period of treading water and lack of passion for about three years. I saw in him a great entrepreneur, full of energy and passion, building schools and hospitals and businesses by getting nonprofits and churches to help him.

I thought, "What an incredible entrepreneurial guy. Were he running a company, I would want to be his banker. I would want to come in and invest money in his stock." Yet this guy didn't have a stock and was not making money and was operating in this poor place, Rwanda.

That evening got Dale thinking that Bishop John was going to get "a lot of attaboys when he went to heaven." The question nagged at Dale: What was he doing that would get him attaboys in heaven? He realized for the first time that he had played the game other people designed. He wondered what the end game should be. He had no idea that a man of the church from Rwanda would make his life come full circle.

I became very haunted by questions about the purpose of my life. I started looking back on my life at KPMG and at Stephens and TruckPro to get an understanding of how passion came and when it went away, how come I couldn't get it back this time.

I began to realize that passion was a divine gift, a spirit that dwelled in you to energize you and give you drive.

In that thought process, I began questioning a lot of things. If passion is divinely given, then what does God care about? If the deal is, I want You to give me passion, and I know You hold it, then what do I have to do for You to give it back to me? The question, then, is, How do you define success? And the question was kind of odd, you know, because I was 50.

Up to this period, Dale had learned from the people he regarded as the epitome of the successful professionals he wanted to be: Jack Stephens, Sam Walton, and Warren Buffet. He studied their attitudes and lives and their businesses. At 50 years old, he wondered what if he studied Jesus in the same way. What did Jesus value and think was successful? Dale found the answer in the book of Matthew.

Jesus said at the end of time everybody will come to the throne and the son will divide people into goats and sheep. People asked, "How do you get into one category or the other?" This was exactly what I was looking for—how can you measure success?—and he said those people who fed the hungry, who clothed the poor, who helped the sick, who visited people in prison, those will be the sheep, the valuable.

So that seemed pretty clear: What did he value? Caring for people who I had never had any interest in. Poor people, pitiful people, people who made bad choices, people who were sick, who were losers and yet this is what he was saying; this is what he wanted us to invest time and effort into: how to serve these people and take care of them.

The parable before that is about the master who leaves town and to his three servants, he gives talents [a unit of value for commerce], telling them to be productive and fruitful. When the master returns, the first guy says, "I traded with the five talents you gave me, and I am bringing back 10." The second guy says, "You gave me two and I gained two." The third man says, "You gave me one and I buried it, because I was afraid of you and didn't want to take any risks." And the master said to him, "Go away, slothful servant," and to the two first servants he said, "Good job, good and faithful servants."

Well, that said to me, What risk am I taking with what he gave me? None. I am not risking a thing. I decided that my actions and my beliefs needed to line up, that the only way I was going to get passion back was to surrender everything in my life, which was really my time. I decided to realign and find what He wanted me to do.

Dale's recommitment decision is very different from the others in the book yet the same in that it ultimately is a recommitment to self. For some others it's a decision to double down on a singular commitment with renewed purpose, or it's a decision to reverse a setback and achieve what you set out to do. For Dale, it's a decision to align his actions with his changing perspective about his life and his legacy.

At 18, I had come to the conclusion that God would be perfectly okay with me living how I wanted—not being a bad or a selfish person, but He wasn't dictating to me a lifestyle. He had let me drive along as if what I did and how I did it didn't really matter to him because we had a sweet relationship on the side.

Then He took my passion away.

When I was 51 years old, He made it clear to me that He does care how I have lived my entire life. I was so hungry for passion that I asked, "What do you want me to do? How do I get this back?"

Pivot Point: Letting Go Decision

"Now is the time for people who are most alert to their purpose in life and looking for significance in life to find a way to bridge the affluence of the West with the needs of the developing world."

Four years after rejoining Stephens and running its investment banking division, Dale cleared the deck. He knew he could not open his mind and heart to what was in store for him if he went to his office at Stephens every day. He also knew from his hiatus after selling TruckPro that facing a blank calendar did not suit him. But he had to risk something; he made the decision to let go and trust that his calendar would get filled with experiences he needed.

> I had no idea what I was supposed to do. People were always asking me to look at a charity, and I had lived my whole life basically stiff-arming those people. Now I made the decision to go with an open hand and go wherever I was led.

To find your calling is, for most people as for Dale, both attractive and mystifying. What's more comforting than to do what one is meant to do? But how do we really know what we are meant to do? What's the difference between a calling and a fitting opportunity? The answers, for Dale, were revealed only after he made the decision to let go of his ideas and expectations. He would simply participate, neither lead nor follow. This was a new role for him: just to be keenly present, and without a motive, to the people and happenings around him. This experience, coincidentally, is sometimes ascribed to the process of creativity, innovation, and serendipitous discovery.

Dale then experienced a confluence of events, so unusual and unexpected, that it makes anyone wonder if there is indeed a master script at work. One incident following another built up to a profound moment of clarity and belief. It started with Bishop John coming back to town six months after Dale left Stephens and about a year after their first meeting. Dale had been desperately trying to figure out how to get his passion back.

> I saw Bishop John again; I said, "I don't know how I can help you, but I have a clean slate, I have 24/7 to figure out what I am supposed to do. What can I do for you?"
>
> He said, "In Rwanda, I am most concerned that we have a vibrant economy. No matter how much we spend on education, if there aren't opportunities for building businesses for these young people to support their families, then the best and brightest will end up in North America and Europe. All those going to school will bear no fruit in Rwanda. You are a business guy; you have spent your whole life financing and building businesses, why don't you spend the rest of your life building businesses in Rwanda?"
>
> That was a suggestion out of the blue; I couldn't believe he even said it. The audacity to suggest that I would go to Africa,

much less invest capital in it. That was the first inkling of what ultimately I was called to.

Three months later, a friend invited Dale and his wife to go to a weekend conference of Opportunity International in Boca Raton, Florida. Dale found out through Google that it was about microfinance, a term he had heard before but didn't really know anything about or have any interest in. But Boca Raton was where all of the KPMG partners' meetings had been, so he thought that it would be nostalgic to go back. He went.

At the dinner reception, he sat down at a table in a big ballroom filled with 300 people, and two women sat next to him. It turned out that Dale had bought TruckPro from the uncle of the woman on his right. The woman on his left had run Beatrice Foods when she became the widow of the owner, who was one of the most successful African American leveraged buyout leaders in the 1980s. Taken completely by surprise that successful businesspeople were at this meeting with the desire to serve the poor, Dale got his second inkling of what he was called to do.

The next morning, the meeting kicked off with a video showing a woman from the Philippines, married with three children, living in the slums of Manila. She gets up at three every morning to go to the farmers market, buys what she can, and sells the goods on the streets of Manila. Watching this video with 300 people in the auditorium, Dale started to cry.

Well, when my dad was seven years old, his mother would wake him up at three in the morning to go to the farmers market. In a horse-drawn wagon they rode all around Lubbock, Texas, selling fresh fruits and vegetables. This was my dad's first job. The earlier you got up, the better chance you had to claim the horse and wagon that would go to the most prosperous areas and make more money. I had heard this story my entire life. My dad used to wake me up every morning by walking in and saying all of the other boys are already up and ahead of you.

When that video came on, the thing that rushed to my head was, "These are the most fundamental values in my life—family and hard work." This woman in Manila was exactly like my father and mother and grandparents.

It felt like Jesus was leaning into my ear and whispering, "You do realize that I have literally been preparing you since the day

you were born for this work, that there are billions of people in
the world who are not losers, who are not pitiful, who simply don't
have an opportunity to work hard enough to earn money to take
care of their families. And you can make a difference to them."

It was like that flame of passion just exploded inside of me
and it said I could become the world's best expert in microfinance. That this is what was calling me. He prepared me my
whole life to create opportunities for people to earn money and
take care of their families. That was it. That lit the flame on that
morning and it has been burning like that since March of 2004.

Dale's life-altering experience at that Opportunity International
meeting removed the blinders that, since college, had blocked out anything that did not help his career. Now seeing the wholeness of his life
and world, Dale was stunned to see how everything came together in a
perfect fit for his calling.

I mean I didn't know that it would be that cool. The door swung
open and I walked through it and I thought, "Oh, now I get it."
I have a purpose that He cares about, and He has equipped me
with what I need to do. That was unbelievable to me, like the
wind ripped through the sails and filled them up with air and
I sailed off on this course.

I wanted to learn everything there was to know about microfinance and business in developing countries and the poor and
how they made money, how they supported their families, what
they valued, what they cared about. I had so much to learn. I had
never been to a developing country; I had never been around
the poor; I didn't know anything about aid.

That was actually kind of exciting that I knew so little. It was
like sitting down at a great big feast. I couldn't pick up anything that
wasn't rich with learning. I got on the plane and went to Rwanda.

Dale learned about the horrific 1994 genocide in Rwanda and the
aftermath and about the dramatic progress the country has made from
staggering devastation to a stable government and social order. He learned
about President Kagame, the leader of the Rwandan Patriotic Front that
had seized control of the country and stopped the genocide. After the

massacre of 1 million Rwandans in 100 days, visionaries and everyday heroes made extraordinary commitments to help a country that needed everything. Kagame has played an astute role in mobilizing people and resources all over the world to achieve his goal of lifting Rwanda out of poverty in one generation. The more Dale learned about Rwanda and its president, the more he felt surprisingly at home.

> President Paul Kagame and Bishop John Rucyahana don't need me for vision; they have plenty of vision and plenty of drive. The value that I bring to them is simply seeing what they see and being creative about helping them understand how to get what they want.
>
> There is something as an investment banker and even as a partner in KPMG, but particularly as an investment banker, that is about understanding someone who is just as driven and just as talented as you are—understanding their vision and being that person they can trust and rely on to help them get it done. At Stephens, the part I loved was that role that helps others achieve their visions. I think that's one of the reasons I am uniquely positioned to do what I am doing in Rwanda.
>
> I also realized that what I found rewarding at Stephens was not about being a shrewd guy doing transactions and making money; it was being involved in building something over time. What I found most satisfying was being associated with something that grows, and the development of young people into professionals and the kind of team that gets things done.

Dale applied these experiences to forming a vision of bridging the wealth and abundance of the West with the poverty and scarcity of the developing areas of the world. Bridge2Rwanda, formed in 2007, builds that bridge for foreign direct investments, for a global network of friends of Rwanda, and for study abroad for Rwandan students. He built a small organization of people living and working in Rwanda for delivering services as well as a husband-wife team in the United States for financial and administrative management. For several years, Dale knew the goal and grand vision but had to try different approaches. The successful dealmaker learned to accept failure as part of being a pioneer.

Then in 2011 Bridge2Rwanda found a highly effective way to develop the next generation of Rwandan entrepreneurs and leaders that became the B2R Scholars Program. How the program developed illustrates what Dale means when he says his role now isn't to build organizations but to be an encourager and activator.

It started with a request from President Kagame. The Rwandans had observed that almost all successful business leaders in Asia have studied abroad at some point in their lives. So the Rwandans created the Presidential Scholars Program in 2006–2007. They identified the country's top 100 math and science high school graduates and asked Dale and some other friends of Rwanda to find universities in North America and Europe that would offer tuition scholarships to these top students, and the Rwandan government would pay for room and board and everything else. That program launched with a dozen students; within a couple of years, it provided almost 90 scholarships. The schools abroad welcomed the Rwandan students' work ethic and performance. The Rwandan government, however, couldn't afford 90 scholarships a year.

President Kagame asked Dale to start an alternative program as they started downsizing the Presidential Scholars program. The new program had to prepare Rwandan students to apply and compete for full university scholarships, which meant training for the Test of English as a Foreign Language (TOEFL), the English proficiency exam, the Scholastic Assessment Test (SAT), admissions interviews, writing essays, and filing applications. The young woman who took this project came from Dale's home state of Arkansas through Bishop John. After meeting Bishop John and mentoring a couple of Rwandan students studying at the University of Arkansas, Anna Reed decided that she was called to Africa. She left her job as a speech pathologist at Arkansas Children's Hospital, working with deaf children who could for the first time hear after cochlear implants. Anna moved to Rwanda in 2009, spent a year and a half teaching English, TOEFL, and SAT and determined that it was going to take a gap year between high school and university to make the Rwandan students internationally competitive for admissions.

Anna recruited Richard Siegler, a Fulbright scholar, to help her. They started the program in 2011 with 15 students and got them all scholarships; the next year 350 students applied for 24 positions, and 21 of them got scholarships; and the third year 1,200 students applied for 35 positions. They've raised over $6 million in scholarship money, mostly in the United States but also in Canada, the United Kingdom, France, and Germany.

> When Anna put this scholar program together and we saw the impact it could have, we just quit doing everything else. We said, "We have finally found the program that identifies the best and the brightest, invests so intensely in them and creates an opportunity they couldn't possibly get otherwise."
>
> Part of it is simply Anna. We have a leader in her who is passionately committed and knew these kids. We said, "Let's focus our resources to make this better and bigger."

The last step in the strategy is to create jobs and opportunity in Rwanda. In this work, Dale's role, again, is to encourage people to develop an idea and facilitate connections and the process. After years of experimenting, Dale has discovered that he needs to find entrepreneurs who will bring a lot of resources to build their businesses in Rwanda.

For example, Dale helped Donny Smith, CEO of Tyson Foods, start a mill feed business in Rwanda. Donny called Dale and said he and his wife wanted to do something for African farmers. They had tried unsuccessfully to do something in Malawi and another country, and someone suggested Rwanda and talking with Dale. They met during the summer and in October they flew to Rwanda to meet with the minister of agriculture and the head of the Rwanda Development Board. Donny talked about building a model farm that could train farmers.

> The minister of agriculture said, "That would be great but if you really want to help, we could really use a commercial feed mill. If we're going to increase milk, meat, and egg production, an animal can only produce as well as it is fed. We don't have a commercial feed mill. Our farmers have to go buy all the ingredients and mix them manually. The nutritional quality is uneven as are prices."
>
> The next morning Donny said, "Okay, scrap the farm; we're going to build a feed mill."
>
> I said, "Obviously, you know how to build feed mills. Tell me how much you think it will cost to do this and how much you're

going to put in, and I'll see about raising the rest of the money. I think this is a viable project."

He said, "I'll put up all the money, personally."

We found one of our Rwandan scholars who had just graduated from the University of Arkansas in Little Rock, and Donny hired him for a yearlong internship at Tyson. He went through Tyson's management boot camp, spent six months learning how to run a feed mill and he returned to Rwanda and he's going to be the operations manager. So we have a Rwandan, college educated in the US and interned at Tyson, who will be the operations manager. The mill will open first quarter of 2014.

These are examples of how Bridge2Rwanda resources inspire other resources, and needs point to other needs, and Dale's network works in inspired ways that for-profit businesses can only emulate. Dale's role redefines his leadership because as a leader among leaders—there are no leaders and no followers—his role connects expertise and activates the network to inspire each other in developing sustainable solutions.

Things like this just happen. Things fall into your lap but you're preparing yourself, your network and friends for a long, long time. That's why I've learned to plan less and less. I know what to do when that opportunity walks in the door.

Ten years after leaving the for-profit world, Dale's passion is stronger than ever for social entrepreneurship. He no longer thinks about the mysteries of passion.

I feel I have discovered a truth in life and that is that business enterprise is transformational, that the creation of private enterprises to address social needs is a big answer to a huge problem. There's a wonderful book I read by Jim Clifton, CEO of Gallup. Gallup started a survey of the entire world, finding that the most universal need is to have a good job. There are 3 billion people on the planet who are of the age and in a place where they really want or need a good job. They define a good job as working for an employer for at least a 30-hour week. There are currently 1.2 billion good jobs out there, leaving the world with 60 percent unemployment. So we have 1.8 billion people in the world who need a good job.

If you're a leader, what does that tell you to work on? And who creates jobs? You can take the top 1,000 local companies in the world and their total employment stays the same year to year. If there's new growth, it's going to come from small to medium size private businesses. Who has the most power to transform the world? It's the entrepreneurs who understand how to grow a business. That's the truth I feel I have discovered.

The only thing I know how to do is to build businesses and to train and develop young people to be entrepreneurs and business managers. So this truth is so relevant to me because it's the only thing I know how to do.

THE LEADER'S LEGACY

Although Dale recounts his career as two halves, the first half in corporate America and the second half in nonprofit work in Rwanda, it was one developmental journey to be the natural leader he was called to be.

Both parts were essential to the whole of his journey. In his for-profit career, he acquired valuable skills and confidence as a business leader who gets the job done. He was well rewarded for his hard work and hunger for learning, from his first professional job at KPMG, to his dream job at Stephens, to what he thought was his ultimate aspiration of owner/CEO of TruckPro. In his nonprofit career, Dale completely recalibrated his expectations and goals, exploring what he had closed off during his climb to success. He found an equilibrium that gave him a deeper sense of flourishing than he had known with conventional measures of success. This has given him a different kind of confidence; his skills and leadership now flow naturally according to the needs of a mission defined by his ingenuity and personal accountability. He is more comfortable getting things done through meaningful relationships than organizational structures. In a sense, he has returned to his roots in Snyder, Texas, and the family business.

The outcome of Dale's letting go decision was reclaiming his core self that had lain dormant during his career climb. Once he opened his mind to the world he had left unexplored, he found that his early decision to go into business instead of the humanities no longer had to be an either/or choice. He could be the highly skilled business professional and serve humanitarian goals.

> I've been doing this for 10 years and my passion hasn't dissipated because there's an enormous global need and I get to be a player, a tiny player, and I am uniquely qualified to help. If I can help create a model where in 10 years, Rwanda can look like Singapore, that model can accelerate a movement in other countries. It's a very dynamic model, nobody has drawn the plan here; I'm still making it up as I go along.
>
> In my life today, I feel I am an actor on a stage and I have a director who hands me the pages of the script a day at a time.

Dale wants his legacy to be the impact made by people he influenced, that he made a difference by coaching them to play to their strengths, that he made an impact on their career choices by getting them involved in a mission. His dream is that younger generations will advance social entrepreneurialism into a viable long-term career.

> The two big things that I regret not having done until I was 50 years old are not being exposed to the poor of the world and not investing time in maintaining and growing networks of friends. I discovered late in life that your network of friends is your greatest treasure.
>
> With that said, at both Stephens and TruckPro there was an opportunity to create something that was outstanding. I invested a lot of myself in recruiting people, establishing values, setting up performance measures and processes, shaping culture and attitudes. When I moved on, both organizations actually grew to be significantly bigger and better because of the foundation laid. I loved having done that.
>
> At the end of my life I want to look back and say that I helped create something similar for Rwanda and Africa as well as the generation of people in America who were called to get involved with those parts of the world; that I really did build this bridge that transformed lives at both ends.
>
> I push people harder than I used to. The opportunity to find a calling that matters and renews your passion is available to

everybody. I don't cut anybody slack anymore. I believe everyone can have it. I don't believe the right thing to do is go to Africa; I believe the right thing to do is to find what you are passionately called to address. The goal is to find that which you are called to serve and that plays to your professional strengths and talents.

The art of leading, on Dale's journey, developed into a leadership model that transcends organizations. Although organizations are necessary to provide structure for the work, the real investment is in the group of people the organizations influence. For Bridge2Rwanda, the real assets extend way beyond the organization. "I'm comfortable that my role is a catalyst and an encourager and that I don't know where these seeds spread today will sprout tomorrow."

CHAPTER 7

Lessons from the Journeys of Five Leaders

WHAT DO LEADERS HAVE IN COMMON?

The subject of leadership continually arouses debate. Are leaders born or made? Does the leader make the job, or does the job make the leader? Can training make leaders? What differentiates leaders from others?

The leaders featured in these chapters and their pivotal decisions demonstrate that leaders develop and evolve, even if they are born or raised to lead. All, in fact, turned insecurities into drivers of achievement, examples of how a relative disadvantage can serve as a powerful motivator. The spark of born leaders, in any case, must be lit by experiences that, in these stories, are the pivot points. The spark becomes a fire that, with decisive action, turns potential into reality.

If there is a secret successful leaders have, it is this: Leading is about creating the job and the leader's value to the mission. This is a very different approach from conventional thinking that success comes with doing what worked for others. Leaders want to know how others handled similar situations and their outcomes. However, leaders take that as a creative spark and adapt it to their own goals and methods. Leading, for them, is figuratively writing their own book. Each book is unique, because, as a client says, much of leadership is influencing the river of events that aren't, and can't be, planned.

In all the leadership journeys in this book, the leader made the job and the job made the leader. They routinely went outside of their comfort zones to advance their business agenda. The five pivotal decisions stand out from hundreds or perhaps thousands of decisions made on the job because these are the ones that influenced the river of events, made them grow as leaders, created the future, and differentiated the leader's vision and accomplishments.

Their natural demeanors are very different but all project an assured-ness of mission. John Rogers is a quiet leader to the point of being underestimated in the first impression, but those who know him would never underestimate what this highly disciplined and competitive busi-ness leader can accomplish. Al Golin has no trace of self-importance, but he speaks with authority whenever he asserts his opinion. Bud Frankel works a room like a caring uncle, but those close to him know the dif-ficulty of meeting his high standards. Glen Tullman shares his passion for changing and improving things in the manner of an inspired teacher, but there's no question that a deep need to achieve goals for significance drive his strategic decisions. And Dale Dawson enjoys connecting with people in a kind and laid-back way, yet everyone he meets recognizes his unspoken expectations for a purposeful relationship.

On their journeys they learned how to handle the paradoxes that make leadership more art than science. There is art in achieving a balance between confidence *and* humility, particularly important at the launch-ing and turning points. The tipping point decision needs the leader to act with conviction yet be flexible. The recommitment decision calls for steadiness *and* risk taking with bold goals—more difficult now because there is more to lose than at earlier stages. At the letting go point, there is art in the balance between continuing to care yet letting people find their own way and learn from their own mistakes. By finding this delicate balance, mature leaders can establish cultures larger and stronger than they might have imagined, producing a new generation of leaders.

Built-in paradoxes make leadership a complex subject of study. Leadership theories abound because none has established a direct causal relationship between specific leadership variables and business perfor-mance and workplace satisfaction. Until the 1940s, the belief prevailed that people were born with traits that destined them to lead. Then two landmark studies in the 1940s from the University of Michigan and Ohio State University found that behaviors, not inborn traits, deter-mine leadership effectiveness. Those studies found that successful leaders exhibited employee-oriented behaviors and/or task-oriented behaviors. Then situational theories combined the trait and behavioral approaches, studying which traits and behaviors are more effective for different situations. Later theories emphasized the importance of the leader-subordinate relationship. But we still don't understand what effective leaders have or do that nonleaders don't have or do and what causes better performance and job satisfaction.

These theories start with a leader-centric perspective, attributing success to the individual's control of self and environment with trainable skills and innate traits. In the extensive interviews with each leader for this book, however, not a single one saw himself as having control over conditions for success. Not a single one saw himself as having any special traits or characteristics or exceptional skills. All talked about working hard and believing their work mattered. All talked about responding to environmental conditions that became pivotal decisions.

The lessons from these leaders are twofold. First, as conveyed in the leaders' playbooks, they were guided by clear values that shaped them. Values served as the platform for their leadership and vision. Each leader's values differed, so leadership does not require adherence to a universal set of values. But all leaders had a values-based platform. Second, their stories show how they became great leaders over the long haul through a series of decisions that forced leaps—not incremental steps—in learning and growth. The circumstances and pivotal decisions differed, but the framework for connecting five clear pivot points makes sense out of how they handled the ups and downs of careers and businesses in a way that distinguished them as leaders.

Let's review the overarching themes that emerge from their different playbooks. One clear theme pertains to the question of how successful leaders spot leaders they want on their team. They look for people who care about the purpose served by the business and by new ideas rather than about what's in it for them. They look for people who do the right thing versus compromising their judgment and actions for office politics and self-promotion. They look for people who think like owners—people who think about turning potential into reality, get it done right, make the investment, and take the risks. They look for people who have innate curiosity and are driven by a natural passion for purposeful work. And, they look for people who have motivated others, and themselves, to do their best work.

This is the way leaders think—in terms of how to serve more than self and in terms of a purpose that others can share, which inherently means a bigger purpose than one's own success. This kind of thinking dispels several myths created by our cultural obsession with success formulas and lifestyles of the rich and famous.

In fact, these themes actively resist groupthink. They stand the test of time. Great leaders know that the challenge is making time-tested truths one's own and that is their competitive edge.

Leading Edge

It's not about authorized power; it's about personal power.

Signs of problems with leadership include people stuck in endless meetings that produce no discernable decisions and results; teams stuck with the same problems for months, years, even decades; and complaints about a dysfunctional culture that end up making a culture of "Why bother?" In this situation, workers regard executive decisions as optional and decision makers get little support. This vicious cycle means that people with appointed power and authority are not leading.

In contrast, true leaders tap personal power to make an impact, whether they have authorized power or not. Throughout their stories, these leaders took personal responsibility to make something important happen. They tapped every internal and external resource available, no matter how limited, to find a way. Leading from personal power helped them direct others to be part of something meaningful, solve problems, and raise the performance and development of the team.

Personal power turned Bud's idea into the largest independently owned marketing agency in the country. The idea propelled Bud to make his launching decision, and the idea never stopped inspiring him, which makes this the most important of his pivotal decisions. Under the same circumstances, another person would have complained about the boss's resistance to change and left it at that while feeling unmotivated and deflated, perhaps not raising his or her hand again.

Personal power gave Glen the fortitude to turn around a business devastated by the burst of the dot-com bubble. Another person would have shut down and blamed bad timing. With bold leadership, Glen used what resources he could salvage—which was mainly his personal power—to reinvent Allscripts and, in the process, form a clear vision for improving health care, making the turning point decision the most important of his career.

John Rogers applied his personal power to making Ariel the platform on which he would demonstrate the strength of diversity in his leadership team as well as in the mutual fund marketplace. This brought his leadership and Ariel to a tipping point as well as made him resolute in his recommitment decision when the Great Recession of 2008 battered the firm. John's personal power to establish a diverse leadership team beyond himself makes the tipping point decision his most important legacy.

Personal power turned Al's misery working for new owners into the opportunity to apply all his hard-earned lessons and fulfill a clear leadership role and need. Taking a firm stand for what he believed in and risking being fired by the chief executive officer (CEO) of the parent company, Al made a resolute recommitment decision when the other option was to retire. It set the leadership agenda of his later years to grow GolinHarris into a global public relations (PR) firm serving the world's leading companies while retaining the culture that was integral to the firm's success.

Personal power guided Dale through an angst-filled decision to leave Stephens without any plans in search of what might reignite his passion. His belief that passion is a divine gift over which he had no influence or control made his letting go an act of faith as well as an act of personal power to seek in places he had never ventured. When he experienced that decisive moment at the Opportunity International conference, he used personal power to create something from nothing. Only by making a well-considered letting go decision did he discover that his entire career was preparing him for developing skilled and entrepreneurial leaders in Rwanda. Only by letting go could he have a new beginning with passion.

Personal power equalizes the opportunity to be a leader. Personal power does not require elite degrees, personal wealth or prestige, or a high organizational title or social status. All of these certainly can make the journey easier from the start but are not the source of personal power. People can start with practically nothing and achieve much. A powerful example is a young man I met in Rwanda. Collin lost both of his parents by age 16, leaving six younger siblings under his care. Thirteen years old at the time of the horrific genocide in Rwanda, he set off to college in Kenya. He paid for college by selling collages he made from scraps and whatever he could find. He turned to painting because tourists could more easily carry home a rolled-up canvas than a collage. Entirely a self-taught artist, he returned to Rwanda, a poor country still struggling from the genocide, and opened an art studio that attracted other artists.

The art studio is an accomplishment, but there is more. He decided that the poor children he passed every day needed something to do. He started free dance lessons for the local children to learn traditional African dances from four instructors paid for by the sales of his paintings. Soon, the lessons drew 80 children. When dancing, the children were no longer poor and no longer aimless; they had purpose. *This 28-year-old young man saw these children on the street corner and decided to do something.*

There's more. He heard about a world children's festival in Holland and sent a video of his dance troupe. The festival selected them to represent Africa at the festival. In May 2009, Collin accompanied eight children to perform at the Via del Mondo Festival. Collin may have created a turning point in these children's lives.

The mission statement for the art studio is simple and powerful: "Using art to change lives." Collin is doing it. With extraordinarily devastating life circumstances, Collin had only his artistic talent and his personal power. It's hard for us to fully appreciate just how bold his vision and efforts are. The great majority of us have far more resources and a far more advantageous environment than Collin. The simplicity of this story about an artist in Rwanda makes it very clear that what stands between us and all that our personal power can achieve is only ourselves.

Leading Edge

It's not about career planning; it's about making pivotal decisions.

For every career plan that works, there is one or more that doesn't. Life is too dynamically in motion for any plan to anticipate everything. Some people swear by having a plan and by strict focus on it. They may attain their goal but they also may miss greater possibilities. In all these stories, situations developed and decisions were made either to capitalize on opportunities or to change the narrative from a certain negative outcome that, if allowed, would have naturally unfolded. No one talked about being the mastermind of a 10-year plan or any long-term plan that defined every stage of growth and its timeline.

Pivotal decisions more often than not were decisions not to follow the plan. Bud's plan was to be a top producer for his boss and be made a partner; instead his boss's dismissal of his idea for change galvanized Bud to start his own marketing agency. Glen's plan was to join an established company in the growing computer industry; instead he joined a start-up in software working for his brother and became a software entrepreneur. Al's plan was to do the work he loved for several more years and retire quietly and comfortably; instead culture clash with new owners provoked him to risk his lifework as well as his retirement. Dale's plan was to be a successful wheeler-dealer Dallas style; instead, he discovered his calling for nonprofit work in Rwanda.

If they had stuck with their plans, all of them would have done well enough, but none would have experienced what became his proudest work.

Leading Edge

It's not about personal gain; it's about personal responsibility.

All the leaders consistently stepped up to the next challenge out of personal responsibility when their abilities and commitment were tested. Personal responsibility pushed them forward, come what may, instead of withdrawing during the darkest hours. Some of those efforts involved 10 or more years of implementing and adjusting; others took only a couple of years. They were in it for the duration, as long as they had control of their personal destiny.

For example, Glen stands out from legions of highly capable executives. Why? Because his sense of personal responsibility to improve delivery of medical services makes him tirelessly committed to the mission. He transformed a failing business model, stood up to Wall Street when taking risks to get closer to a vision they didn't understand, and made bold bet-the-business decisions to become an industry leader. In all these decisions, his overriding sense of personal responsibility to achieve the goal predisposed people to want to believe he could pull it off, and his use of personal power got people to invest in his leadership. Personal responsibility turned Glen's passion for change into improving health care. When he stepped down from Allscripts, Glen knew it was time to let go.

Al could have retired when harsh pressures made him compromise his principles and leadership to deliver a profit margin that was destroying the culture. Out of a deep sense of personal responsibility to clients, staff, and the company's future, Al put his convictions and legacy on the line. That pivotal moment gave him clear vision about the past, present, and future. He was taking personal responsibility for it all.

Personal responsibility turned John from a good teammate to increasing the financial literacy of African Americans and youth. And personal responsibility made Bud always work extra hard to bring in more business to replace a lost account rather than cut payroll as was the general practice in the advertising industry. Personal responsibility opened Dale's mind to serving others in a cause literally and figuratively foreign to him.

These leaders show that personal responsibility activates personal power. Feeling personal responsibility but not taking action results in worry and guilt that does not meet anyone's needs. Taking personal responsibility and exercising personal power to do something about the issue, ultimately, separates leaders from everyone else.

Leading Edge

It's not about style; it's about authentic caring and what fits the moment.

These five leaders dispel the notion that has been in vogue that leadership style is a key determinant of leadership effectiveness and that has everyone claiming to have a collaborative or consensus-building style and a coaching style. Each of the featured leaders has an authentic and unique way of being an effective leader that includes bandwidth and acumen to calibrate his style to fit the need and the relationship.

There is a time and place for every leadership style. These seasoned leaders know there are situations that require a command-and-control style, others that require a collaborative style, and yet others that are better led with a facilitative style. A leader calibrates style and tone to the situation, which also means having the capacity to vary style and tone.

For example, John's natural style is coaching, but with the uncoachable, he can be commanding. In times of market volatility and economic crisis, he leads with a very deliberate calm. He does everything he can to have a stabilizing influence with anxious clients, stressed staff, and provocative journalists. When it is business as usual, John strictly enforces timeliness and thoroughness, and the lack thereof brings a flare of impatience from an otherwise even-tempered man.

Al broke away from his natural collaborative style to do something out of character when he rebelled against Shandwick's CFO. And he knew when to set aside his nice-guy style and make the tough firing decisions.

The twists and turns in Bud's story demonstrate how fluid a leader needs to be in his or her composure. When the top three people responsible for Frankel's largest account defected to work on a competitor's account, Bud led with a facilitative style to help the remaining account team rise to the occasion. During a period of so much growth that he halted efforts to win new business, Bud led with a collaborative style to allow people to do their jobs right and well. During the period of preparations for an initial public offering, Bud led with a commanding style to address the clashing of different interest groups.

Leading Edge

It's not about having money; it's about having choices.

Although all these leaders have reaped handsome financial rewards, none of them consciously considered money to be his objective. For all, the importance of money is that it affords more options. And more choices enable them to pursue a vision that really matters, one that is more than about survival and making a living.

Al's story clearly demonstrates that the role of money must be viewed over the long run. After selling the company, he realized that he had sold too soon and it was a bad money decision. In the ensuing 14 years under two different owners and years of struggling with the second, Al emerged a stronger leader with more clarity about his business goals and life goals. Under the third and current owner, Al leveraged the greater resources of its owner to turn GolinHarris into a global leader. As the 84-year-old chairman of the firm, Al no longer regrets a bad money decision, taking immense pride in knowing that GolinHarris is doing award-winning work, has earned enduring client relationships, and is sustainable with a global footprint.

Leading Edge

It's not about you; it's about the work and doing the right thing.

For all the leaders, neither problems nor solutions were about *them*. The power of the idea, says Bud, had its own life. His job was to make sure that decisions supported and fulfilled the integrity of the idea and commitment to the idea guided all its thinking and practices. He started with an idea, and the dynamic marketplace was ready for Bud's dynamic leadership to develop it into an innovative approach to marketing.

The idea drove his development as a leader, perhaps even more than his leadership drove development of the idea. By focusing employees and clients on the power of the idea and how to keep taking it to the next level, Bud made a lasting impact on how people did marketing that was more far reaching than he ever imagined.

John knew from the outset that the mutual fund industry is all about performance numbers. His job was to make sure the firm was doing everything it could to rank in the top 25 percent of return on investment of mutual funds. His success depended on building a team and doing rigorous proprietary research that could pick winning stocks. John never lost sight of the real work and vigorously avoids distractions. He knows the line that he won't cross in his support of civic activities and political campaigns. He knows that duty to Ariel comes first and nearly always trumps his personal interests.

They were all in, through good times and bad. Work became their passion. Their passion was their work. A good illustration of the power of this belief in the work itself is Dale's experience. When he found his passion gone at 50 years old and was disquietingly without direction, he was desperate to find a purpose to which he could feel genuine devotion. He completely surrendered himself and his ego to the journey of life.

LEADERS CONTINUALLY CREATE THEIR JOBS

The leaders in this book all started with a strong work ethic, a healthy dose of ambition, and a competitive drive. Wouldn't they have succeeded at whatever they did? Very likely. Wouldn't they have become leaders in whatever they did? We can only speculate. Remember, however, there are many people who work hard, have ambition, have competitive drive, and are not proven leaders. The fallacy of studies of successful people that focus on the traits they have in common, explains statistician Nassim Nicholas Taleb in his best-selling book, *The Black Swan* (Random House, 2007), is that millions of unknown others have the same attributes but get significantly different results.

What we do know is that these promising and determined individuals made pivotal decisions that turned potential into reality. They kept looking into the future and raising the bar. They didn't think about leadership as a position or a career goal; they simply tackled each new set of lessons and tests. Their goals kept evolving into bigger ones; then one day they realized just how much they had achieved. Their competitive drive spurred them on through occasional failures and saved them from defeat. In this organic process, Bud turned from a marketing pro and small business owner into a leader who changed an industry. Al turned from a PR man into an industry legend. Glen turned from a software executive into a health care leader. John turned from a money manager into a business and civic leader. Dale turned from a successful financial executive into an entrepreneurial philanthropic leader.

Pivot points and decisions propelled these people into real-life situations that revealed their priorities, values, commitments, and abilities under pressure. Each decision point presented tough decisions, obstacles, and complexities on progressively grander scales. Each decision helped them learn to discern from the noise their own true voice and which other voices mattered. That explains the riveting power of these and other successful leaders and artists who did it their way. They continually inspire with new ideas, new goals, new lessons, new visions, and bring people along to the next level.

CHAPTER 8

Lessons from Survey Findings

In examining the five pivotal decisions of the five leaders, the crucial, if obvious, question is whether the same decision-making strategy applies to the general population. If this has broad application, then, what can we learn from this about leadership development and its relationship to organization performance and the course of careers?

As mentioned in the first chapter, the empirical study tested three hypotheses about leadership. First, there are five pivotal opportunities to make decisions that determine the course of a career. Second, accountability and ingenuity drive leadership behavior. Third, when accountability and/or ingenuity fall short in decision making, other behaviors produce less successful outcomes.

A 15-minute questionnaire was administered via an Internet research panel to 500 adults who met our screening criteria: older than 21 years of age; graduated from college; in professional occupations, including small business owners; and specific employment status. To qualify for the survey, respondents had to be working full-time or if working part-time had to be older than 25 years of age. Unemployed respondents had to meet one of the following conditions: unemployed and looking for work, unemployed and not looking for work (if 25 or older, for example, a full-time mother), unemployed and a full-time student (if 25 or older), or retired.

Respondents who met these criteria represent 16 percent of adults in the United States, which translates to 37 million people. Within this group, the following characteristics emerged:

- Age distribution: 70 percent were older than 45 years, having more career experiences.

- Household income: 62 percent had household incomes of more than $75,000.
- Education: 55 percent had more than a university bachelor's degree.
- Employment status: Only 1.48 percent were unemployed and looking for work.
- Occupation: Nearly 40 percent had a professional position in a company, 22 percent in professions requiring graduate degrees, and nearly 20 percent were vice presidents through chief executives.

DO PIVOT POINTS OCCUR IN MOST PEOPLE'S CAREERS?

To determine whether many people experience the five pivotal decisions as we defined them, the survey provided brief descriptions of the five decision points. The questionnaire contained four questions about each pivotal decision the respondent experienced: whether you experienced the decision, and if yes, your age at that time, the success of the outcome, and your decision-making behaviors. To gather data about behaviors used in decision making, we asked respondents to indicate degree of agreement with behavior statements provided in the questionnaire.

Study Findings

Pivotal decisions are a common career experience and mark career stages related to age.

Pivotal decisions occur for almost everyone, with 78 percent of respondents saying they had made at least one such decision. That represents 29 million adults in the United States. Across the age-diverse sample population, the average person has faced two pivotal decisions so far.

The pivotal decisions experienced by the most respondents were the launching and turning point decisions in an expected age-related progression of the decision types. (See Figure 8.1.)

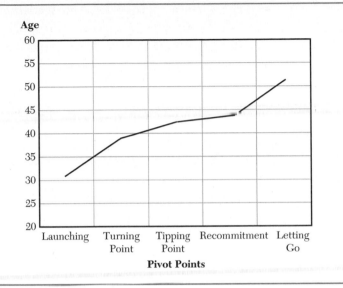

FIGURE 8.1 Age-Related Progressions When Making Five Pivotal Decisions

- Most launching decisions occur in the 20s to early 30s (mean age 31 years).
- Turning point decisions peak at 35 to 44 years old (mean age 39 years).
- Tipping point decisions mainly occur at 35 to 54 years old (mean age 42 years).
- Recommitment decisions begin a sharp increase at 40 years and peak at 45 to 54 years old (mean age 44 years).
- Letting go decisions peak heavily at 55 to 65 years old (mean age 51 years).

Study Findings

The respondents who never made a pivotal decision (22 percent) show a low tolerance for risk.

Of those who qualified for the survey, 22 percent said they had never made a pivotal decision. Analysis shows tolerance for risk as the meaningful difference between the 22 percent of respondents who had never made a pivotal decision and the 78 percent of respondents who had made at least one pivotal decision. Their demographic profiles did not substantially differ, although the 22 percent who hadn't made pivotal decisions tended to be slightly younger.

The group who had never made a pivotal decision had substantially lower agreement with statements such as "When making a decision, I love the challenge," "I'm excited by change," and "When confronting a big decision, I look at it as an opportunity and not as an obstacle." This suggests that these respondents may have faced pivot points but reacted negatively at decision points and made a decision, just not a pivotal decision. In truth, making the choice to stick with the status quo and not make a pivotal impact is still a decision not to take a new course of action. We'll see later in the next study finding that even many of the pivotal decisions that were made ended up rated less than "very successful."

The 22 percent who actively avoided making decisions that involved new challenges and opportunities represents one in five people in professional careers. Leaders must be able to identify those who avoid pivotal decisions accurately so that these people are not put in roles with meaningful decision-making responsibilities. Because pivotal decisions affect not only individual careers but also the work team and company, employers need to understand how this individual behavior influences the work environment. We also need to understand better how the work environment influences this avoidant behavior. Often, both the environment and the individual have a part in a mutually reinforcing problem of resistance to change.

Study Findings

Outcomes of pivotal decisions were more often successful than not. Decision makers rated 25 percent of decisions "somewhat successful" and 41 percent "very successful."

It's essential to understand that the survey collected two sets of data. One set of data is about *the people who made pivotal decisions*—500 respondents who represent 16 percent of US adults (37 million people), whom we've been talking about up to this point. Another set of data is about *the decisions made*—our respondents made 805 pivotal decisions. How respondents made each of their decisions is where the findings get interesting.

Although two out of three decisions were perceived as successful (66 percent), fewer than one in two decisions were rated as "very successful." The good news is that making a pivotal decision has a two-in-three chance of resulting in some degree of success—those are good odds. However, for decisions that loom large in the trajectory of careers and businesses, less than a 50/50 chance for clear success does not exactly invoke confidence. Also, human nature is to feel failure more intensely than success, amplifying the effects of the 30 percent of unsuccessful outcomes (12 percent very unsuccessful, 7 percent somewhat unsuccessful, and 11 percent mixed). (See Figure 8.2.)

These data suggest there is a major opportunity for improving how pivotal decisions are made and suggest how to support the decisions that really matter in developing leaders and businesses. Although much attention goes to career planning and business planning, most planning processes neglect to locate the decision at hand *accurately* on a *clear*

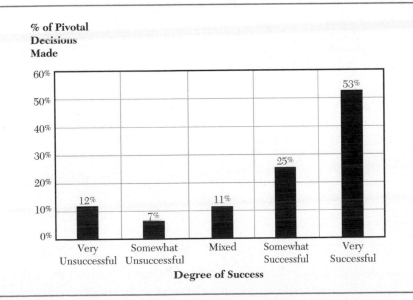

FIGURE 8.2   Success of Pivotal Decision Outcomes

road map of where decision makers were, where they are, and where they want to go with a wider perspective than the immediate goal. The whole framework of five pivotal decisions can help by putting each decision in a big-picture perspective marked by developmental guideposts. I will address this in the book's final chapter.

Findings from the study get interesting in how success varies by type of decision. We found a strong correlation between how people approach pivotal decisions over time and the success rate of types of decisions. Let's look at the success rate of the five decisions and then how decision-making styles relate to the success of outcomes.

Study Findings

Launching point decisions were believed to be the most successful. Tipping point and recommitment decisions were regarded as the least successful.

Respondents rated on a 5-point scale the perceived success of each decision outcome. The most successful across all respondents is the launching decision, with 79 percent of decisions regarded as "very successful" and "somewhat successful." And the least successful is the recommitment decision at 46 percent. Table 8.1 breaks down the success ratings for each decision, and Figure 8.3 shows what percentage of each decision was regarded as "very successful."

When we factor in the age-related progression of pivotal decisions, these findings indicate that people need the most help in midcareer—not when younger and less experienced, as some might think. Looking at the mean age of 42 when making a tipping point decision and the mean age of 45 when making a recommitment decision, we find the age range of 40 to 48 most susceptible to making decisions that end up with less-than-successful outcomes.

Contributing factors include the narrowing pyramid that makes competition increasingly difficult; more personal responsibilities, including family considerations; and more challenging work

TABLE 8.1   Degree of Success of Each Pivotal Decision

	Very Successful	Somewhat Successful	Total
Launching Decision	53%	26%	79%
Turning Point Decision	47%	25%	72%
Tipping Point Decision	26%	26%	52%
Recommitment Decision	21%	25%	46%
Letting Go Decision	45%	24%	69%
Average of All	41%	25%	66%

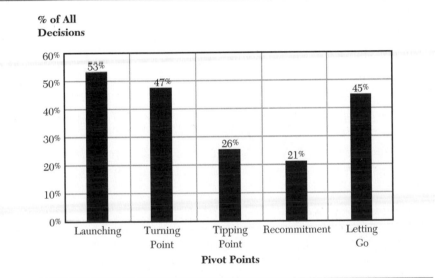

FIGURE 8.3   Very Successful Outcomes of Each Pivotal Decision

responsibilities and situations. Also, as one rises in the organization and has more visibility, the opportunities and threats intensify pressures and increase risks. Of course, complacency, disillusionment, or plain inertia can also creep in or suddenly occur in midcareer. Whatever the reason, this is a critical time to take a hard, honest look at where you are and where you want to go.

So far we reviewed key findings about the pivotal decisions made. Next, we examine findings about how people make pivotal decisions.

HOW DO PEOPLE MAKE PIVOTAL DECISIONS?

In exploring how people make pivotal decisions, we studied how the five leaders featured in this book made their pivotal decisions. They held themselves accountable to make something important happen different than could be expected from the usual course of the status quo. They had ideas, took action, and produced desired results. They demonstrated courage, risk-taking, confidence, creativity, and hard work. But people can express any of these qualities in non-leader activities, so we eliminated such traits as important but only descriptive and not what truly differentiates leaders. These leaders fulfilled and exceeded significant goals, which others can't or don't, because they used ingenuity and moved forward with accountability. Ingenuity set the direction while accountability guided the actions of their pivotal decisions.

The quantitative study then tested whether high accountability and strong ingenuity drive leadership decision making among the broad range of professionals included in the research sample. And, if so, we wanted to know the incidence and success of decisions according to different degrees of accountability and ingenuity. To reduce social bias of answers, nowhere in the study was it mentioned that this was a study about leadership.

To explore how people went about making pivotal decisions, we developed 40 statements of various decision-making behaviors that reflected various facets of accountability and ingenuity we had heard from the interviews of the featured leaders. Respondents used a 5-point agree/disagree scale to indicate how much each statement reflected their experience when making each of the five pivotal decisions. The 40 statements showed various degrees of accountability for holding oneself accountable and various degrees of ingenuity in terms of having ideas, solutions, and overarching vision.

Again, to reduce social bias, nowhere in the study did we use the words *accountability* and *ingenuity*. These statements were designed to indicate the degree of excitement versus dread, the degree to which the decision was viewed as an opportunity versus a problem, the balance between future-directed work and daily demands, the amount of second-guessing, the desire to delegate or avoid making a decision, the number of options explored, the amount of deliberation versus decisiveness, and the amount of consensus building.

The 40 items were then clustered, using a multivariate statistical approach called variable cluster analysis. In this analysis, items that are

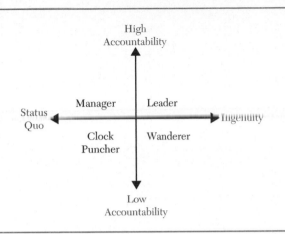

FIGURE 8.4   Four Types of Decision-Making Behaviors

highly correlated form groups or *clusters*. From this analysis, four clusters emerged, which I call leader, manager, wanderer, and clock puncher. (See Figure 8.4.) The four clusters can be visually plotted on the matrix formed by ingenuity on the horizontal axis and accountability on the vertical axis. On the ingenuity axis, the right end marks innovative thinking that generates new ideas, solutions, and vision; the left end marks conventional thinking confined by the status quo. On the vertical axis, accountability is high on the top end and low on the bottom.

The findings about these behaviors reflect data about the decisions, not about the decision maker. That is to say, the same person can make one pivotal decision like a leader and make another like a clock puncher. Remember, these are types of behaviors, and the same person can exhibit all, some, or none of them at different times.

Study Findings

When confronted with a pivotal decision, a person applies—for better or for worse—one of the four postulated approaches to make the decision.

Findings validated the quadrant of four behavior sets based on the degree of accountability and degree of ingenuity activated in the approach to decision making. One way or another, 78 percent of respondents made a decision. Of the pivotal decisions made, 36 percent involved

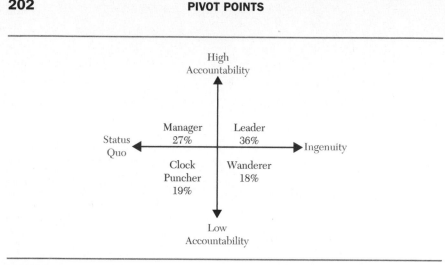

FIGURE 8.5   Percentages of All Decisions Made with These Behaviors

high accountability and strong ingenuity; 27 percent high accountability and weak ingenuity; 19 percent low on both dimensions; and 18 percent low accountability but strong ingenuity. (See Figure 8.5.)

Of all the pivotal decisions made, roughly one in three qualifies as a leadership decision by optimizing both accountability and ingenuity. Most bosses would find this low rate unacceptable because these data are just about decision making and not about the success or failure of actual results. Furthermore, this is about *important strategic decisions* that are recognized as having a pivotal role.

It's also noteworthy that more of the decisions made focus on accountability than on ideas and innovation. Adding the two quadrants scoring high on accountability, two-thirds of decisions were made using the approaches of leaders and managers. On the other hand, only half of decisions scored high in ingenuity, using approaches of leaders and wanderers.

Study Findings

These data suggest that most organizations run primarily on accountability; ingenuity and innovation lag significantly behind.

We need more research about the reasons accountability plays a significantly more dominant part than ingenuity in pivotal decisions. Possibilities include short-term focus of management objectives, personal compensation tied to short-term objectives, organizational resistance to new ideas, and low tolerance of risk. Also, decision makers may want to make their jobs and lives easier by staying within the status quo.

This confirms what every leader knows: Leading change and innovation are among the toughest challenges and often fail. This study clearly differentiates leadership decisions from managerial decisions. Accountability for activities that only maintain the status quo, on a continuous basis, does not call out a leader, even when there is a reputation of hard work and meeting short-term financial targets.

With the rapid pace of change technology and globalization brought, success increasingly depends on a balance of ingenuity and accountability. This points to the importance of addressing the degree of accountability and ingenuity a person demonstrates in hiring, training, and performance evaluations.

Study Findings

Decisions made with leader behaviors are regarded more often by decision makers as more successful.

Analysis indicates that the different approaches to making a pivotal decision increase or decrease the likelihood of a successful outcome. The data on the perceived success of decision outcomes strongly correlate with decisions made within the leader quadrant. With the exception of the letting go data, both comprise similar declining curves and percentage ranges. Table 8.2 compares these numbers.

The decision where success is less correlated with leader style was letting go. Although letting go had the fewest decisions applying the leader style, it was viewed as having a high rate of success—almost the same as for turning point decisions. Spiking at 55 to 65 years old, the letting go decision is not approached as an opportunity or with an investment of effort to explore options or build understanding.

TABLE 8.2 Leader Style Correlates with Success of All Pivotal Decisions

Decision	Decisions Leader Style	Decisions Rated Very Successful
Launching	45%	53%
Turning Point	36%	47%
Tipping Point	34%	26%
Recommitment	31%	21%
Letting Go	25%	45%

The data about letting go seem to indicate that letting go is not usually thought about as involving accountability and vision. The reality of organizations, however, requires a strategic letting go that empowers other people and is done in a way that helps others succeed. To remain successful, organizations need a succession plan with a perspective for the future. For the organization, truly successful letting go is a challenging part of leadership that needs further exploration.

For the individual, there is an opportunity for people to make this decision more strategically, realizing every ending is also a beginning, even if it is retirement.

Study Findings

On average, people are inconsistent in their approach to pivotal decisions. Of those who made more than one pivotal decision, 12 percent consistently did so exhibiting leader behavior.

We analyzed the data for consistency in how people made pivotal decisions and how many consistently optimized accountability and ingenuity in decision making across all the decisions they made. Among the people in the study who had made any pivotal decisions, 61 percent had made more than one decision and hence could be examined for consistency. Within that group, 76 percent were inconsistent—for example, they acted like a manager at one pivot point and as a leader at another. The other 24 percent were consistent.

Of those who were consistent, only 12 percent, or half of those who made more than one decision, did so in a leader-consistent fashion. If we looked at the people who consistently behaved like leaders as a percentage of the entire qualified sample population, only 7 percent consistently exhibited leadership decision making. The others either were inconsistent or were consistent but not in a leader-oriented manner.

Study Findings

The approach to decision making varies by the type of pivotal decision. Over time, fewer decisions are made with leadership accountability and ingenuity.

The leadership approach is most often applied to launching decisions and, second, to turning point decisions. (See Figure 8.6.) A dramatic drop in the use of leadership behaviors occurs when making tipping point decisions and recommitment decisions. There is another decline for letting go decisions.

At first glance, it is surprising that leadership behavior in making decisions at pivot points decreases over time, when you would expect it to increase with experience and maturity. But this correlates with the finding discussed earlier that the success of decisions declined at the tipping point and recommitment decisions.

The reasons for the declining leadership curve may be the same reasons that these midcareer decisions are less successful. They include the narrowing pyramid, more family responsibilities, more risk in challenges and opportunities, and perhaps disillusionment and tiring of one's career.

The success curve by decision type follows the leader curve, except at the letting go decision as already noted. (See Figure 8.7.)

This chart clearly shows that the incidence of *very successful outcomes declines over the series of pivotal decisions as do decisions made with leader behaviors*, with the exception of letting go decisions. This is contrary to our own expectation that leadership behaviors increase

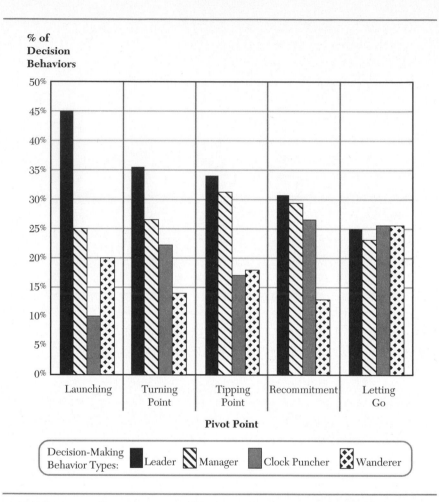

% of
Decision
Behaviors

FIGURE 8.6   Percentage of Decision Behaviors by Pivot Point

in decision making when one has more experience, skills, and understanding. The success line actually is an inverted pyramid; as competition
progressively narrows at the top, fewer decision makers and decisions
succeed. The declining success curve also suggests that less-than-successful outcomes over career stages result in the individual adopting
clock puncher and wanderer approaches to pivotal decisions.

Furthermore, the four decision-making styles peak at different
decision points: leader at launching, manager at tipping point, clock
puncher at recommitment, and wanderer at letting go. The behavioral
pattern starts out with new ideas and accountability and then shifts to

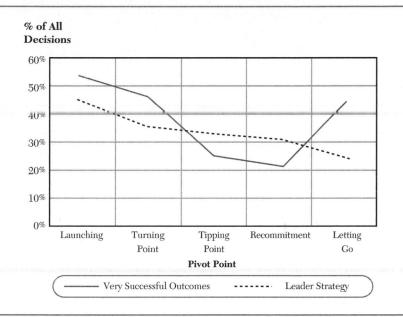

FIGURE 8.7   Correlation of Leader Behavior with Very Successful Outcomes

favor accountability over ideas. As people make pivotal decisions with less leadership vision, they default to making managerial decisions. (See Figure 8.8.) From there, many people over time demonstrate less accountability and ingenuity in their decision making, making decisions more as a clock puncher, somehow doing just enough to keep their jobs. Later, they drift to wanderer behaviors that center on ideas over accountability.

In other words, the average person's decision making becomes more conservative over time. The pattern of behavior moves progressively away from new ideas and toward the status quo, then to less accountability, and finally to having ideas but not holding oneself accountable to make them happen. This pattern says that the more we have to lose, the more we try to play it safe. It may also say that negative experiences over time, whatever their nature, wear many people down, and they go down a path of retrenchment rather than recovery.

The findings of this innovative study give an enlightening context for the leadership journeys of the five leaders featured. The study shows that the person who makes all five pivotal decisions and makes them

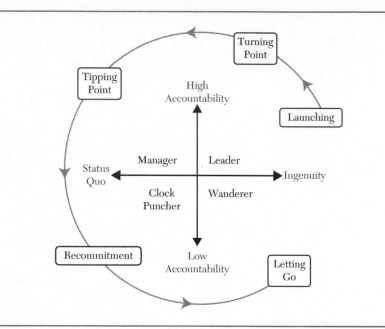

FIGURE 8.8   Path of Decision-Making Behaviors

consistently with high accountability and strong ideas is rare and stands out as a true leader with a career record of both measurable and harder-to-measure qualitative performance outcomes.

TO LEAD IS TO CREATE

When all eyes are on the leader, there is no leadership guidebook or how-to manual that can help. Everyone successful in a job at the top eventually realizes that leading requires charting your own path, not trying to step into another's shoes. That's what makes leading a coveted job, yet nothing really prepares one for it—an unsettling feeling for all newcomers facing all those expectant and critical eyes looking to you for decisions and direction that they will quickly judge.

The five-pivotal-decisions framework identifies stages of preparing a leader for progressively bigger challenges and opportunities. The decision point does not announce itself as a pivotal one. That's why it is so important to understand the drivers of successful outcomes when these decisions are made.

It's all part of the developmental process. What may appear at the time as a trivial decision, perhaps not even a decision, may be one of the most important decisions of one's life. A good example is Al Golin's decision to make a phone call when a friend gave him a sales lead. Ray Kroc, just starting McDonald's, personally answered Al's call. That call launched a relationship that was the foundation of the growth of Al's public relations firm and which has continued for 55 years. Al could not possibly have anticipated that call meant he would grow with the most successful quick-service restaurant in history and that the simple decision to make a cold sales call would shape not only his leadership and his firm but also the public relations industry. Behind that call was Al's decision to create his own success as a junior partner in a small firm rather than have to depend on the decisions of a large company as in his previous jobs.

Great outcomes and great leaders arise from pivotal decisions made with high accountability and strong ingenuity. Because it's hard to know in advance that a decision can be pivotal, you must always approach decisions—big or small—with a high degree of accountability and ingenuity. And this is why, as the examples of our five leaders show, leadership is more a state of being than a set of skills or traits. Over the course of five pivotal decisions, leaders create and fulfill a singular role and write their own book, figuratively, on leading.

In the next chapter, we take a closer look at the four decision-making behaviors and how you assess where you are in your pivotal decisions.

CHAPTER 9

Your Pivotal Five

A New Career Road Map

The framework of five pivotal decisions can help you increase self-awareness by understanding where you've been, where you are currently, and how you got here—for better or for worse. Doing a career path checkup that examines your pivotal decisions, motivations, and goals can help you formulate, refine, or overhaul your career goals. This appraisal can illuminate a path into the future—and motivate self-management and inspire self-development for future pivotal decisions.

Clarity about your real aspirations, apart from institutional career advancement paths, will help you look in the right places for your next pivot point. As Sam Phillips, the father of rock and roll, purportedly said to an unknown Elvis Presley imitating Dean Martin in his early auditions, "I don't record singers, I record souls." Elvis then delivered what became his signature sound and style. Likewise, pivotal decisions at their best are expressions of souls, what we mean in the phrase "Follow your passion."

Before taking a look at the questions that will help you construct your career road map, let's review a few guidelines for answering them.

First, most people would include family responsibilities in their answers; just make sure you also think more broadly and answer these questions about more than just your family goals and commitments. Second, depending on your life situation and priorities for the future, answers can center on income-earning careers or volunteer community involvement. Third, when answering these questions, remember that pivotal decisions build on each other; for example, to have a tipping point decision typically depends on a preceding turning point decision. Consequently, you may need to consider at least two pivot points at the same time; for example, to answer the question about the turning point, consider at the same time your answer to the question about the tipping point.

Take time to reflect before answering the questions in this chapter. You may or may not be able to answer with specific details. The five-pivotal-decisions framework is not a crystal ball for seeing the future, but it is a diagnostic to enhance self-awareness. Pivotal decisions ideally develop our singular strengths and interests, so you want to be able to look squarely in the eye of your private self and be able to envision facing decisive moments. Those are the moments when you, and only you, know what you must do and take full responsibility for making the pivotal decision and handling the consequences. Being able to express in words this authentic pivotal self is a catalyst for action—words have power. They will direct your personal power to act on opportunities and challenges that become the dots that connect over time and build real, and at times, unstoppable momentum.

Steve Jobs, in his 2005 commencement address at Stanford University, said: "You can't connect the dots looking forward; you can only connect them looking backward." Jobs laid out his personal story, connecting seemingly unrelated events, starting with his biological mother's decision to give him up for adoption to dropping out of Reed College and then to designing fonts for the first Macintosh computer. He ended his story with this advice: "So, you have to trust that the dots will somehow connect in your future, you have to trust in something—your gut, destiny, life, karma, whatever—because believing that the dots will connect down the road will give you the confidence to follow your heart, even when it leads you off the well-worn path, and that will make all the difference."

Certain dots stood out as the five proven leaders featured in this book recounted their stories. They didn't connect the dots as five pivotal decisions, but they recalled the experiences that made the biggest difference in their careers. These dots, remembered as if they occurred yesterday, reveal the essence and maturing of the leaders and what they led. When each read his story in the narrative framework of five pivotal decisions, every one of them gained useful insights for their continuing journey.

To understand the decisions you want to be able to make in the future, objectively assess where you are on your own road map of pivotal decisions. Pivot points focus on these five questions you must ask yourself about your career. Thought starters for each question will help you answer them as clearly as you can. You may want to take the Decision-Making Quiz further in this chapter before answering these questions.

CONNECTING YOUR DOTS: YOUR PIVOTAL DECISIONS

Your Pivotal Five

1. What subject and skills have you mastered or do you want to master, and what is worth massive amounts of your time and energy?

- What do you find comes easily to you? What do you pursue with natural curiosity and interest? At which activity do you consistently obtain excellent results?
- Do you identify with this as one of your key strengths?
- What would you spend a lot of time on, and pursue with excellence, even if you weren't paid to do it? (Do not focus your answer on activities you value as purely recreational, for example, improving your golf game.)
- If it is true that "What I do is who I am," how would you answer "What do you do?" (Your answer can in fact be the case or can be aspirational.)
- What degree of expertise do you want in this area? What do you need to do to acquire that level of expertise? How long will it take?
- Are you willing and able to devote the years needed to attain real mastery? (Your answer should reflect years already spent as well as years you're willing to spend to get there.)
- In your work experience, which aspect of the work have you enjoyed the most? At which aspect of the work have you excelled?
- If you already have mastery in this area, do you continuously keep your expertise current and competitive? If not, what can you do to refresh your skills?

- Is there a different way to apply your strengths that you could find more interesting and challenging?

2. What problem do you want to solve or condition do you want to improve?

- Once you have attained a degree of mastery, how would you like to differentiate more clearly what you offer from others with the same level of mastery?
- What experience do you need that would establish your competitive differentiation?
- What stands between you and doing what you admire in others in your field of expertise? Is it an internal insecurity or fear, or an external situation? Identify specific obstacles that hold you back. How would you like to change the narrative?
- What conventional thinking or practices in your work environment would you like to improve and innovate?
- What ideas do you have for making an improvement or innovation in your current work or area of passion?
- What is a key obstacle that you need to get past or break through to reach your tipping point? (You may want to first answer the next question about your desired tipping point.)

3. What would you like to be your tipping point and is there a fundamental barrier to break through to achieve that tipping point?

- Envision your most respected mentor presenting you at an important industry event. Write one paragraph for what your mentor says to introduce you—this can be based on your actual experience or on your aspirations—that summarizes your greatest achievements and character.
- Write another paragraph about what you would have done that built the momentum toward that tipping point—when a powerful wave of events enabled peak performance and achievements.
- Read those two paragraphs aloud. I recommend that you videotape your reading and review it.
- What are the key words in those paragraphs about what you want to be known for?
- What are two or three action steps that would be milestones for accomplishing each of those goals?
- What do you see as the biggest risk to get to the tipping point?
- What do you need to do to make the risk manageable?
- Who do you need to help you?

4. What is worth renewing your commitment and seeing it through?

- What is your purpose—the difference you can still make that would make your career worth even more than all the time and effort you have already invested? Does your answer apply to your current role?
- What is your purpose that you could achieve better in a different role? What are one or two of those other possible roles?
- What are the main reasons for not making a recommitment to your current role?
- What are the reasons that would make recommitment the best decision?
- What do you still need to do to feel completion and not carry forward any regrets? Which of these steps do you want to take?
- Does that relate to your current job? If not, what does it relate to?
- If you face the decision to recommit to your current work environment or make a change, was there a triggering event that has made you emotionally reactive? If so, which options may burden you with unfinished business? Which options are more likely to allow you to go forth with your self-worth intact?
- What would make you the most proud for the next generation of leaders to carry forward as your work? Is there more for you to do to ensure that legacy?
- Is there something you've always thought you would try when you had the time and financial security? Would you regret it if you never tried?

5. How do you both leave a legacy and personally move on?

- In what tangible ways can the best of your life work carry on?
- What are your criteria for when it's time to let go of important responsibilities and give others growth opportunities?
- What are your criteria for when it's time to let go in terms of leaving the job?
- Do you have individuals who are ready to carry the torch?
- What do you want or need to do to prepare the next generation of leaders after you?
- What do you need to do to leave on your terms when it's time to go?
- How much time could it take to prepare for the day you can confidently leave responsibilities in other people's hands?

- What's next that makes letting go easier? Write the outline of the next chapter of your story.
- If you are facing retirement, how will you make the transition from the current structure of your work and lifestyle to the next stage without the structure your job has provided? What will you structure your daily life around?

Your Pivotal Plan

For each of the five pivot points, identify the things you can do to prepare and position yourself for seizing opportunities that align with your answers. Make an action plan that includes these activities:

- Participate in education, training, and conferences.
- Develop or strengthen your network and relationships.
- Conduct research and due diligence. Read books.
- Identify and engage resources and mentors.
- Redefine or clarify your desired role.

These questions help you determine what have been your pivotal decisions so far and locate where you are in your career stage. Next, you will assess how you made those pivotal decisions. From there, you can decide how you want to improve your future decision making.

CONNECTING YOUR DOTS: YOUR DECISION-MAKING BEHAVIOR

If you like, you can take a short version of the survey we conducted for our research, as explained in Chapter 8, and use your test results to help construct your career road map. Although the survey study used 40 statements to assess decision-making behaviors, we applied a statistical method called discriminant analysis to find the statements most effective in separating leaders, managers, clock punchers, and wanderers. Twelve statements emerged as the most important in distinguishing one style of decision making from another. Here they are.

Decision-Making Quiz

Instructions. At various points in your career, you may have made one of the types of pivotal decisions described in this book. This quiz can help you understand the decision-making behaviors you used when making that decision. That is, did you make the decision like a leader, a manager, a wanderer, or a clock puncher? To find out, think back to a pivotal decision you've made, and try to remember what you were thinking and experiencing during the decision process. Think only about that one decision, not other decisions in your career. You can come back and repeat the process with another pivotal decision later.

With this one pivot point decision in mind, indicate how much you believe each statement listed describes what you were thinking and experiencing at the time of this particular decision. You can do this by using a scale from 1 to 10, where a 10 means you agree strongly that the statement describes what you were thinking and experiencing and a 1 means you disagree strongly with the statement. Of course, you can choose any number from 1 to 10.

Rating 1–10	Statement
	1. At the time, the demands of performing properly in my existing role cut short the time I could spend really thinking through my vision and adequately informing it.
	2. When making this decision, I invested the time and effort to explore a variety of options.
	3. When making this decision, I spent a lot of time considering all the reasons why a change would not be good.
	4. At the time, I probably didn't invest as much as I should have in my current position—I was too excited about the possibilities that might lie ahead with the decision I was trying to make.

(continued)

(continued)

Rating 1–10	Statement
	5. I found the whole process of making the decision stressful and unnerving.
	6. Once I realized I needed to make this decision, I avoided getting overly immersed in the day-to-day work of my current position and instead devoted significant time and energy to make sure to do things that gave me time to get new perspectives and to reflect.
	7. At the time, I worked hard to build consensus and enthusiasm for my decision among people in my organization (or new organization) who would be affected by what I was trying to do.
	8. When making this decision, I was so busy with day-to-day work that I didn't have enough time to think strategically.
	9. At the time, I constantly second-guessed myself and tried to talk myself out of making a change.
	10. At the time, I worked hard to make sure that everyone involved in or affected by the decision understood my thinking.
	11. At the time, I found it very easy to set aside what I was supposed to be doing in my current role and spend lots of time thinking about my vision and the decision I was making.
	12. At the time, the role I was in and the nature of the business was very fluid and constantly changing. So I had to expend a lot of intellectual effort staying on top of the day-to-day work.

Determine Your Score. To find out what decision-making style you adopted for one particular pivot point decision, take the scores for items 3, 5, and 9, add them together, and put that number in the box that follows labeled *clock puncher*. Then take the scores for items 1, 8, and 12, add them together, and put them in the box below labeled *manager*. Take the scores for items 4, 6, and 11, add them together, and put them in the box labeled *wanderer*. Finally, take the scores from items 2, 7, and 10, add them together, and put them in the box labeled *leader*.

	Clock Puncher	**Manager**	**Wanderer**	**Leader**
Enter Your Scores →	Add scores from Q3, Q5, and Q9	Add scores from Q1, Q8, and Q12	Add scores from Q4, Q6, and Q11	Add scores from Q2, Q7, and Q10

Once you have the four total scores entered into the boxes in the grid above, you can determine your decision-making style for one particular pivotal decision by following the steps below.

1. If your leader total is greater than or equal to 15 **AND** your clock puncher total is either the lowest or tied for the lowest of the four scores, then you deployed a **LEADER** style, and you can stop here. If this was not the case, continue to the next step.

2. If your clock puncher total is either the highest or tied for the highest of the four scores, then you deployed a **CLOCK PUNCHER** style, and you can stop here. If not, continue to the next step.

3. If your manager total is greater than or equal to 13, then you deployed a **MANAGER** style. If your manager total is less than 13, then you deployed a **WANDERER** style.

You can now pick another pivot point decision you have made, and repeat these instructions.

As a word of caution, simplifying the scoring for this self-quiz decreases accuracy from when applying true statistical methods for scoring.

Let's next take a close look at these four types of decision-making behaviors.

LEADER, MANAGER, WANDERER, AND CLOCK PUNCHER

To understand better how everyone can apply pivotal decisions to his or her own singular journey, let's take a closer look at each of the four decision-making approaches.

Decision-Making Behaviors

Leader: High Accountability and Strong Ingenuity

When people make a decision using leader behaviors, they particularly agree with the following statements. Furthermore, they agree with these statements significantly more often than other behavior types do:

- When making this decision, I loved the challenge that was involved and found the process, the opportunity, and the risks exciting.
- At the time, I worked hard to build consensus and enthusiasm for my decision among people in my organization who would be affected by what I was trying to do.
- When making this decision, I consulted with a lot of knowledgeable sources and people to gain good insight and advice.
- When making this decision, I invested the time and effort to explore a variety of options.
- At the time, I worked hard to make sure that everyone involved in or affected by the decision understood my thinking.

The statements reflect a decision-making process that places high importance on gathering information on ideas and resources, as well as high accountability for exploring and gaining support of other people who would be affected. In the research study, we found that building consensus occurred significantly more often for turning point and tipping point decisions than the other pivotal decisions.

All the leaders in this book were very consistent over the long haul in terms of accountability and ingenuity, even when they experienced catastrophic setbacks. When most people would retrench and lose their verve, these leaders continually held themselves accountable. They reached for bold solutions, which energized them and helped them keep their verve through all five pivotal decisions. They were able to see them through because they brought people along their journeys.

These experiences both revealed and built leadership character. When competition between Bud and his business partner made them behave more like sibling rivals than leaders, Bud made the difficult decision to split up the 20-year partnership. Building his vision for the company as its solo leader engaged people on his MBWA rounds. When John suffered his first devastating setback, in part because of his decision to change distribution strategy, he built up his leadership team at a time he could least afford to—and that helped him pass the test of survival. When Al recognized that the firm was too dependent on one client—and practiced what he preached about fixing things before they break—he built a wonderful new partnership with Tom Harris and, together, they grew the firm and its reputation beyond a single industry.

More examples include pivot points driven by personal needs. Driven to prove his abilities away from the business his brother had founded, Glen decided to leave CCC for his first chief executive officer role in the health care sector, having explored options where he could make a significant impact. Dale made the decision to devote himself to rediscovering passion when most others in the same kind of situation settle for the easier path. He sought out new people, experiences, and ideas. He explored new options and fields of expertise. He built consensus among people who captured his imagination about how he could contribute the most value.

Decision-Making Behaviors

Wanderer: Low Accountability and Strong Ingenuity

When people make a decision like a wanderer, they particularly agree with the following statements:

- When confronting this decision, I looked at it as an opportunity, not as a problem.
- When making this decision, I loved the challenge that was involved and found the process, the opportunity, and the risks exciting.
- At the time, I found it very easy to set aside what I was supposed to be doing in my current role and spend lots of time thinking about my vision and the decision I was making.
- Once I realized I needed to make this decision, I avoided getting overly immersed in the day-to-day work of my current position and instead devoted significant time and energy to make sure to do things that gave me time to get new perspectives and to reflect.
- When making this decision, I invested the time and effort to explore a variety of options.

Wanderers can look like leaders; they agree with a few of the same statements to the same extent. People can make the mistake of seeing wanderers as leaders upon first impression and in job interviews. Wanderers offer imaginative ideas and speak with passion about them. Their passion for ideas can make them dynamic and particularly attractive to teams that need innovative thinkers. Also, wanderers can give a lot of thought to how the idea looks and feels and all its functions and benefits. Everyone gets lost in his or her idea at some point in time, but wanderers don't switch back to practical needs as leaders do. Wanderers forget that great thinkers also need to be great doers. A wanderer can create, and have others create, plenty of presentations, but very little of it translates into action and progress.

The idea of ideas drives wanderers. They like the excitement they feel when thinking about creative possibilities and ignore the practical needs and hard work of execution. They also end up not being accountable for their usual responsibilities. They assume that other people will somehow fill in for them. Wanderers end up not producing pivotal outcomes.

Decision-Making Behaviors

Manager: High Accountability and Low Ingenuity

When people make a decision like a manager, they particularly agree with these statements:

- At the time, the role I was in and the nature of the business was constantly changing. So I had to expend a lot of intellectual effort just staying on top of the day-to-day work.
- I was very torn between maintaining a good performance level in what I was currently doing versus trying to envision and think through the decision properly.
- I focused more on delivering what I needed to deliver in my existing role—I didn't spend enough time building a long-term vision for where I wanted to go next.
- When making this decision, I was so busy with day-to-day work that I didn't have enough time to think strategically.

Managerial decision making is driven by time. This decision maker has high accountability for the job at hand but makes little time for thinking about strategy, improvements and innovation, and vision. Managerial decision making is the opposite of the wanderer type.

Often managerial decisions and leadership decisions are both referred to as simply senior management decisions. A clear distinction should be made between them. Managerial decisions are part of a leader's job and might sometimes produce pivotal results, but leadership decisions elevate the idea or purpose of work, standards, and performance. Managerial decisions make things run smoothly—keep well-maintained trains running on time—a necessary function that enables everyone, including leaders, to do their jobs. A leadership decision, on the other hand, pulls self and others forward to achieve a vitally important shared goal beyond business as usual.

In the real life of organizations, executives who are great managers are often put into leadership roles. Unfortunately, managing is not leading. Over time, people realize decisions are not being made to address strategic issues about competition, changes in the marketplace, and organizational effectiveness. Whole organizations of people constantly make internal presentations and attend meetings. Without clear vision and clear accountabilities, these companies end up talking to themselves, underachieving, and losing their best people. It takes leadership with distinctly different approaches from managing to keep people fully engaged, stretching their talents and skills, and producing results in which they take pride.

Decision-Making Behaviors

Clock Puncher: Low Accountability and Low Ingenuity

When people make a decision like a clock puncher, they particularly agree with these statements:

- I found the whole process of making the decision stressful and unnerving.
- When making this decision, I often found myself thinking about how easy it would be just to leave things as they were and not make a change.
- When making this decision, I spent a lot of time considering all the reasons why a change would not be good.
- At the time, I constantly second-guessed myself and tried to talk myself out of making a change.

All these statements see the status quo as the easiest and most comfortable option. Their comfort zone drives clock punchers. The commitment of clock punchers is to getting a paycheck with as little stress and risk as possible. Risk-taking and change are very stressful to some, while others are critics and cynics.

They can be very smart and high functioning. But they want the safe and easy path. They resist change without even considering the idea. They actively avoid accountability and new ideas while lobbying for maintaining the status quo.

Clock punchers don't invest in people and help them grow. Although they can fulfill basic job requirements, the more problematic clock punchers can obstruct other people's work and progress.

Clock punching behavior is like being a renter versus a homeowner. Renters don't think about making capital improvements to the property whereas owners invest in it as an asset. When there are problems, renters call the property owner; owners fix the problem. When renters find a better deal, they simply move; owners juggle a complex equation that includes financial and emotional investments. When renting, one invests little effort and does just enough to meet his or her needs.

There is a time and place for renting; most of us have been renters at some time. So it is with careers. Most of us, when we were young, had jobs we were just trying out. We were employees, thinking like renters and not as owners. For some, this can last decades. Even at the senior level, people can drift into the clock punching mode; wanting to detach from the caring and stress of ownership, they pull back and work to support a comfortable lifestyle.

For the leaders featured in this book, once they started thinking and behaving like an owner, there was no turning back. For entrepreneurs like Bud and Al, sometimes that meant not taking a paycheck for months at a time but paying their employees and suppliers. This kind of thinking and behaving, which is not for everyone, focuses on commitments as a covenant with themselves and others on the shared journey.

So, you might ask, how would wanderers and clock punchers slip through the gates and get to executive positions? It's because everyone experiences all these behaviors to different degrees with different frequency and durations. These categories are not lifetime sentences.

As we saw in the research findings, people slip in and out of all these modes, but they also tend to default to one mode often. Most people make some pivotal decisions in different quadrants of behaviors, traversing the path, shown in the research, that over time moves away from leader strategies. Strong leaders can shift from one mode to another; however, when it comes to pivotal decisions, they consistently display high accountability and ingenuity.

WARNING SIGNS

If you found yourself not making pivotal decisions consistently as a leader, you may want to find ways to make your future decisions with more accountability and ingenuity. If you scored lower than you expected on the questionnaire for your current career situation, you may have landed unwittingly in a career trap.

First, the status quo can be a trap of complacency. It's simply easier not to rock the boat. New ideas take work and face too many skeptics.

Insular thinking sets in, making ideas more safe than imaginative and solutions more recycled than on target. But a key finding in our study is that people who focus only on the day-to-day issues even with diligence and excellence don't get the successful outcomes leaders get. In comparison, manager style decisions for the launching and turning point decisions did not correlate with the success curve, as did the leader style. Leaders welcome the challenge and risk of a new opportunity and actively seek new ideas. They actively avoid complacency and insular thinking. They see solutions and options others miss. To stand out as a leader, make appointments with yourself—literally, block out time on your calendar—to brainstorm on a regular basis about forward-looking needs of your team and business.

Another trap that almost everyone falls into on occasion is busyness. Being so busy getting through a day can leave no time for matters that need careful thought. Daily interactions at the office become primarily transactional, such as project and information updates. Ideation and problem solving become work done solely in scheduled meetings and the annual planning process. There's no other time to discuss new perspectives and ideas with colleagues and customers. It becomes a way of life and years pass since you had an idea that truly excited you. Our study found that leaders make the time to talk with a variety of people to explore a number of options and to gain support for ideas. So I often advise people to make the time to have lunch once a week with someone other than daily contacts to have conversations that explore new ideas and options.

A third common career trap is having more concern for keeping your job than for doing your job. The job of meeting expectations can turn into managing by a checklist. While it's certainly important to deliver according to agreed upon goals and expectations, the job of the leader also includes inspiring others through example and outlook. All five of the featured leaders were passionate about their work, cared about their people, and believed in an exciting future. People want to be part of something that engages the passion and optimism of their leaders. They want their leader to care about the work more than they care about profits. They want their leader to care about what the team thinks. Our empirical study found that leaders worked hard to build enthusiasm and to make sure that everyone affected by a major decision understood his or her thinking.

Overall, the most important differentiator of leader decision making is reaching out to people, listening to them, understanding the problems people struggle with in their jobs, and building awareness and support for decisions. Often, people lend support simply because they feel treated with respect and appreciation when they were asked to give their perspective. Accountability for rallying support is so important—it can make the difference between success or failure of a decision—that, if you do nothing else differently, do this as a regular part of your job and you'll likely see more consistently successful outcomes.

Often, it seems that the last person to know that people see him or her struggling in the job is the individual in it. The individual can explain every problem, never thinking he or she has responsibility for the problem. And when a position is eliminated or a person is passed over for a promotion, the individual believes his or her contributions went unrecognized and underappreciated. Such individuals can believe their quiet style made them overshadowed by more aggressive and outgoing types, or, feel set up for failure by a difficult assignment or situation. It's often referred to as office politics, which is a real problem but not as often as perceived.

However, as leaders in this book and many examples around us show, at the center of effective leadership is a spirit of personal responsibility and accountability for worthy ideas and accountability for making them reality.

People often confuse working hard with performance, their efforts becoming blinders to the purpose of their hard work. Results may not be commensurate with efforts. We all have worked with someone who believes they have good reasons to explain every delay, stumble, and lifeless project. They need to ask for feedback from those they trust to see what others see, which usually is a defensive person who is not dependable. People are often surprised that even a few seemingly minor stumbles combined with their excuses tarnished their reputation. Accountability to most teams and bosses mean consistent delivery plus taking responsibility for the stumbles. It pays to get feedback and gauge your accountability quotient as others see you.

Coming up short on ingenuity, the other key measure of leadership decision making, can also be a blind spot for many people. Often, people fail to see the extent to which they stay within the comfort zone of the status quo. They don't know what they don't know. From the vantage point of his or her comfort zone, new ideas appear as more work and disruptions than they are worth. Some people show chronic resistance to new ideas. There is a clear difference between disagreement about a specific change and resistance to change itself. In disagreement, you are fully engaged in researching and thinking through the matter at hand. In resistance, you see new ideas in a negative light. Instead of offering alternatives, you complain and ignore the matter. These people can fulfill responsibilities of executive roles but often his or her career has stalled. Nonetheless, he or she can't understand when passed over for bigger jobs. These individuals need to redefine their contributions and value, ideally, before a disappointment. Usually, pushing forward involves leaving the protection of his or her comfort zone, and exploring new ideas and solutions with the intention to take a risk.

The challenge is to recognize in your own career these warning signs. It's difficult to see yourself as others see you. It's easy to trade off effectiveness for efficiency just to get through a day, especially when technology and globalization enable constant connectivity. This makes it perhaps more important than ever to look truthfully at the trade-offs we've made and which of them we want to reclaim, where we are, and where we want to go, and take action on closing the gap. Who can give you honest and trustworthy feedback? Which two or three areas need the most self-management to help you address where you are stuck? What self-development activities will open new possibilities and expand your comfort zone? What will make you accountable for taking these actions?

As the journeys of the five leaders show, pivot points can recharge a career. As Dale Dawson said, "There is real power in doing a self-assessment." Continually evaluating what works and what doesn't, building on one's strengths, and compensating for weaknesses evolves into an authentic and effective leadership style. Along the journey, the leader increasingly knows what he or she stands for with full accountability and pride.

YOUR AUTHENTIC PATH

Each leader in this book built his leadership on a different platform. That platform started as an idea and evolved into a core value that built the house, so to speak, inspiring and informing pivotal ideas and decisions in the process of building. Each leader defined his value and key to success in different ways. Glen defined his leadership platform as change that solves important problems. Al's platform proved the economic value of trust and culture. Bud's platform was commitment to an idea about how companies can better connect with customers. John made being a good teammate a platform for actualizing the strength of diversity. Finally, Dale's platform of passion for building businesses and developing managers worked in investment banking and in addressing poverty in Rwanda. As different as their leadership agendas were, pivot points defined their very different journeys. With pivotal decisions, they created situations and conditions for hope and progress through engagement and collaboration of many people.

That is the spirit in which the featured leaders share their experiences and reflections. They respect the individual journeys of leadership. They hope to inspire readers to act on their own possibilities and to navigate through the difficult times. They don't think they have a formula for success or for leading. They know that the all-encompassing nature of a leader's job depends on genuine caring and an agile mind. It brings to mind a popular saying during the early years of Internet adoption and the crazy pace of dot-com growth: "The challenge is like changing the tires while you're going 120 miles an hour."

Understanding their journeys gives us different perspectives to apply leadership to our own situations and goals. Aspiring executives can see in their own career experiences and life situations their own decisive moments. Young managers can reflect on their own beliefs, values, and goals. Students can find direction from the range of leaders and industries. Aspiring entrepreneurs can draw their road map for the true journey of creating real and sustainable economic value.

Take the insights you may have gained about leadership and yourself and traverse your own authentic path. Write your own leadership playbook. Play to your strengths. Find a profession to which you want to be devoted. Find the challenges that excite you as opportunities. Make a commitment to an idea that is worth all of your energy. Live up to your commitments because they matter to you. Then, you too will be the leader you *want* to be.

About the Author

Julia Tang Peters, founder and principal of Leadership Effectiveness Quotient LLC, is a business consultant who helps chief executive officers and heads of teams make, or clarify, pivotal decisions that really matter in the success of their people and organizations. Before LEQ, she held leadership positions in major companies. Julia earned a master of management degree from the Kellogg School of Management at Northwestern University in 1984. She also earned a master of science degree from the School of Education and Social Policy at Northwestern University in 1993 and a bachelor of arts in history from Lake Forest College in 1975. She has a certificate in family therapy from The Family Institute, affiliated with Northwestern University, conferred in 1993. Julia, a licensed family therapist, had a past practice at Northwestern University and the Family Institute. Julia lives in Chicago with her husband and has four adult children.

Index